POLITICAL WOMEN

POLITICAL WOMEN

BY

SUTHERLAND MENZIES

IN TWO VOLUMES

VOL. II

KENNIKAT PRESS
Port Washington, N. Y./London

POLITICAL WOMEN

First published in 1873
Reissued in 1970 by Kennikat Press
Library of Congress Catalog Card No: 78-112815
ISBN 0-8046-1082-7

Manufactured by Taylor Publishing Company   Dallas, Texas

CONTENTS OF VOLUME II.

—·—

Contents.

PART III.

BOOK I.

PRINCESS DES URSINS.

BOOK II.

BOOK III.

Contents.

BOOK IV.

BOOK V.

(Continued.)

POLITICAL WOMEN.

CHAPTER III.

THE STRUGGLE BETWEEN CONDÉ AND TURENNE AT PARIS—
NOBLE CONDUCT OF MADEMOISELLE DE MONTPENSIER—FALL
OF THE FRONDE.

THE second-rate actors in this shifting drama presented no
less diversity in the motives of their actions. Beaufort, who
commanded the troops of Gaston, and Nemours those of
Condé, although brothers-in-law, weakened by their dissen-
tions an army which their concord would have rendered
formidable. The necessity of military operations required
their absence from Paris; but they preferred rather to there
exhibit themselves to their mistresses, decked out in a
general's uniform, and grasping the truncheon of command.
No greater harmony existed between the Prince de Conti
and Madame de Longueville than when La Rochefoucauld
severed them. At Bordeaux they favoured opposite parties,
and contributed to augment the discord prevailing, and to
weaken the party of the Princes by dividing it. The Duchess
de Longueville, when no longer guided by La Rochefoucauld,
did not fail to lose herself in aimless projects, and to compromise herself in intrigues without result. On Nemours
being wounded, his wife repaired to the army to tend him,
and the Duchess de Châtillon, under pretext of visiting one

of her châteaux, accompanied her as far as Montargis ; thence she went to the convent of Filles de Sainte-Marie, where, believing herself quite incognita, she went, under various disguises, to see him whom she had never ceased to love. These mysterious visits soon became no longer a secret to any one ; and then Condé and his sister could convince themselves how different are the sentiments which love inspires and those which self-interest and vanity simulate. The great Condé, by his intelligence and bearing, had all the means of pleasing women ; but obtained small success notwithstanding. Mademoiselle Vigean excepted, he appears to have been incapable of inspiring the tender passion, in the truest acceptation of the phrase. He went further than his sister, it seems, in the neglect of his person. It was his habit of life to be almost always badly dressed, and only appeared radiant on the field of battle. So that the Duke de Nemours was not the only rival with whom Condé had to contend for the favours of that beauty for whom Louis XIV. in his boyish amusements had shown a preference, and which has furnished a theme for some agreeable trifling to the sparkling muse of Benserade. An abbé, named Cambiac, in the service of the house of Condé, balanced for some time the passion to which Nemours had given birth in the bosom of the Duchess de Châtillon, and the jealousy of Nemours failed to expel Cambiac. The Duchess kept fair with him as the man who had obtained the greatest sway over her relation, the Princess-dowager de Condé. The condescension of the Duchess de Châtillon towards this intriguing and licentious priest procured her, on the part of the Princess-dowager, a legacy of more than a hundred thousand crowns in Bavaria, and the usufruct of an estate worth twenty thousand livres in rent per annum. Cambiac, however, retired, when he knew that Condé was his rival. But the victor of Rocroy had more address in winning battles than in conducting a love intrigue. He was clumsy enough to employ as a go-between in his courtship of his new mistress a certain gentleman named Vineuil, who was, it is true, one of his most skilful and attached followers, but whose good looks, agreeable and satirical wit, and enterprising character rendered him a very dangerous emissary among women. He had even acquired some celebrity through his successes in that way. Madame de Montbazon, Madame de Mouy, and the Princess of Wurtemberg had successively experienced the effects of his seductions. Vineuil made himself very agreeable to Madame de Châtillon, and if Condé were wronged by him in that quarter, he never knew of it; for Vineuil was always in great favour with him. Nemours excited his jealousy, and Nemours only dreaded Condé. However, shortly before, in the month of March, 1652, the Marquis de la Boulay and Count de Choisy, both enamoured of this Queen of Hearts, were bent on fighting a duel about her. A rumour of their intention got wind. The Duchess de Châtillon heard of it, and appeared unexpectedly on the spot fixed by the two adversaries for a rendezvous; and at the very instant they were about to unsheath their swords, she flung herself between them, seized each by the hand, and led them into the presence of the Duke d'Orleans, who charged Marshals l'Hospital, Schomberg, and d'Etampes, then in Paris, to arrange that affair and prevent a duel. In this they succeeded, but these rivalries and gallant intrigues very sensibly weakened Condé's party, and hindered there being anything secret or combined in the execution of projects determined upon in the councils of its chief.

In the meantime, the siege of Etampes had been raised;

and the army of Condé had issued forth, probably with the intention of attacking Turenne if he were found engaged with the Duke de Lorraine. On its approaching Paris, Condé took the command of it, and fixed his head-quarters at Saint-Cloud, in order to manœuvre on both banks of the Seine. The proximity of his camp to Paris did him far greater harm than even a defeat would have done. With but a scanty commissariat, Condé was of course obliged to permit every sort of licence. All the crops were ruined in the neighbouring fields; the peasantry were plundered, injured, and their domestic peace destroyed; and the country-houses of the rich Parisians were pillaged and burned in all directions. The evils of civil war now came home to the hearts of the people of the capital, and, forgetting how great a part they themselves had taken in producing the results they lamented, they cast the whole blame upon Condé, and regarded him thenceforth with a malevolent eye.

That prince was distracted with different passions and different feelings. He was himself desirous of peace, and willing to make sacrifices to obtain it. His fair mistress, the Duchess de Châtillon, linked with La Rochefoucauld and the Duke de Nemours, confirmed him in seeking it; but, on the other hand, his sister, who sought to break off his connection with Madame de Châtillon, joined with the Spaniards, to whom he had bound himself by so many ties, to lead him away from Paris, and to protract the war. Gaston's daughter, too, Mademoiselle de Montpensier, mingled in all these intrigues, and took the same unwise means to force herself as a bride upon the young King, which De Retz took to force himself as minister upon his mother. But while these separate interests tore the capital, the peril of the army of Condé became imminent. Turenne having brought the Court to St. Denis, caused a number of boats to be drawn up from Pontoise, and commenced the construction of a bridge opposite Epinay.

Condé, betrayed on all sides, could at length perceive what an error he had committed in quitting the army only to lose himself amidst a series of impotent intrigues, and in having preferred the counsels of such a fickle mistress as Madame de Châtillon to those of a courageous and devoted sister such as Madame de Longueville. Towards the end of June, he got on horseback with a small number of intrepid friends, and rode forth to try for the last time the fate of arms.

It was too late. Marshal de la Ferté-Senneterre had brought from Lorraine powerful reinforcements to the royal army, which thereby amounted to twelve thousand men. That of the Fronde had scarcely the half of that number, and it was discouraged, divided, incapable of giving battle, and could only carry on a few days' campaign around Paris, thanks to the manœuvres and energy everywhere exhibited by its chief. It was evident that no other alternative remained to Condé but to treat with the Court at any price, or to throw himself into the arms of Spain, and the famous combat of the Faubourg Saint-Antoine, seriously considered, was only an act of despair, an heroic but vain protest of courage against fortune. Success would have remedied nothing, and a defeat might have been expected, in which Condé might have lost his glory and his life. It was no slight error of Turenne to risk a combat against such an adversary without a disposition of his entire force, for at that moment La Ferté-Senneterre was still with the artillery before the barrier Saint-Denis. Reunited, the Queen's two generals might overwhelm Condé; separated,

La Ferté-Senneterre remained useless, and Turenne left alone might purchase his victory very dearly. The latter therefore required that La Ferté should hasten to join him by forced marches, and that the attack should not be commenced before he arrived. But the orders of the Court admitted of no delay, and the Duke de Bouillon himself advised an immediate attack, in order to avoid having the appearance of manœuvring with Condé. Hence the fatal combat of the 2nd of July, 1652, in which so many valiant officers, of whom the army was proud, perished uselessly.

Historians in relating the details of that deplorable day have dwelt upon the courage and talent displayed by Condé within that narrow arena, that small space of ground which extended from the barrier du Trône, by the main street of the Faubourg Saint-Antoine, in front of the Bastille. As usual, he had formed a picked squadron which he led on all points, himself leading the most desperate charges. He had posted himself in front of Turenne, disputing foot to foot with him the *Grande Rue Saint Antoine*, and during the intervals of relaxation of the enemy's attacks, he rode off towards Picpus to encourage Tavannes, who was repelling with his customary vigour every attack made by Saint-Mégrin, or to hold in check, on the side of the Seine and Charenton Navailles, one of Turenne's best lieutenants. It was in the *Grande Rue* where the rudest shocks were delivered. Turenne and Condé there rivalled each other in boldness and obstinacy, both charging at the head of their troops, both covered with blood, and unceasingly exposed to the fire of musketry. Turenne, far superior in numbers, was rapidly gaining ground, when Condé suddenly, sword in hand, at the head of his squadron of fifty brave gentlemen, forced him to fall back, and the affair remained undecided until Navailles, who had just received a reinforcement with artillery, overthrew all the barricades in his path, and in advancing, threatened to surround Condé. The latter, throwing himself quickly in that direction, saw on reaching the last barricade his two friends, Nemours and La Rochefoucauld, the one wounded in several places and unable to stand, the other blinded by a ball which had passed through his face just below the eyes, and both in immediate danger of being made prisoners. All exhausted as he was—for the fighting lasted from morning till evening,—Condé had still heart and energy to make a last charge for their rescue, and to place them in safety within the city. He felt the old flame of Rocroy and Nordlingen firing his blood, and he fought like the boldest of his dragoons. The citizens on the ramparts beheld with emotion the Prince, covered with blood and dust, enter a garden, throw off his casque and cuirass, and roll himself half-naked upon the grass to wipe off the sweat in which he was bathed. Meanwhile, La Ferté-Senneterre had come up. From that moment all gave way, and the Prince, feebly seconded by his disheartened soldiers, with the greatest difficulty reached the Place de la Bastille. There he found the gates of Paris shut. In vain did Beaufort urge the city militia to go to the assistance of that handful of brave men on the point of succumbing: wearied with three years of discord and manipulated by Mazarin, it no longer responded to the summons of its old chief. Splendidly dressed ladies waved signals to their champions and lovers below, and the streets became alive with the shouting of armed citizens, who desired to be let out to the aid of their defenders, and could not see with cold blood the slaughter of their friends. Thousands went to the Luxembourg to beseech Gaston to open the gates of the city for the reception of the wounded and the protection of the over-matched. Long trains of wounded and dying young men began to be carried in ; the groans and blood were horrible to hear and see ; and the women of all ranks and ages were frantic with sympathy and grief. De Retz and terror had so chilled the Duke d'Orleans into inaction that he would have let Condé perish, had not Mademoiselle de Montpensier, who was at that time smitten with Condé, wrung indignantly from her father, by dint of tears and entreaties, an order to open the gates to the outnumbered Prince.

Mazarin, from the heights of Charonne, where he had stationed himself with the young King, might well have thought that it was all over with his worst enemy; and, when startled to hear that Mademoiselle herself had even ordered the cannon of the Bastille to be fired upon the royal army, exclaimed, " With that cannon-shot she has slain her husband," making allusion to the ambition which the Princess d'Orleans always had to espouse the youthful Louis XIV. True, on that same day, Mademoiselle destroyed with her own hand her dearest hopes ; but that trait of generosity and greatness of soul has for ever honoured her memory, and shields it from many errors and much ridicule. After having solemnly pledged itself to Condé, it would have been the height of opprobrium for the House of Orleans to let Condé fall before their eyes : better to have perished with him, and at least saved its honour.

Mademoiselle has related in what condition she found Condé, when having placed herself at the window of a little dwelling near the Bastille, in order to see the troops pass as they entered the city, the Prince hurried for a moment from the gate to speak to her. He neither thought of himself, all covered with blood as he was, nor even of his cause, very nearly hopeless : he thought only of the friends he had lost. It did not occur to him that they were those who had embarked him in negotiations the results of which had proved so fatal : he thought only that they had died for him, and his anguish grew insupportable. " He was," says Mademoiselle, " in a most pitiable state ; he was not wounded himself, yet he was covered from head to foot with dust and blood, his hair all disordered, his face flushed with exertion, his cuirass battered with blows, and having lost the scabbard of his sword in the fight, he held the blade naked in his hand." As he entered, the memory of all those he had seen fall around him seemed to rush suddenly upon Condé, and casting himself upon a seat, he burst into tears. " Forgive me," said the great soldier, " I have lost all my friends —the gallant young hearts that loved me." " No, they are only wounded," said his cousin, " and many of them not dangerously ; they will recover and love you still." Condé sprang up at the good news, and rushed back into the fight. At the head of all his effective cavalry, he made one desperate, long-continued charge, and drove the enemy backward for a mile. In the meantime, the gates were opened wide, and, file after file, the weary soldiers marched into the city ; and dashing homeward after his brilliant assault, Condé and his squadron galloped in the last : but when the ponderous bars were once more drawn across the portals, it was felt that the combatants indeed were saved, but that the Fronde was destroyed.

CHAPTER IV.

THE DUKE DE NEMOURS SLAIN IN A DUEL BY HIS BROTHER-IN-LAW, BEAUFORT.

SOME few days after the fierce fight of the Faubourg Saint-Antoine, Condé had an interview with the Duke d'Orleans, " who embraced him with an air as gay as though he had failed him in nothing." * Condé uttered no word of reproach out of respect to his daughter. He did not behave exactly in the same way towards Madame de Châtillon. She had addressed a note to him begging him to visit her. She showed this effusion to Mademoiselle, saying, " He will at least see from that the uneasiness which is felt for him." But Condé's mind was disabused, and when he met her who had been his ruin, " he cast upon her, we are told, the most terrible glances conceivable, showing by the expression of his countenance how much he despised her." † Well would it have been if soon afterwards the grand-nephew of Henry IV. had not lent anew his ear to the song of the syren and resumed the slavery of her dishonouring fetters!

It is not to our purpose to retrace the melancholy scenes of which, after the combat of Saint Antoine, and during the remainder of the month of July, 1652, Paris was the theatre. It would be only to dwell upon the sad spectacle of the agony and supreme convulsions of a beaten

* Mademoiselle de Montpensier, tom. ii. p. 148.   † The same.

party, struggling in vain to escape its fate, and seeking safety in excesses which only served to precipitate its destruction.

Condé left no violent extreme untried to determine Paris to make further sacrifices for his cause. Dissatisfied with the deliberations of the Hôtel de Ville, he caused it to be carried by assault by the populace, who killed several of the *échevins*. The Fronde, however, was approaching its last agony. Divided amongst themselves by selfish interests, and outwearied with endless intrigues, the majority of the Frondeurs only awaited a fitting opportunity of treating with Mazarin. An amnesty soon made its appearance, and the Cardinal took the step of quitting France once more in order to facilitate a reconciliation. But Condé, on his side, was very little disposed thereto, for he had gone very far indeed to retrace his steps. Furious at having failed to reach the object which he had thought to attain, exasperated by the abandonment of his partisans, by the sarcasms of pamphleteers, he demanded securities and large indemnifications; and proposed such hard conditions that all accord with him became impossible. Thereupon he collected some troops around his standard, a tolerably large number of gentlemen, and rejoined the Duke de Lorraine, who was advancing upon Paris. Their united forces amounted to eighty squadrons and eight thousand infantry. Turenne had scarcely half that strength; but he manœuvred so skilfully round Paris, that they failed to get any advantage over him. Condé withdrew; and when the King, on his return to the Louvre, published a second amnesty (October, 1652), the Prince had crossed the frontier, after having taken several strongholds in his line of march. Shortly afterwards, he became generalissimo of the Spanish armies, whilst a decree of the parliament declared him guilty of high treason and a traitor to the State.

Previous to Condé's departure from Paris, intense indignation had been excited in every well-balanced mind by a shocking event—the Duke de Nemours having been slain by the hand of his brother-in-law, the Duke de Beaufort, in an abominable duel. From De Nemours the provocation had come, and all the wrong was on his part; but as the victim, he was deplored by all those who were ignorant of what had contributed to bring about the affair, and for some time the new governor of Paris (Beaufort) could not show himself in public.

In the Dukes de Nemours and La Rochefoucauld, Condé had lost his two pacific advisers. In vain had he offered to La Rochefoucauld the post of Nemours, the command under him, and thus to be the second authority in his army. La Rochefoucauld had excused himself on account of his wound, and Condé gave the vacant command to the Prince de Tarente. Henceforward, Madame de Châtillon quite alone was unable to counterbalance the counsels and influence of Madame de Longueville, and Condé plunged deeper than ever into the Spanish alliance and the war waged by that nation against France.

Whilst all these events were happening, Bordeaux had become the theatre of continued troubles. Madame de Longueville no longer agreed with her younger brother; the inhabitants of the city, who had only entered half-heartedly and been almost forced into rebellion, became impatient to extricate themselves from the constrained position in which they were held. As the sequel to negotiations which the city carried on with the Duke de Vendôme, who blockaded it, there was a general amnesty.

When Condé retired to the Netherlands, it was not long before it became known, to the national humiliation, that the best soldier of France, a prince of the blood and protector of the people, had followed the recent example of his conqueror, and sold his services to Spain. The young King made his triumphal entry into Paris, accompanied by his mother and Turenne. He convoked the Courts, and received them into favour, " provided they returned within the limits of their duties, and abstained from interfering with the government." Gaston was sent into honourable exile, to his castle in the beautiful town of Blois, and the Cardinal-Archbishop, the evil spirit of the Fronde, was received with apparent cordiality, and began to entertain hopes of supplanting his rival; but when he had fallen into disrepute with the citizens, he was quietly carried off to Vincennes, and left to meditate on his plots and schemings within the bars of his solitary apartment. The Parisians were now so changed from what they had been, that they received their old enemy, the Cardinal Mazarin, with demonstrations of delight, when he made his solemn entry into the repentant city with young Louis as an attendant at his side.

CHAPTER V.

THE TRIUMPH OF MAZARIN.

MAZARIN might well have claimed the right of accompanying to Paris, on the 21st October, 1652, Louis the Fourteenth and Anne of Austria, and to share the joy of their victory over the Fronde, for he was the true achiever of it. It was he who, by retiring so opportunely, by leaving the Fronde to itself, had allowed it to exhibit at its entire ease its fury and impotence; it was he who, from the depth of his exile, disquieted by the success of Châteauneuf, had collected troops, rallied round him experienced generals, raised the banner of the monarchy, and from one vantage ground to another had carried it forwards even to Paris. But by reappearing there prematurely, Mazarin might have risked the rekindling of animosities scarcely yet extinguished. It was his own advice he followed—to second the effect of the amnesty by a momentary absence, in order to leave no pretext to those who had so often promised to yield if he quitted the kingdom. Sure of the young King, surer still of his mother, leaving with them his instructions and approved advisers, Mazarin had disappeared, withdrawing at first to Bouillon, across the frontier; then, as by degrees the King's government became consolidated at Paris, he drew nearer and moved to Sedan; next, he went openly to join the royal army, taking with him powerful reinforcements, munitions, provisions, and money. Admirably commanded by

Turenne and La Ferté-Senneterre, it had forced the little army of Condé and the Duke de Lorraine to slowly beat a retreat in the direction of the Netherlands. Active, resolute, indefatigable, he did not hesitate to prolong the campaign beyond its ordinary limits, until the end of December, and even up to January, 1653. He had only quitted the army on beholding the enemy abandon French territory, and after having made the frontier of Champagne and Picardy secure from any chance of a return of offensive operations. It was then that he put his troops into winter quarters, and that he himself, heralded and sustained by these solid successes, had taken the road to Paris.

On the 3rd of February, 1653, he therein made a truly triumphal entry. The young King, accompanied by his brother the Duke d'Anjou, went out for more than a league to meet him, received him with the greatest apparent affection, took him into his carriage, and two hours afterwards they entered by the Porte Saint-Denis, in great pomp, amidst the joyous shouts of that same populace which, two years previously, had pursued him with imprecations. The Cardinal was thus enthusiastically conducted to the Louvre, where Anne of Austria awaited him.

He there beheld once more that courageous Queen, whom history, misled by the impostors of the Fronde, has too much misconceived, that stanch friend, an example among all queens, and almost among all women, of a constancy equal to either fortune; who, in the early days of 1643, had discerned the great abilities of Mazarin, and seen in him the only man capable of properly conducting the affairs of France; who, after having owed to him five long years of glory, had in 1648 and 1649 defended him against the aris-

tocracy, the parliament, and the people united; who later
had only consented to his retirement because he himself had
judged it necessary; who during his absence had alike resisted every species of seduction, every kind of menace, and
had never ceased to be governed by his counsels; who, at
Gien, learning the rout of her troops at Bleneau whilst at
her toilet, went on with it calmly, when everyone else spoke
of flight, rivalling Mazarin himself in courage and coolness.
On finding themselves once more together under the roof of
royalty after so many long and sorrowful separations, after
seeing each other so often on the very verge of ruin, they
might well be proud of their mutual constancy, which had
deserved and brought about the halo of prosperity surrounding that auspicious day, and together look forward for the
rest of their lives with the solid hope of sharing a glorious
repose.

Around the Queen, the Cardinal was welcomed by a
brilliant array of great nobles and fair ladies, formerly the
bitter enemies of Richelieu's successor, but who were there
assembled to compliment him upon his happy return.

Amongst those ladies foremost in their congratulations
was the Princess Palatine, with whom we have already made
some acquaintance—Anne de Gonzagua, one of the most
eminent personages of the seventeenth century. Of an admirable beauty, which served in some sort as a setting to an
intellect the most solid, she was as capable of taking part in
the deliberations of statesmen as in the assemblies of wits
or in gallant intrigues, seeking, it is true, her advantages, but
not by the betrayal of any one; who, without treason to
royalty, had given advice the most judicious to the Fronde,
and would have saved it, if the Fronde could have been
saved. As she had never ceased to keep up the best under-

standing with Mazarin, she could very well associate herself with his triumph.

She was there also, that other famous female politician, of a grade still higher, as beautiful and as gallant, of a less gracious, perhaps, but yet stronger disposition, more capable still of grand enterprises, and never suffering herself to be stayed by any danger or any scruple—the widow of the Constable de Luynes, Marie de Rohan, Duchess de Chevreuse, who formerly had lent a hand to every plot concocted against Mazarin, and in concert with the Palatine had proposed, as we have seen, the sole measure which could bring together all the Cardinal's enemies, and form a great aristocratical party strong enough to make head against royalty:—the marriage of Condé's son with a daughter of the Duke d'Orleans, and that of her own daughter with the Prince de Conti. This latter match having been broken off in a manner the most outrageous to her feelings, Madame de Chevreuse had separated from Condé with éclat; and, too experienced to ally herself with the sort of *tiers-parti* which Retz had proposed, but allowing herself to be gently and skilfully guided by the Marquis de Laignes, whom Mazarin with his usual adroitness had known how to win over, she had returned to the side of her early friend, Anne of Austria, and became resigned to the power of a man who at any rate knew his own mind, and whose robust ambition never wavered at the breath of vanity or the gust of momentary passion. The fame and honour that she might expect from the Fronde had been offered to her by Mazarin, and in return Madame de Chevreuse had brought to royalty the declared support of the three illustrious families, the Rohans, De Luynes, and the Lorraines. It was she who, ever puissant over the Duke de Lorraine, had negotiated a secret treaty between him and the

Cardinal, and who by turns had made him act in such contrary directions. Restored entirely to the Queen's favour, Madame de Chevreuse was at her side in the Louvre, to welcome warmly the return of the prosperous Cardinal.

After Madame de Chevreuse, Mazarin had had no adversaries more dangerous than the Vendômes and Bouillons. And yet on that memorable day of February 3rd, 1653, he could consider the heads of those two powerful families as the firmest supporters of his greatness.

Cæsar, Duke de Vendôme, natural son of Henry the Fourth, was much more formidable by his intelligence, his valour, and his craft than by his birth. There was nothing —even to the virtues of his wife, a reputed saint,—which was not put to the profit of his ambition. His daughter, the beautiful Mademoiselle de Vendôme, had married that brilliant Duke de Nemours, who had come to such a miserable end. His eldest son, the Duke de Mercœur, was a sagacious and estimable prince, and the Duke de Beaufort, his youngest, was the idol of the populace of Paris. It was Beaufort who, in 1643, urged by the two duchesses De Montbazon and De Chevreuse, had formed the design of assassinating Mazarin. The Duke de Vendôme had been suspected of being implicated in that affair; he had at least given shelter in his château at Anet to all the accomplices of his son ; and, forced to quit France to avoid the arrest with which he was threatened, he had wandered for several years through Italy and England, everywhere stirring up enemies against the Cardinal. The latter saw clearly that it was better to acquire a son of Henry the Fourth at a given price, than to prosecute him without the slightest advantage. After all, what did the Duke desire, and what were his demands when Mazarin became prime minister ? Either that the government of Brittany, which his father, Henry the Fourth, had destined for him, and that his father-in-law, Philibert Emmanuel of Lorraine, held ; or that the Admiralty, one of the highest posts in the state, should be given him. Mazarin had repulsed these pretensions in 1643, but looked upon them favourably in 1652 ; he therefore made the Duke High-Admiral, even conferred upon him the title of State Minister, with a seat at the council-board, after being assured that Vendôme, having secured that which he had always sought to attain, would serve him as firmly as he had formerly opposed him. He had an infallible pledge for his fidelity. The Duke's eldest son, the loyal and pious Duke de Mercœur, had married one of the Cardinal's nieces, the amiable and virtuous Laura Mancini, so that the house of Vendôme was interested in and inseparably united to Mazarin's fortunes. Therefore, on the 3rd of February, 1653, the High-Admiral Cæsar de Vendôme, engaged in pursuing the Spanish fleet in the sea of Gascony, entered the Gironde, and threatened the relics of the Fronde at Bordeaux. On his part, the Duke de Mercœur, named governor of Provence, watched over that important province for the King and Mazarin, whilst the Duke de Beaufort, who earlier had been desirous of laying violent hands on the Cardinal, and who yet quite recently had shown himself as his implacable enemy, covered and protected by the services of his father and brother, retired to Anet, without being the least in the world disquieted ; satisfied with beholding Madame de Montbazon satisfied because plenty of money had been given her, and awaited quietly the moment at which he should succeed his father in the command of the fleet, and shed his blood in the service of his King.

The Bouillons were of little less importance than the

Vendômes.   The Duke was a politician and a soldier of the
first class, capable of conducting a government or leading an
army, and who had only one sentiment or thought in heart
and head—the aggrandisement of his house.   Already sovereign prince of Sedan, urged by his wife, still more ambitious than himself, he had in 1641, in the hope of securing fresh territorial acquisitions, treated with Spain, taken
part in the revolt of the Count de Soissons, and won the
battle of La Marfée against the royal army.   In 1642, he
had entered into the conspiracy of the Duke d' Orleans and
Cinq Mars, and, arrested, thrown into chains at Pierre-
Encise, he had only saved his head from the scaffold by
abandoning his principality.   Ever since, he had not ceased
to agitate for the recovery of that which by treason he had
lost.   He had again demanded Sedan from Mazarin in 1643,
and not being able to obtain it at the hands of that great
servant of the Crown, that, in order to satisfy a private
interest, France should renounce one of its best strongholds on the frontier of the Netherlands, he had ranked
himself among the Cardinal's enemies, and forced at first
to flee, like the Duke de Vendôme, had scarcely returned
to France ere he embraced with ardour the Fronde, though
without the slightest conviction, be it understood, and in the
sole hope of easily obtaining from it what he could not
snatch from royalty.   He had enlisted with him in the
Fronde his brother Turenne, of whom he disposed absolutely, and who was equally ambitious, and equally covetous
of the grandeur of their family, but after his own fashion,
and the mould of his frigid, reflective, and profoundly dissembling character.   At the peace of Ruel, in 1649, the Duke
de Bouillon had demanded "his re-establishment in Sedan, or
if the Queen preferred to reimburse him for it at an estimated

price, with the possessions promised and due to his house; for himself, the government of Auvergne; for his brother that of Haute and Basse Alsace, with that of Philipsbourg and the command of all the armies of Germany." Mazarin had then committed the error of not satisfying this ambitious and powerful house; hence, in 1650, the conduct of the Duke in Guienne and that of Turenne at Stenay and in Flanders. In 1651, the Queen treated seriously with the Duke, and on his return Mazarin succeeded in entirely gaining him over. Not desiring at any price to restore Sedan to him, he granted the equivalent demanded—a great domain at Château-Thierry, much richer than that of Sedan, and, without effective sovereignty, that title of *Prince*, so dear to the vanity of the Bouillons, which the head of the family could not only transmit to his children, but which could descend also to his brother Turenne. The Duke de Bouillon having once taken the part of abandoning Condé, in spite of all his engagements, and of serving royalty, did it with the same energy which he had displayed at Paris and Bordeaux. He never afterwards forsook Mazarin, but assisted him with his advice, and suffered even more than once in person, by acting with his customary vigour, and the obstinate ardour of his country and race. It was he who, on the night of the battle of Bleneau, brought reinforcements to Turenne, and enabled him to stop Condé. It was he, again, who, on the 2nd of July, 1652, to let Mazarin see that he had gained him for good and all, joined with the Cardinal in pressing Turenne, against all the rules of war, not to wait the coming up of the troops of La Ferte-Senneterre. A truthful witness, and one of the principal actors in that sanguinary drama, Navailles, even affirms that the Duke de Bouillon took part in the affair, and

that he was at the attack in which Saint-Megrin perished. If
Bouillon had lived, with his immeasurable ambition and his
capacity equalling his ambition, would he have been contented with the second rank, and would he always have remained the devoted servant of the Cardinal ?

None can say : for the Duke de Bouillon was cut short in
his ambitious career; he died on the 9th of August, 1652,.
without having enjoyed those possessions and those honours
which he had so greatly coveted ; but ere closing his eyes he
saw them pass to his children. Turenne, carefully conciliated
and caressed, was made, on his brother's death, governor of
Auvergne, and the viscounty of Turenne erected into a prin-
cipalty. Very shortly afterwards he also received the post
of minister of state. Mazarin went even still further : desirous of heaping up benefits upon the illustrious soldier whose
honesty and ambition he had so long known, desirous at the
same time to attach in his person all the Protestant party by
decisive acts, which would show in a conspicuous manner
that whosoever should serve him well would be faithfully re-
compensed, without distinction of religion, the skilful and
politic Cardinal made the Duke de la Force, a Protestant and
the father-in-law of Turenne, Marshal of France, as his father
had been. Thus, on the 3rd of February, 1653, Turenne
was likewise at the Louvre at Mazarin's side, as the representative of all his family, and already occupied with preparation for the campaign that was about to open in the spring
in the Netherlands, and where he was to take command of
the French army.

But if Mazarin had taken care to win over successively
those chiefs of the Importants and the Frondeurs in whom
his experienced eye had recognised as sincerely disposed to
a loyal submission, he had this time taken care not to allow

himself to be betrayed by false appearances, and did not fail
to strike at, or at least banish from Paris, those whom he
despaired of acquiring. He had lent himself with good
grace to the reconciliation sought by the Duke d'Orleans;
as it was not his wish to give to France and Europe the appearance of ill-treating the King's uncle, and constrain him
perhaps once more to go in search of a foreign asylum;
but by conciliating him in the most suitable way, he had
taken surety of him, and being convinced that too much
lenity would only embolden him to mix himself up in
fresh intrigues, he did not permit him to remain in Paris,
when the King returned thither, for fear lest in his palace of
the Luxembourg, surrounded by perfidious advisers, whilst
lavishing great marks of deference upon the Queen and the
young King, he might cherish and rekindle on occasion the
hopes of the Fronde. Therefore, it was arranged that the
Duke d'Orleans should quit Paris on the day previous to
that of the King's entry, and consequently he retired at first
to Limours, then to Blois, the ordinary refuge of his treason
and faint-heartedness, where, in nowise persecuted, but
watched and kept within bounds, he passed amidst general
indifference the remainder of his contemptible career. Mademoiselle remained also for some time in disgrace at St.
Fargeau, and consoled herself by degrees for the ruin of her
divers pretensions with her large fortune and small court.
The Cardinal de Retz putting a good face upon a losing
game, and especially desirous of receiving from the King's
own hand the cardinal's hat granted him by the Pope, in
order to claim the right of wearing the dress and of enjoying
the honours and privileges attached to that high dignity, had
been among the first to meet the King at Compiègne at the
head of the clergy of Paris, and had addressed him in a bold

and artful speech, in the style of that of Cæsar in the affair
of Cataline, skilfully covering the defeat of his party, recom-
mending the policy of moderation, referring more than once
to the conduct of Henry the Great towards the Leaguers,
and through fear lest it should not be sufficiently understood
that he was speaking about himself, citing the pacific words
of Henry to his great uncle, the Cardinal de Gondi. In that
oration he had also insinuated some high compliments to the
Queen, as though he had resumed his former hopes. The
next day, at mass, the King placed the red hat upon his
head, and henceforward De Retz assumed and wore the dress
of cardinal. After the King's return, he had carried his
audacity so far as to present himself at the Louvre to
pay, as a faithful subject, his homage to their Majesties.
On the 1st of December, he preached with great effect at
Notre Dame, and recommenced his old course of life of
1648, making pious sermons in the intervals of his gallant
rendezvous, devoting the morning to preaching at church,
the evening to *bonnes fortunes,* and reknitting in the dark
the meshes of his old intrigues. But Mazarin knew him
thoroughly: he was persuaded that De Retz was incapable of
confining himself to his ecclesiastical functions, incompatible
as they were with his dissipated and licentious habits, with
his restless and factious disposition, and so under his
minister's advice on some slight suspicion arising, the King
had him arrested even in the very Louvre, on the 19th of
December, 1652, and conducted to the donjon of Vincennes.

Mazarin was too cautious to treat La Rochefoucauld after
the same fashion. He knew marvellously well that, separated from Condé and Madame de Longueville, who constituted all his importance, La Rochefoucauld was no longer to

be dreaded, and that he was not of a humour to make himself the champion and martyr of a vanquished party. The serious wound which he had received in the combat of Saint Antoine turned him, so to speak, to advantage. Struck by a ball which had traversed both cheeks and temporarily deprived him of sight, it was impossible for him to continue in active service and to follow the army. He did not therefore play false to Condé in not accepting the command of such troops as remained to the Fronde—a command which, on his retirement, was offered to the Prince de Tarent. It was absolutely essential that he should be speedily cured of his wound; and that real motive covering his weariness and long-felt disgust, he did not, like Persan, Bouteville, and Vauban, join the Prince in Flanders. On the other hand, he had not objected to the amnesty, and therefore could not be included in the royal declaration issued on the 13th of November against Condé, Conti, Madame de Longueville, and their chief adherents. But Mazarin took good care not to pursue him, and La Rochefoucauld, after allowing the first outburst of the storm to pass over, retired to his estates to bury himself in obscurity for a few years, and to taste that repose of which he had so great need. Then he quitted his retreat and reappeared at Paris. It must have been necessary for him to go very far in conciliation to be received again into favour. He succeeded in it, however, by saving appearances, to use a modern phrase, and in skilfully managing the transition. He made his peace with the politic and gracious Cardinal, rode in his carriage, saying with as much reason as wit, "Everything happens in France!" He managed to get his son into intimacy with the young King, and, wonderful to relate, he obtained from Mazarin, in indemnification for the losses he had experienced in carrying on war against him, a thumping pension of eight thousand livres.

If space permitted us thus to run over successively the list of all the great nobles who had previously had a hand in the Fronde, it would be easy to show that on the 3rd of February, 1653, the most ardent and the most illustrious of those we have cited, and many others, such as the Duke d'Elbeuf and Marshal Houdancourt, both generals of the Fronde at Paris in 1648 and 1649, the Duke de Guise, so strongly bound to Condé, almost all, in short, were ranged round Mazarin, and fought with him and for him, and that for one sole but very sufficient reason—which was that the clever Cardinal knew how to make them understand wherein lay their true interests.

Self-interest, self-interest, such was, with very few exceptions, the unique mainspring of the aristocracy in the Fronde, and La Rochefoucauld has only erected into a maxim and even generalised into excess the principle which he had seen practised everywhere around him.

It may thus be judged whether, as some writers have asserted without the slightest knowledge of the facts, the Fronde was a great and generous cause which failed of obtaining success. On the contrary, it was simply a powerful coalition of individual interests, and if considered under the aspect of an abortive anticipation of the French revolution, and some general design sought for therein in one way or another, it would be rather that of stifling in its cradle the principles of that revolution.

Is it true that the Fronde, as has been asserted, was a counterpart, a sort of miserable imitation, of the revolution which was then convulsing England? Not the least in the world. That other error, still stranger than the preceding, rests upon a false and deceitful analogy—that common shoal of historical considerations and comparisons. At bottom, the earlier part of the English revolution was almost entirely of a religious character, whilst in the Fronde the religious element did not intervene at all, thanks to the enlightened protection enjoyed by the Protestants. It seemed, indeed, like a demoniacal caricature of our British troubles at that moment. No sternness, no reality ; love-letters and witty verses supplying the place of the Biblical language and awful earnestness of the words and deeds of the Covenanters and Independents ; the gentlemen of France utterly debased and frivolised ; religion ridiculed ; nothing left of the old landmarks ; and no Cromwell possible. All sense of honour disappears when conduct is regulated by the shifting motives of party politics. The dissensions of the Fronde accordingly produced no champion to whom either side could look with unmingled respect. The great Condé and the famous Turenne showed military talent of the highest order, but a want of principle and a flighty frivolity of character counterbalanced all their virtues. The scenes of those five or six years are like a series of dissolving views, or the changing combinations of a kaleidoscope ; Condé and Turenne always on opposite sides—for each changed his party as often as the other ; battles prepared for by masquerades and theatricals, and celebrated on both sides with epigrams and songs ; the wildest excesses of debauchery and vice practised by both sexes and all ranks in the State ; archbishops fighting like gladiators, and intriguing like the vulgarest conspirators ; princes imprisoned with a jest, and executions attended with cheers and laughter ; the highest in the land caballing, cheating, and lying, but keeping a firm grasp of power:—no country was ever so split into faction, or so denuded of great men.

But, while all these elements of confusion were heaving and tumbling in what seemed an inextricable chaos, the monarchical principle, strange to say, still burned brightly in the hearts of all the French. Even in their fights and quarrelings there was a deep reverence entertained for the ideal of the throne. The King's name was a tower of strength; and when the nation, in the course of the miserable years from 1610 to 1661, saw the extinction of nobility, religion, law, and almost of civilised society, it caught the first sound that told it it still had a King, as an echo from the past assuring it of its future. It forgot Louis the Thirteenth, the Regency, and the Fronde, and only remembered that its monarch was the grandson of Henry the Fourth, when it witnessed in his reign the culmination of the French monarchy, and the splendid intellectual development with which it was simultaneous.

And that brilliant day of Mazarin's triumph was shadowed by no eclipse. It was not one of those lucky freaks of fate often followed by long disgrace: no, that Minister's triumph rested on solid foundations. Not only he saw at his feet, in the Louvre, all his former enemies vanquished, but not one of them able to rise again in enmity, for all their strength was exhausted. The wearied citizens wanted repose, and placed all their hopes in royalty. The parliaments, ashamed of having allowed their ancient loyalty to be surprised by the deceitful caresses of the discontented nobles, returned voluntarily within the prudent limits of their institution, satisfied with having seen the government recognise all their legitimate complaints, and bind itself to respect their just and necessary independence. The aristocracy thought itself still more fortunate at having thus been extricated from this last defeat. It left, it is true, upon the field of battle some few of its feudal pretensions, but in exchange, titles, honours, and wealth were lavished upon it, and its vanity could at any rate console its ambition. The good fortune of Mazarin opened the eyes of everyone to his merit. No one could refrain from applauding his firmness and his capacity. Had he proved unsuccessful, he would only have been looked upon as a second Concini; victorious, he was another Richelieu to whom it was necessary to succumb, but who might be served without loss of honour, because, after having shown that he was as firm in his principle of government as his imperious predecessor, he did not play the tyrant; and, far from making the weight of his power felt, he forced himself rather to disguise it under flattering words, did not show the least resentment for former injuries, extended a hand to everyone who came to him, listened to every complaint that had anything legitimate in it, entertained every pretension that was at all reasonable, and seemed disposed to base his government upon skilful concessions and not upon useless rigour. His star was believed in, his moderation inspired confidence, and people grew eager to participate in his triumph. Already at Vendôme, a grandson of Henry the Great had espoused one of his nieces; the proudest among the French nobility were soon about to contend for the hands of the others; and the man whom the Fronde had so persecuted was about to place his family upon the steps of the throne. The solemn reception which the King and Queen gave Mazarin at the Louvre on the 3rd February, 1653, was not therefore an idle pageant or empty ceremony. That same day, Mazarin could understand that a new era had arisen for him, more brilliant and more secure than that of 1643, after the defeat of the *Importants*, and that that sterile and sanguinary halt upon the road of reform and the civilising march of monarchy known in history under the name of the Fronde was at last and for ever terminated.

BOOK VI.

CLOSING SCENES.

CHAPTER I.

HAVING rapidly summarised the fate and fortunes of the leading male actors who figured in the Fronde, we will now glance briefly at the closing scenes in the careers of the fair politicians whom we have seen playing such brilliant and prominent parts in that curious tragi-comedy.

To high-born French women—princesses and duchesses—the revolt of the Fronde especially belonged. They were at once its main-springs, its chief instruments, its most interested agents ; and among them Madame de Longueville, who enacted the most conspicuous part, was by its events the most ill-treated of all.

We have seen her the heroine—or, perhaps the adventuress—of the civil war, rushing into dangers and mixing herself up in intrigues of every kind, in order to serve the interests of another. She was not a consummate politician like the Palatine, for she had no real business tact. Her true character and the unity of her life should be sought where they were really shown—in her devotion to him whom she loved. It is there—in that devotion wholly and always the same, at once consistent, yet absurd, and very touching even in its downright follies.

All her eccentric movements were attributable to the restless and fickle spirit of La Rochefoucauld. Solely occupied with his own interests, it was he who drew her into the vortex of party politics and civil war, with a view to his own self-aggrandisement. It was for love of him that she sacrificed domestic peace, repose, and reputation.

At Bordeaux Madame de Longueville had at first enjoyed the same popularity as that which she had acquired in Paris at the commencement of the first Fronde. Upon that section of the second Fronde which had its head-quarters in the South, the Duchess, after its chief, the Prince de Conti, was the most likely person to exercise a decisive influence alike by the clearness of her intellect, the firmness of her character, and the great confidence with which she had inspired the entire party. In 1650 she had covered herself with glory at Stenay, and the eyes of not only France, but the whole of Europe, were fixed upon her. She was unable to play the same part at Bordeaux. Invested at Stenay with supreme authority, she had been compelled, as it were, to display all the intelligence and energy she possessed: at Bordeaux she was only an adviser indifferently well listened to. And moreover, in 1650, her frame of mind was widely different. With a sincere attachment to the interests of her party and her house, another and more intimate sentiment animated and sustained her: she loved and was beloved. A reciprocal devotedness justified in some measure that passion which had already passed through three long and trying years, and found its aliment and its strength in common sacrifices. In fact, if Madame de Longueville had braved in Normandy all kinds of danger and even death to cross the sea in order to reach the Netherlands and unfurl at Stenay the banner of the Princes, La Rochefoucauld, too, it must be remembered, had been continually in arms. That interval was the golden era of their lives. They suffered and combated for each other. They had the same cause, the same faith, the same hopes. Their hearts were never more united than during that cruel year when, separated by civil war, they could scarcely, from the furthest extremities of France, address each other, amid risks innumerable, in a few apparently insignificant lines, but through which, nevertheless, there breathed a tenderness and confidence proof against everything. Now all was changed. As we have said, La Rochefoucauld had grown wearied of the Fronde, into which he had hopefully flung himself in 1648. In 1651 he became desirous of reconciling himself with the Court, and making a pact which would have infallibly separated them, since M. de Longueville, irritated with all that had at length reached his ears, had summoned his wife in a menacing tone to join him in Normandy. It was she who then, in her turn, was compelled to draw over La Rochefoucauld. He continued to follow in her footsteps through the sentiment of devotedness that still lingered in his heart, but without conviction, and with a lukewarmness which deeply wounded Condé's high-souled sister. She felt that she was no longer loved commensurately with the heroic and tender ideal of which she had dreamed, and that a struggle with fortune, too long continued, had cast down his inconstant and wavering spirit. Hence also arose that momentary error which we have neither disguised nor excused. Love enfeebled and discouraged had delivered her up once more to her natural coquetry, and coquetry stimulated by politics had made her brave the semblance of an infidelity towards La Rochefoucauld and herself. Without being hurried away in the slightest degree by the senses or the heart, in her endeavour to carry off the Duke de Nemours from Madame de Châtillon and the peace party, and engage him more deeply in that of the war and Condé, she had slightly compromised herself; and La Rochefoucauld, influenced by an implacable resentment, instead of breaking with her openly, had, at Paris, entered into a shameful league with Madame de Châtillon and his pretended rival, the Duke de Nemours, in order that they might rob the poor Duchess of her last consolation, the esteem and affection of Condé. Left in Guienne, without any great or engrossing occupation, with a vacant mind, discontented both with others and herself, Madame de Longueville was no longer the brilliant Bellona of Stenay, but her pride and dignity, which she could not lose, never failed to sustain her. She therefore resolved to remain even unto the end faithful to that brother whose heart was sought to be steeled against her by the whispers of calumny: to remain in Bordeaux as long as possible, without recoiling from any means which necessity might prescribe. Not for a single day, not for an hour, did she dream of separating her fate from that of Condé, and of bending the knee before his victorious enemies.

At length, however, it was her inevitable fate to yield to the star of Mazarin and Louis XIV., who having obtained the mastery over the South as elsewhere, she was compelled to quit the factious city, and repair, by command of the Court, to Montreuil-Bellay, a domain belonging to her husband in Anjou. Shortly afterwards she obtained permission to go to Moulins, where her aunt, the inconsolable widow De Montmorency, was superior of the convent (*Filles de Sainte-Marie*). From that visit to Moulins may be dated the conversion of the beautiful and adventurous princess. On emerging from such a chaos of turmoil and commotion, in that calm and holy retreat, her thoughts reverted to the pure and innocent period of her youth, to the brilliant and tumultuous past, to the sorrowful and disenchanted present.

Embroiled with the Court and her brothers, abandoned by La Rochefoucauld, in the decline of her beauty, upon the eve of maturity, she saw in Heaven alone a refuge against others and herself. But the Divine grace had to be awaited as well as prayed for, the prickings of conscience were succeeded by relapses—the ties to be broken were still so strong! At length, one day when engaged in reading, "a veil, as it were, was drawn from before the eyes of my mind," she wrote, in that somewhat hyperbolical style of which she was fond; "all the charms of truth, concentrated upon one sole object, presented themselves before me. Faith, which had remained dead and buried beneath my passions, became renewed. I felt like a person who, after a long sleep in which he has dreamed of being great, happy, esteemed, and honoured by everybody, awakens all on a sudden to find himself loaded with chains, pierced with wounds, weighed down with heaviness, and pent up in some dark prison." To that conviction she remained faithful until death, and expiated her six years of deviation by a penitence which lasted for five-and-twenty, and continued ever on the increase.

The first act of the Duchess, after her conversion, was to implore pardon of her husband. M. de Longueville behaved generously, and went to meet her at Moulins, and took her back with him to Rouen with every mark of delicacy and distinction. Reverting to the aspirations of her youth, Madame de Longueville placed herself in active communication with the good Carmelites, whom she had never entirely forgotten. She was constantly writing to Mademoiselle du Vigean, the *sous-prieure*, for guidance in her new way of life; for she had need of spiritual advice, and cried out for help, and help came through the good offices of the Marquise de

Sablé, who had herself withdrawn from the world to Port-Royal, and supplied the want felt by her illustrious friend by placing her in the hands of one of the great spiritual guides of that day, M. Singlin. Between the ghostly adviser and the fair penitent there ensued frequent conversations curiously flavoured with a spice of romance. Persecution had already attacked Port-Royal, and M. Singlin, in order not to be recognised, went to the Hôtel de Longueville disguised as a doctor, his features being concealed by an ample wig. M. Singlin strove to fix limits to the ardour by which Madame de Longueville was carried away, he counselled her to remain in the outer world, to which her husband and children bound her, and in which her salvation, he said, might be as surely accomplished by exacting more vigilance than it would be found necessary to exercise in the retirement of the cloister.

Madame de Longueville's piety had been generally subordinated to the vicissitudes of a very agitated existence. Her primitive tendency to devotion was rekindled on every occasion that she experienced a trouble, a disenchantment, or any failure of courage. In 1651, when she had been somewhat compromised by the homage of the Duke de Nemours, she had retired to the Carmelite convent at Bourges; then towards the end of her sojourn in Guienne she had sought refuge among the Benedictines at Bordeaux. But all these gleams of repentance vanished so soon as some caprice of fortune came to reawaken, by the hope of fresh success, her natural inclination for political intrigue and pleasure. On accompanying her husband to Normandy she appeared wholly resolved not to allow herself to be engrossed by anything save her eternal welfare. However, it appears that her desire to abstain henceforward from all political intrigue was looked upon incredulously for several years; since, in 1659, at the time of the Treaty of the Pyrenees being signed, Mazarin, replying to Don Louis de Haro, who required that the French Minister should restore Condé "to all his birthrights," still placed, as we have noticed, Madame de Longueville among the feminine trio, who, said he, "would be capable of governing or of overturning three great kingdoms." Yet Mazarin yielded, and Condé returned to France.

The long and rigid penitence which she imposed upon herself, and which Madame de Motteville characterised by the expressive term—"very august," restored to her somewhat of that importance which she was desirous of renouncing through humility. But the world is ever distrustful on the score of a repentance which has some tinge of ostentation about it. One historian remarks that "the Duchess de Longueville being unable to dispense with intrigues, after she had renounced those of love and politics, found sufficient to satisfy her in devotion." This sentence, read aright, would mean that the schisms of Catholicism gave her an opportunity of playing a considerable part in taking under her protection the persecuted party of the Jansenists. Madame de Longueville, on whom was bestowed the designation of "Mother of the Church," and who in that quality recovered some reputation at the Court of France, and acquired a very great one at the Court of Rome, rendered an eminent service to the Jansenists by obtaining for them from the Pope, in 1668, that theological transaction which was called "The Peace of Clement the Ninth." It would, however, be unjust to tax her with hypocrisy. All that was extreme in the pious practices to which she devoted herself

must be attributed to her exalted nature, which mingled
passion with every sentiment of her soul.

When the Duke de Longueville died in 1663, the Duchess
availed herself of the state of independence in which her
widowhood placed her to give herself up wholly to exercises
of piety and penitence, and the education and care of her
children. The latter occupation caused her much grief—
the Count de Dunois, by his bad conduct and imbecility, and
the Count de Saint Paul himself, the son so dearly beloved,
by his precocious debaucheries and fiery impatience of character. Then, as by degrees they had less need of her care,
she devoted herself deeper and deeper to expiation, lavishing
her fortune to repair in the provinces ruined by civil war the
evils she had helped to inflict, weeping and humbling herself
in her efforts to subdue that pride which was the characteristic of her race, receiving outrages and insults uncom-
plainingly, accepting them as the just chastisement of her
sins, and forgiving those who dealt her the most cruel
wounds. And so, in austerities and self-mortification she
ended her days, sharing them between the Carmelites, in
whose convent she had an apartment, and Port-Royal des
Champs, where she had built a wing—having a preference
for Port-Royal. She was always naturally disposed to
favour the rebellious, and these rebels, it must be remembered, were the persecuted for conscience' sake. Madame de
Longueville's protection was extended to the principal Jansenists, whom she sheltered in her chateau, and her influence
at length brought about that peace in the Church, which, so
long as she lived, gave calm and security to the sacred community. Notwithstanding her predilection for Port-Royal,
she continued to inhabit her hôtel, which she did not quit
until after the death of the Count de Saint-Paul (1672),

killed so unfortunately by the side of the Great Condé at the passage of the Rhine.

That blow was the last of Madame de Longueville's earthly troubles—it overwhelmed her. Madame de Sevigné has depicted in a few touching sentences the scene which was witnessed when the fatal tidings reached the wretched mother : " Mademoiselle des Vertus returned two days since to Port-Royal, where she is constantly staying. They sent M. Arnauld to fetch her, that she might break the terrible news. Mademoiselle des Vertus had only to show herself; her hurried return was the certain signal that something sad had happened. In fact, as soon as she appeared, she was greeted with : ' Ah ! mademoiselle, how is my brother ? ' Her thoughts dare not venture further question. ' Madame, his wound is going on favourably.' ' There has been a battle ! and my son ? ' No answer. ' Ah ! mademoiselle, my son, my dear boy, answer me, is he dead ? ' ' Madame, I cannot find words to reply to you.' ' Ah ! my dear son ! did he die upon the spot ? Was not one single moment given him ? Ah ! *Mon Dieu !* what a sacrifice !' And thereupon she sank down in bed, and of all that the most poignant anguish could exhibit in convulsions and swooning, and in dead silence and stifled groans, by bitter tears and appeals to Heaven, and by tender and pitiful plaints, she went through them all. She sees certain persons, she takes broths, because it is the will of God ; but she gets no rest ; and her health, already very bad, is visibly shaken. For myself, I wish she may die, not believing that she can survive such a loss." Some few days afterwards Madame de Sevigné. writes : " There exists in the world one man not less touched by this blow : it has occurred to me that if they had both met each other in the first burst of grief and no one else had been present, all other feelings would have given place to tears and moans re-echoed from the depths of both their hearts."

With this young Duke de Longueville disappeared the last witness to bygone errors. The last link was broken, and, from that day, Madame de Longueville belonged no more to this world. She died on the 15th April, 1679, at the Carmelites, where her remains were interred ; her heart being taken to Port-Royal. A year afterwards, in the same convent of Carmelites, the Bishop of Autun, Roquette, whom Molière had in view when drawing the character of Tartuffe, pronounced her funeral oration. Madame de Sevigné, who was present at the ceremony, says of the orator : " It was not a *Tartuffe*, it was not a *Pantaloon :* it was a prelate of distinction, preaching with dignity, and going over the entire life of that Princess with an incredible address ; passing by all the delicate passages, mentioning, or leaving unmentioned, all the points that he ought to speak or be silent upon. His text was " Fallax pulchritudo, mulier timens Deum laudabitur." Assuredly many delicate points must have presented themselves in the life of a princess who had been a politician and a Frondeuse, a gallant woman, and a Jansenist. Yet Father Talon, a Jesuit, who was present at her death, was fond of repeating on fitting occasions : " Jansenist as much as you will, she died the death of a saint."

There were three well-defined periods in the agitated life of the Duchess de Longueville—and happily the end was conformable to the beginning, to neutralise, as it were, the censurable middle part. But admitting such condonation, does not that same *mezza camin* constitute the seduction which that brilliant period exercises over almost every writer who seeks to portray it, over those even who indulge in ecstacies on the score of her penitence ? So the prestige of beauty and the charms of mind traverse centuries to win unceasingly posthumous admiration ! These are the qualities which give a more undying interest to the career of Madame de Longueville even than the grandeur of her soul; for that is an incontestable feature which all must recognise, whether partisans or adversaries :—in spite of her errors and deviations, she certainly possessed greatness of soul. If a terse judgment then were summed up of her character, it might be said without flattery that, take her all in all, she was not unworthy of being the sister of the great Condé.

With the opinions of such astute statesmen as Cardinal Mazarin and Don Louis de Haro upon the mischievous tendencies of political women, it may be well, in the instance of Madame de Longueville to couple the sentiments of an acute and highly intellectual writer of our own day, who showed herself a subtle analyst of character. Mrs. Jameson, discoursing upon the characteristics of Shakespere's women (in the form of a dialogue between Alda and Medon) calls them " affectionate, thinking beings, and moral agents; and then witty, as if by accident, or as the Duchess de Chaulnes said of herself ' Par la grace de Dieu.'

" Or," retorts *Medon*, the male interlocutor, " politicians to vary the excitement ! How I hate political women !

" *Alda.* Why do you hate them ?

" *Medon.* Because they are mischievous.

" *Alda.* But why are they mischievous ?

" *Medon.* Why?—why are they mischievous ? Nay, ask them, or ask the father of all mischief, who has not a more efficient instrument to further his designs in this world than a woman run mad with politics. The number of political, intriguing women of this time, whose boudoirs and drawing-rooms are the *foyers* of party spirit, is another trait of resemblance between the state of society now and that which existed at Paris before the Revolution."

In another place, however, the same judicious and usually discriminating writer is betrayed into giving — more from conjecture, it would seem, than close acquaintance with the facts of her life—an historically false and singularly unjust estimate of Madame de Longueville's character.

"*Alda.* Women are illustrious in history, not from what they have been in themselves, but generally in proportion to the mischief they have done or caused. * * * Of those which have been handed down to us by many different authorities under different aspects, we cannot judge without prejudice ; in others there occur certain chasms which it is difficult to supply ; and hence inconsistencies we have no means of reconciling, though doubtless they might be reconciled if we knew the whole, instead of a part.

"*Medon.* But instance—instance !

"*Alda.* Do you remember that Duchess de Longueville, whose beautiful picture we were looking at yesterday ?—the heroine of the Fronde ?—think of that woman—bold, intriguing, profligate, vain, ambitious, factious !—who made rebels with a smile ; or if that were not enough, the lady was not scrupulous,—apparently without principle as without shame, nothing was *too* much ! And then think of the same woman protecting the virtuous philosopher Arnauld,[*] when he was denounced and condemned, and from motives which her worst enemies could not malign, secreting him in her house, unknown even to her servants—preparing his food herself, watching for his safety, and at length saving

* The Jansenist.

him. Her tenderness, her patience, her discretion, her disinterested benevolence not only defied danger (that were
little to a woman of her temper), but endured a lengthened
trial, all the ennui caused by the necessity of keeping her
house, continued self-control, and the thousand small daily
sacrifices which, to a vain, dissipated, proud, impatient
woman, must have been hard to bear. Now, if Shakespere
had drawn the character of the Duchess de Longueville, he
would have shown us the same individual woman in both
situations :—for the same being, with the same faculties and
passions and powers, it surely was : whereas in history, we
see in one case a fury of discord, a woman without modesty
or pity ; and in the other an angel of benevolence, and a
worshipper of goodness ; and nothing to connect the two
extremes in our fancy.

"*Medon.* But these are contradictions which we meet
on every page of history, which make us giddy with doubt
or sick with belief; and are the proper objects of inquiry for
the moralist and the philosopher."

With a true eye for the refined and the beautiful, and that
honestly sympathetic nature without which it is impossible
to discriminate between what is noble and what is mediocre,
still Mrs. Jameson, in the above reflections upon the character of Madame de Longueville, was obviously led to draw
hasty and erroneous conclusions either from a superficial
glance at detached passages in the Duchess's extraordinary
career with regard to the dates of which she is widely in
error, or others during which her conduct and actions were
but too easily susceptible of misrepresention and distortion
at the hands of partisan writers. Such unjust judgment
would most probably be formed by accepting anecdotes, like

those contained in Tallemant's scandalous chronicle or Bussy Rabutin's "Letters," as historic truths; or by placing implicit faith in every statement made by De Retz or La Rochefoucauld, given as both were to exaggeration and over-colouring, and whose object, moreover, was not so much to tell the truth as always to exalt themselves, sometimes by its suppression, at others by downright falsification.

Without attempting to extenuate the errors of Madame de Longueville, moral or political, it has been the author's endeavour to reconcile the apparent contradictions in her character, imputed in the passage above cited, by assigning the different incidents, which have doubtless caused an intelligent woman to falter in her judgment, to their proper place in the order of time. For as, during the Olympian contests, swift-footed Spartan boys, to typify the transmission of Truth, ran with a lighted torch, and, as each fell breathless, another took up the flambeau and bore it on, bright and rapid, to the goal, so should the light of History be passed steadily and carefully from hand to hand, and its sacred flame—the Truth —be kept ever burning clearly onward in the course of time.

CHAPTER II.

THE DUCHESS DE CHEVREUSE.

SIDE by side with the two great statesmen, Richelieu and Mazarin, the clever, daring, vivacious, charming Marie de Rohan occupied a more elevated position, and certainly played a more extended part, than any other of the political women who were her contemporaries during the stirring times of the first half of the seventeenth century.

Seductive, with irresistible fascination of manner, singular grace and animation; of pregnant wit, though quite uneducated; devoted to gallantry, and too high-spirited to heed propriety; obeying no control save that of honour; despising, for those she loved, danger, fortune, and opinion; rather restless than ambitious; risking willingly her own life as well as that of others; and after having passed the best part of her existence in intrigue of every kind—thwarted more than one plot—left more than one victim on her path—traversed nearly the whole of Europe, by turns an exile and a conqueress who not unfrequently dazzled even crowned heads; after having seen Chalais lay his head on the block, Châteauneuf turned out of the ministry and imprisoned, the Duke de Lorraine well-nigh despoiled of his territories, Buckingham assassinated, the King of Spain embroiled in a war of ever-recurring disasters, Anne of Austria humiliated and overcome, and Richelieu triumphant; sustaining the struggle, nevertheless, even to its bitter end;

ever ready, in that desperate game of politics—become to
her a craving and a passion—to descend to the darkest
cabals or adopt the rashest resolves ; with an incomparable
faculty of discerning the actual state of affairs or the predominant evil of the moment, and of strength of mind and
boldness of heart enough to grapple with and destroy it at
any cost ; a devoted friend and an implacable enemy ; and,
finally, the most formidable foe that Richelieu and Mazarin,
in their turn, encountered :—such was the celebrated
Duchess de Chevreuse whom we have seen alternately
courted and dreaded by the two great political master-spirits
of her time, the founders of monarchical unity in France.

When the Fronde broke out, that ardent factionist rushed
once more to Brussels, and there brought over to her party
the support of Spain, together with her own long experience.
She was then nearly fifty years old. Age and sorrow, it is
true, had dimmed the lustre of her beauty ; but she was still
abounding in attraction, and her firm glance, her decision,
her quick and accurate perception, her dauntless courage
and genius, were yet entire. She had there also found a
last friend in the Marquis de Laigues, captain of the Duke
d'Orleans' guards, a man of sense and resolution, whom she
loved to the end, and whom, after th decease of the Duke
de Chevreuse in 1657, she linked probably with her own
destiny by one of those " marriages of conscience " * then
somewhat fashionable. It was not our purpose to follow her
step by step through the last civil war, and so plunge the
reader into the labyrinth of the Fronde intrigues. Suffice
it to say, therefore, that she played therein one of the most

* See "Memoirs of Brienne the Younger," tom. ii. chap. xix., p. 178.
" Le Marquis de Laigues qui certainement étoit mari de conscience de la
Duchesse."

prominent parts. Attached, heart and soul, to that faction and its essential interests, she steered it through all the shoals and quicksands which encircled it with incomparable skill and vigour. After having so long enlisted the support of Spain, she knew the proper moment to effect a timely separation from it. She always preserved her great influence over the Duke de Lorraine, and it is not difficult to recognize her hidden hand behind the different and often contrary movements of Charles IV. She had a principal share in the three great movements which mark and link together the entire history of the Fronde between the war in Paris and the peace of Ruel. In 1650 she was inclined to prefer Mazarin to Condé, and she ventured to advise laying hands on the victor of Rocroy and Lens. In 1651— an interval of incertitude for Mazarin, who very nearly ensnared himself in the meshes of his own craftiness and a too-complicated line of conduct—a great interest, the well-founded hope of marrying her daughter Charlotte to the Prince de Conti, brought her back once more to the Condé party, and hence the deliverance of the imprisoned Princes. In 1652, the accumulated blunders of Condé brought her back again and for ever to Anne of Austria and Mazarin. She did not endorse De Retz's foolish idea of constructing a third party during the revolt, nor dream of a government shared between Condé and Mazarin, with a worn-out parliament and the fickle Duke d'Orléans. Her politic instinct told her that, after an intestine struggle so long sustained, a solid and durable power was the greatest necessity of France. Mazarin, who, like Richelieu, had never opposed her but with regret, sought for, and was very glad to follow her advice. She passed over, therefore, with flying colours to the side of royalty, served it, and in return received its services. After Mazarin, she predicted the talent in Colbert, before he was appointed to office ; she laboured at his elevation and the ruin of Fouquet : and the proud but judicious Marie de Rohan gave her grandson, the Duke de Chevreuse, the friend of Beauvilliers and Fenelon, to the daughter of a talented burgess—the greatest financial administrator France ever had. Thenceforward she readily obtained all she could desire for herself and for her family ; and thus having reached the summit of renown and consideration, like her two illustrious sister-politicians, Madame de Longueville and the Princess Palatine, she finished in profound peace one of the most agitated careers of that stormiest of epochs —the seventeenth century.

It is said that the Duchess also, towards the close of her earthly pilgrimage, felt the influence of divine grace, and turned heavenwards her gaze, wearied with the changefulness of all sublunary things. She had seen successively fall around her all whom she had either loved or hated— Richelieu and Mazarin, Louis XIII. and Anne of Austria, the Queen of England, Henrietta Maria, and her amiable daughter the Duchess d'Orléans, Châteauneuf, and the Duke of Lorraine. Her fondly loved daughter had expired in her arms, of fever, during the miserable war of the Fronde. He who had been the first to lure her from the path of duty —the handsome but frivolous Holland—had ascended the scaffold with Charles I. ; and her last friend, much younger than herself, the Marquis de Laigues, had preceded her to the tomb.

Arrived at length but too clearly at the conviction that she had given up her mind to chimeras and illusions, and seeking self-mortification through the same sentiment which had brought about her ruin, the once-haughty Duchess became the humblest of women. Renouncing all worldly grandeur, she quitted her splendid mansion in the Faubourg St. Germain, built by Le Muet, and retired into the country —not to Dampierre, which would have only too vividly recalled to her remembrance the brilliant days of her past existence—but to a modest dwelling at Gagny, near Chelles. There she awaited her last hour, far from the world's observation, and ere long expired in tranquillity at the age of seventy-nine, the same year as Cardinal de Retz and Madame de Longueville. She desired to have neither solemn obsequies nor funeral oration, and forbade that any of those lofty titles which she had borne through life and had learned to despise should accompany her to the grave. It was her wish to be buried obscurely in the small and ancient church of Gagny; and there, in the southern aisle, near the chapel of the Virgin, some faithful but unknown hand has placed upon a slab of black marble the following epitaph :—

" Here lies Marie de Rohan, Duchess de Chevreuse, daughter of Hercule de Rohan, Duke de Montbazon. She espoused, first, Charles d'Albert, Duke de Luynes, peer and constable of France, and secondly, Claude de Lorraine, Duke de Chevreuse."

CHAPTER III.

THE PRINCESS PALATINE.

THE political importance of the Princess Palatine dates from 1650, when the arrest of Condé, Conti, and the Duke de Longueville urged her, as we have seen, to take part in the struggles of the Fronde. The Duchesses de Chevreuse, De Montbazon, De Guéméné, and other famous feminine factionists of that time, became, in the hands of Anne de Gonzagua, as so many wires with which she moved at her will the men whom these women governed; for the Princess exercised alike over all those men and women that superiority which disinterestedness, good faith, and firmness of decision confer. De Retz, when he discovered her characteristics, was immediately struck with the above-named qualities, especially the two latter. "To have stability of purpose," said he, when speaking of his first interview with Anne, "is a rare quality, which indicates an enlightened mind far above the ordinary class." And further on, "I do not think," he remarks, "that Queen Elizabeth had more capacity to govern a state." Mazarin, too, somewhat later, in alluding to the dread in which he held the famous trio of political women for their capacity to work mischief, remarked to Don Louis de Haro:—"The most turbulent of the male politicians do not give us half so much trouble to keep them within bounds as the intrigues of a Duchess de Chevreuse or a Princess Palatine."

Anne de Gonzagua, the Princess Palatine, lived long after the Fronde in the midst of all sorts of political troubles and diplomatic intrigues : conferences innumerable were held beneath her roof, and in that tortuous labyrinth she wandered and manœuvred to her heart's delight. Sometimes she laboured to reconcile Condé with Anne of Austria, sometimes to reunite Gaston and Condé, or perhaps the Queen and Madame de Longueville. She often failed, it is true, in these attempts, and meanwhile Mazarin, with more address, setting in motion in his retreat beyond the frontier the most powerful machinery, and making magnificent promises, again appeared above the political horizon—winning over his enemies one after another through his secret agents ; at one time it was Châteauneuf, at another Gondi, whom he made for good and all a cardinal ; at another it was Madame de Chevreuse. He had passed his word to the Princess Palatine that he would some day give her the post of superintendent of the young Queen's household : he did so, in fact, but on condition that she should relinquish it two months later to the Countess de Soissons, which she did in all good faith. Then she withdrew from court, somewhat undeceived no doubt touching men and things therein, if it really were the case that she ever had indulged in great illusions concerning court life.

Years rolled away, however : Mazarin died. Court intrigue with her was at an end. The personages who had been mixed up in the Fronde hurly-burly, so menacing in reality, so puerile in aspect, so insignificant as an isolated fact, and so formidable as a symptom, appeared affected by that decay which change of circumstances more than lapse of time imposes upon men and ideas. All that sort of thing was out of fashion. The reign of the

Grand Monarque was in all its heyday.   Besides, the Palatine was no longer young; she had married her daughters,
and dwelt in seclusion.   And it was when living thus
tranquilly that a rapid, unforeseen, enthusiastic conversion
came upon her like a surprise.   For all relating thereto, we
must listen to Bossuet, who dwells upon it in his funeral
oration upon the Princess.   His eloquence revels in relating
the miracles suddenly wrought in such a soul as hers.   He
expatiates on that sudden change with an apostolic joy and
an incomparable majesty: it was a subject worthy of him,
the brilliant narrator of solemn events.   It was exoteric to
that life upon which it was so difficult to pronounce an
eulogium; he was not trammelled in the flow of his diction
by those oratorical precautions which are so distressingly
hampering to an impetuous genius like his.   He celebrated
a victory of grace, and that in accents the most touching
and expressions the most powerful.   It was the hymn of an
illustrious conversion, chanted by the noblest mortal voice
ever heard.

Bossuet relates with inimitable art the Princess's two
dreams; the simple anecdotes are dramatised, poetised—
one might almost say sanctified—in proceeding from his
lips.   But, in short, whether Anne de Gonzagua saw or
thought that she saw that mystical mendicant, and those
symbolical animals, in her slumbers, the truth is that in
soul she was touched, agitated, shaken, overcome.   An
ardent faith, an invincible longing for prayer and penitence,
had obtained the mastery over that rebellious soul.   She
felt once more the enthusiasm of her early youth; she felt
beating once more, at the Divine Master's name, that heart
which had too often throbbed for His creatures only.   Her
scepticism vanished; she had no other ambition left save

that of gaining heaven, and holy tears were seen to dim those eyes wherein it once seemed as though the source of such emotion was dried up for ever. It was done. A great thing was accomplished, whatsoever had been the cause. A soul which incredulity had frozen into apathy became fervent before its Creator. Anne de Gonzagua did not fear to let her repentance be seen ; she desired that the publicity of her penitence might obliterate, if it were possible, the scandal of her past life. Her conscience became tender, even scrupulous. "*Plus elle était clairvoyante,*" says Bossuet, "*plus elle était tourmentée.*" Henceforward she devoted herself wholly to charity and prayer. She became as humble as she had hitherto been proud. She cherished a life of seclusion as much as she had once loved mundane notoriety. She became as sincerely a Christian as she had formerly been an infidel. During the lapse of twelve years this startling confession of faith did not belie itself for a single day. "Everything became poor about her house and person," says her illustrious panegyrist. "She saw with sensible delight the relics of the pomps of this world disappear one after another, and alms-giving taught her to retrench daily something fresh. . . . A person so delicate and sensible had suffered for twelve entire years, and almost without an interval, either the most vivid anguish or languor exhausting alike to mind and body ; and notwithstanding, during the whole of that time, and in the unheard-of torments of her last illness, in which her sufferings were increased to the utmost excess, she had not to repent of having once wished for an easier death. Again and again did she suppress that weak wish by uttering, so soon as she felt it arising, with the Saviour, the prayer of the Sacred Mystery of the Garden, 'Father, thy will, not mine, be done!'"

Such a sight must have moved the least susceptible—to have beheld the Palatine thus redeem her past errors. She was anxious to write with her own hand the account of her conversion, and addressed it to the celebrated Rancé, the Abbé of La Trappe. It was from that narrative that Bossuet drew the source of his own. Some few years previously, with that polished and elegant vein which intercourse with so many superior minds tends to create, she had written, as though she had foreseen that she would not despair of her spiritual future, a short but charming panegyric upon Hope. Bussy-Rabutin has preserved this relic in one of his letters. "I have never in my life," he says, with no doubt a little too much enthusiasm, "seen anything better or more delicately written." There is to be found in it, it is true, a happy inspiration and a passage capable of pleasing minds struggling with difficulties. "It is permitted to us," she says, "to measure our hope by our courage, it is noble to sustain it amidst trials; but it is not less glorious to suffer the entire ruin of it with the same high-heartedness which had dared to conceive it." Those are noble sentiments, and revealing a vigorous mental power. The end of the Princess Palatine (1681) showed clearly that she had not, for the mere pleasure of expressing herself elegantly, vaunted the delights of a saint-like hope. "Ready to render up her soul," says Bossuet, "she was heard to utter in dying accents, 'I am about to see how God will treat me, but I hope for His mercy.'" Such was the close of that life, the piety of which illuminated its latter years; such was the death of that Princess who, after having been remarkable among the women of her time for her beauty, her errors, and, at last, by her penitence, had the rare good fortune to be praised by the most illus-

trious of historians, priests, and authors of the great
century.

Our notice of this celebrated woman would be incomplete
without a passing glance at the singular fortunes of Henri
de Guise, subsequent to his desertion of his first love, Anne
de Gonzagua.

The Duke de Guise, after playing a conspicuous part in
the first dissensions of the Regency, and after having killed
Coligny, had married at Brussels the widow of the Count de
Bossut, with whom he became quickly disgusted, and whose
fortune he squandered. A violent passion next possessed
him for the charming and witty Mademoiselle de Pons, maid
of honour to the Queen. He took it into his head to espouse
her, and " the marriage was spoken of as though he had
never been married before." That phantasy, however, did
not hinder him from taking part, as a volunteer, in the campaigns of 1644 and 1645. Whilst at Rome in 1647, endeavouring to obtain a dispensation to enable him to secure
the hand of Mademoiselle de Pons, the Neapolitans, having
revolted against the Spaniards under Masaniello, elected him
as their leader, and gave him the title of generalissimo of
their army. Brave, enterprising, and born for adventure,
able, moreover, to render available ancient pretensions to
that kingdom, through René d'Anjou, who in 1420 had
espoused Isabelle de Lorraine, encouraged in short, if not
supported, by the French Court, where it was deemed politic
to keep at a distance from it a man bearing the great name
of Guise, so formidable some sixty years before, the young
prince embarked in a simple felucca, sailed boldly through
the naval armament of Don Juan, seized the reins of government, defeated the Spanish troops, and made himself master
of the country. He won all hearts by his address, his gentle-

ness, and his affability. But want of circumspection in his gallantries, the objects of which were not always of a rank equal to his own, caused jealousies and discontent among the nobles. His enemies, profiting by a sortie which he made for the purpose of getting a convoy into Naples, delivered up the city to the Spaniards. His repeated efforts to re-enter the place proved futile. After having defended himself like a lion, he was nevertheless carried prisoner to Madrid. The great Condé, who was then serving the enemies of his country, demanded that Guise should be set at liberty, in the hope that he might foment troubles in France. But the ill-treatment which the Duke had experienced at the hands of the Spaniards left impressions upon his mind which made him regardless of a promise that had been extorted from him. He attempted again in 1654 to reconquer the kingdom of Naples, with the aid of a French fleet, but failed of success. He then went back to Paris to seek indemnity for the loss of his crown. In 1655 he was appointed to the post of grand-chamberlain of France. He figured in the famous *carrousel* of 1663, at the head of a quadrille of American savages, whilst the great Condé appeared as chief of the Turks. On seeing those two personages so pitted, some wit observed, "There go the heroes of history and fable." The Duke de Guise might indeed be very aptly compared to a mythological entity, or to a knight errant of the age of chivalry. His duels, his romantic amours, his profusion, the varied adventures of his life, rendered him exceptionable in everything. He died in 1664, leaving no issue.

CHAPTER IV.

MADAME DE MONTBAZON.

AMONGST the celebrated women of the first half of the seventeenth century, many were, says Bussy Rabutin, " pitiable," whilst some were " brazen." We must assert unhesitatingly that Madame de Montbazon belonged to the latter class. She was " one of those personages, however, who made the most noise " at the courts of Louis the Thirteenth and Anne of Austria, as we are told by Madame de Motteville, and as we have already seen by the prominent political part she played in the factions of the Importants and the Fronde. In summing up her character, we shall be silent upon the subject of many of her faults, though it is not our wish to excuse one of them.

" She was not wanting in wit," remarks Tallemant ; " for she had been acquainted with so many witty people ! " There is a spice of flattery in this, for we must agree with Madame de Motteville and M. Cousin that the wit of the dazzling rival of Madame de Longueville was far from being as delicate and attractive as was her handsome person, though we cannot at the same time look upon Tallemant's phrase as a calumny. Both space and courage would alike fail us, should we attempt to produce a list of all the lovers, titled and untitled, who had peculiar opportunities of sharpening the wit of Madame de Montbazon.

Among the first of her adorers, beside the name of Gaston

d'Orléans, must be cited that of the Duke de Chevreuse, her husband's kinsman. Their *liaison* furnished matter for a ballad, and was very nearly the cause of a duel at the door of the king's apartments, between the Duke de Montmorency and the Duke de Chevreuse ; but that did not hinder Madame de Montbazon from becoming the friend of her step-daughter, who, older and more experienced in the political world than she was, often used her as an instrument. The young Duchess was a more dangerous rival to Madame de Guéméné, her other step-daughter, from whom she carried off, not her husband, but the Count de Soissons. And it was not enough that she obtained an easy conquest over her, for she instigated the Count to add outrage to desertion, and he docilely compromised his forsaken mistress by a gross and shameful perfidy.

But, passing rapidly over the errors of her youth, it is the close of Madame de Montbazon's political career with which we are now concerned. The influence which the gay and gallant Duchess long exercised over the Duke de Beaufort had sometimes proved useful to the interests of the Court, and during the early troubles of the Fronde the Queen and Mazarin took care to keep her favourably disposed towards them. But the importance which Beaufort's infatuated passion gave or seemed to give her, speedily made the Duchess one of the heroines of the Fronde—though, it must be owned, one of the secondary heroines. Her allies were careful not to allow her to take upon herself a part she was unable to sustain. Violent, unreflecting, accessible to the most contradictory suggestions, ready for any turn, and the sport of every caprice, she was wanting in all the better qualities of a political woman. Her indiscretion became formidable on

all occasions when secresy was necessary, and more than
once the Duke de Beaufort was obliged to be excluded from
the assemblages at which the chiefs of the Fronde took
counsel together. It was well known that he dare not keep
anything from his mistress, and it might chance that a
royalist might turn to account the confidence which she
wormed out of her lover, for conformity in political sentiments was not one of the conditions which she imposed upon
the adorers whose homage she welcomed. Her correspondence with Marshal d'Albret exposed her moreover to be
subject to, without being aware of it, the influences of the
Court, and her intimacy with Vineuil tended to make her an
ally, in spite of herself, of the Prince de Condé. Hence it
is easy to explain the mistrust with which she inspired the
Coadjutor of Paris, the future Cardinal de Retz. She herself did not fail to perceive the surveillance which he exercised around her ; and she was irritated to see with what
facility he modified in his own fashion the line of conduct
which she had just previously dictated to the Duke de Beaufort. She was forced to confess that his authority prevailed
over her own. One evening, disheartened by the incapacity
of the grandson of the great Henry, and terrified by the
dangers to which their imprudence exposed the Frondeurs,
and esteeming the political talent of Gondi to be more truly
worthy of her own, she opened her heart to him, and proposed that they should enter into a treaty of alliance. The
gallant Coadjutor would only consent to accept one portion
of the treaty, and, happily for the Duke de Beaufort, who
was busily occupied with a game at chess during that strange
conversation, he stipulated to eliminate from the proposed
association everything that related to politics. But the
Duchess would not consent to those terms.

In love, Madame de Montbazon was very mercenary ; we say it once for all, and beg to be excused from citing proof of the assertion. In politics, she also surrendered herself very willingly to any representation the eloquence of which was aided by crowns or pistoles. It was thus that in the month of August, 1649, she promised that the Duke de Beaufort should not oppose the return of the Court, at the same moment that she opened her hand to receive a considerable sum. It was thus that, the same year, she accepted two thousand pistoles from the Spanish envoys, who, desirous of rendering her favourable, promised besides that the sum of twenty thousand crowns and a pension of six thousand livres if she would secure to them the concurrence of the Duke de Beaufort. But she did not always meet with debtors so honest as Mazarin and the Spanish ambassadors. In 1650, whilst the treaty was preparing which sought to unite the Frondeurs with the Princes, then prisoners at Havre, a negotiation was entered into with Madame de Montbazon in which the Prince de Conti was offered to her as a husband for her daughter. The proposition was not accepted. The proposers were not discouraged, and a sum of a hundred thousand crowns was offered to her. This time the Duchess could not resist, and the treaty was signed in all due form. Unfortunately, when the Princes were liberated, she was imprudent enough to confide her voucher to the Princess Palatine, who, with perfidious haste, had promised to take care of her interests. She never saw the precious contract again, and the Prince de Condé only answered her demands by cruel and cutting jeers. In that adventure, it was not Madame de Montbazon who played the shabbiest part.

The aid which the Duchess had often lent the Court

amidst intrigues the most contradictory, did not preserve her from exile when the King made his entry into Paris, on its definite pacification in October, 1652. She did not return thither till 1657. " She was still beautiful, and as much carried away by vanity as though she had been only in her twenty-fifth year," says Madame de Motteville, when noting her reappearance. " She relied all the same upon her charms," she adds with a somewhat malicious finesse, " for she returned with the same desire of pleasing ; and those who saw her assured me that the mourning garb which she wore as a widow, and to which she added everything in the shape of ornament that self-love could suggest, rendered her so charming, that in her case it might be said that the course of nature was changed, since so many years and so much beauty could meet together." * Thus, by dint of care and art, did Madame de Montbazon succeed in preserving her beauty much longer than she could have hoped for, since, in the pride of her eighteen summers, she declared that old age commenced at thirty, and requested it as a favour that she might be flung into the river and drowned so soon as she reached the dreaded period. Who would have dared to remind her of that imprudent proposal in 1640 ? And who could have refused her a respite even in the latter moments of her existence ?

Permission had scarcely been given her to appear at Court, when she was attacked by an illness which seemed nothing

---

* The same sentiments were thus versified by Loret, when announcing that the Duchess had obtained permission to return to Court :

> " Montbazon, la belle douairière,
> Dont les appas et la lumière
> Sous de lugubres vêtements
> Paraissent encore plus charmants . . . . "

more than a common cold, but which turned out to be the measles. In the course of a few days the malady proved fatal. Three hours only were accorded to this earthly-minded woman to prepare for death. She made confession and received the sacrament with every indication of the most lively piety and the most sincere repentance, saying to her daughter, the Abbess of Caen, "that she regretted not having always lived in a cloister as she had, and that she looked with horror upon her past life." Up to those last three hours, she had refused to believe that there were degrees in the morality of women, and to admit that they were not all equally virtuous.

"She was little regretted by the Queen," Madame de Motteville tells us, " as she had frequently forsaken her interests to follow her own caprices. The minister heard of her death with the feeling one entertains for one's deceased enemy. Her former lovers looked upon her with contempt; and those who admired her still, were but little touched at her loss, because each, jealous of his rival, left tears and grief as the share of the Duke de Beaufort, who was at that moment the most beloved."

On that point Madame de Motteville was in error. Which of the two—M. de Beaufort or M. de Rancé—was most beloved it would be difficult to determine. But this is so far certain, that M. de Rancé, the future founder of La Trappe, was the lover who regretted her the most sincerely. He had hastened to her sick couch so soon as he heard of her illness; and he had arrived, not too late, and only to find himself the spectator of a most horrible sight, as has frequently been related with much romantic and dramatic detail, but soon enough to pass within her chamber the last hours left to her of life. " Already balancing and wrestling between heaven and this world," says Saint Simon, who was in his confidence, " the sight of that so sudden death achieved in him the determination of withdrawing from the world which he had for some time meditated."

Among the different versions of this catastrophe, Laroque asserts that, after an absence on a long journey, on De Rancé's return, he called at the Hôtel Montbazon, and then learned, for the first time, the death of the Duchess; that he was shown into her room, where, to his horror, the headless body lay in its coffin. The head had been cut off, either because the lead coffin was not made long enough or for the purpose of an anatomical study. Some assert that De Rancé took the head, and that the skull of the woman he loved so well was found in his cell at La Trappe. History, however, will not accept this romantic incident.

Touching the fate of De Rancé's rival—when Louis XIV. returned to Paris in 1652, the Duke de Beaufort submitted to the royal authority, and took no further part in the civil war, which the Prince de Condé carried ŏn for several years longer. Later, the Duke obtained the command of the royal fleet. In 1664 and 1665, he was at the head of several expeditions against the African corsairs. In 1666 he commanded the French men-of-war ordered to join those of Holland against England. Finally, in 1669, he went to the aid of the Venetians, attacked by the Turks in the island of Candia. The galleys and vessels, newly constructed in the port of Toulon, disembarked seven thousand men under Beaufort—a contingent too weak for such a dangerous undertaking. That aid only served to retard the taking of Candia for a few days, and was the means of useless bloodshed. In a sortie, the rash and impetuous grandson of Henry the Great was cut to pieces in the most merciless way; and as his body could not be found after the fight, his death gave rise to fables sought to be rendered probable by the remembrance of the eccentric part he had previously played.

CHAPTER V.

MADEMOISELLE DE MONTPENSIER.

ANNE MARIE LOUISE D'ORLÉANS, Duchess de Montpensier, whom history distinguishes by the epithet of *La Grande Mademoiselle*, after telling us in her memoirs, at least twenty times, in order to make herself better known, that she was fond of glory, adds—" The Bourbons are folks very much addicted to trifles, with very little solidity about them; perhaps I myself as well as the rest may inherit the same qualities from father and mother." * With this hint, who-ever scans her portrait may readily read the character her features reveal :—a mind false to the service of a noble and generous heart; an honest but frivolous mind, too often swayed by a bombastic heroism ; a *précieuse* of the Hôtel Rambouillet, whom Nicolas Poilly very happily painted as Pallas, with her helmet proudly perched upon the summit of her fair tresses; an amazon, who bordered upon the adven-turess, and, notwithstanding, remained the princess; in short, a personage at whom one cannot help laughing heartily, nor at the same time help admiring.

Passing by the subject of her numerous matrimonial projects, we hasten on to the commencement of her poli-tical—and perhaps we may add her military†—career, when, in January, 1652, a treaty had been concluded between

* The daughter of Gaston d'Orléans and the charming Marie de Bourbon, she was born in 1627, the same year as Bossuet and Mad. de Sévigné. Her mother died five days after her birth.

† Her father, writing to her companions in arms the Countesses of

Monsieur her father, Condé, and the Duke de Lorraine, the
Duchess d'Orléans had signed in her brother's name, and
the Count de Fiesque in the name of Condé. On her part,
Mademoiselle, somewhat fantastic but loyal and courageous,
had joined her mother-in-law, and declared for the Fronde,
partly through her liking for *éclat* and the notoriety of
parading at the head of the troops, with her two ladies
of honour, the Countesses of Fiesque and Frontenac,
transformed into aides-de-camp; partly by the secret hope
that by Mazarin's defeat and her father's triumph she might
succeed in espousing the young King, and so exchange
the helmet of the Fronde for the crown of France.

It would be a great mistake to attribute to this fair
Frondeuse a liberalism of ideas to which she was most
assuredly a stranger. "It must be," she somewhere remarks, "that the intentions of the great are like the
mysteries of the Faith : it does not belong to mankind to
penetrate within them ; men ought to revere them, and to
believe that they are never otherwise than for the welfare
and salvation of their country." But, however that may be,
it did not prevent the civil war from being a very amusing
thing for Mademoiselle. To hear the drums beating to arms
one fine morning, to see men running through the streets to
defend the barricades as well as their untrained hands could
wield musket and sabre, to lie upon the floor in a large
chamber at Saint-Germain, and to find on awaking that
chamber filled with soldiers in great buff jerkins,—those
were pleasures not to be always found at will, and were to
be made the most of when met with. Such pleasures,
moreover, savouring of the unforeseen, the adventurous,

Fiesque and Frontenac shortly after their entrance into Orleans, complimented them upon their courage, and addressed his letter to *the Countesses
Adjutant-Generals in the Army of my Daughter against Mazarin.*

and the grotesque, solely determined Mademoiselle's conduct in the outset. But on the second Fronde breaking
out, when the struggle of the Parliament with royalty had
become a quarrel between princes and ministers, Mademoiselle felt that the honour of her house was at stake. Gaston,
after having pledged himself to the Prince de Condé, so far
as a man who does not know his own mind can give a
pledge, contented himself with whistling, as he was wont to
do, or to dissertating cleverly without acting. But his
daughter wrested from him an authority to go herself and
defend Orleans against the troops of Louis XIV.; his
daughter, on seeing the unfortunate adherents of Condé
engaged with her in rebellion overpowered at the Faubourg
Saint-Antoine, secured their retreat by ordering the guns
of the Bastille to cannonade the royal forces, although that
cannonade should slay the husband of whom she still
dreamed; that daughter, too, when she heard of the disgraceful scenes of the 4th of July, 1652, boldly did what no
one else dare do,—she flew to the assistance of the victims
of the Hôtel de Ville, without bestowing a thought of the
imminent danger she thereby ran.

But it is in the Princess's own Memoirs that the curious
epopee must be read; and to which a dry abridgment
does injustice. Whether she hold council of war with her
fair *Maréchales de Camp*, without allowing the men folks
to give her their ready cut-and-dried advice,—whether she
be thrust into Orleans through the gap of an old gateway,
and, covered with mud, be seen carried along its streets in
an old arm-chair, laughing heartily,—or when hastening to
arrest the massacre at the Hôtel de Ville, she stops to
look at Madame Riche, the ribbon-vendor, talking in her
chemise to her gossip, the beadle of St. Jacques, who has

nothing on but his drawers,—the reader is always reminded
that he sees and hears the granddaughter of Henry IV.—a
Parisian with a touch of the princess in all she says and
does, and he cannot help asking himself momentarily whether it be all incorrigible frivolity, or some quaint species of
natural heroism which speaks and acts thus strangely.

Heroic or frivolous, Mademoiselle expiated her pranks by
an exile of four years in her manor of Saint-Fargeau.　The
rupture with her father, who drove her out of doors, and
denied her permission to take refuge under any other roof
he owned, her consequent wanderings, at times not a little
affecting, and at others comical, when directing her steps
towards her place of banishment, her arrival at the ruinous
château which has neither doors nor windows, and which is
haunted by ghosts, and the attempts to embellish the
tumble-down place, and people it with gaiety, animation,
and life, are so many scenes to which the piquant style of
Mademoiselle gives singular attractiveness.　Whilst avenues
were being planted and a theatre built, matrimonial negotiations went on as briskly as ever, and pretenders to her
hand abounded—the Elector of Bavaria, the Duke of
Savoy, the nephew of the Duke of Lorraine, the Duke de
Neuborg.　The reception of M. de Neuborg's envoy, an
honest Jesuit, who draws out of his pocket victoriously
two portraits of his good lord, ogles Mademoiselle as long
as he could, and talks " goguette " to her for a whole hour,
is one of the most amusing farces anywhere to be met with.
Unluckily, the farce was not worth the candle in the opinion
of certain judges, and all the diversions of Saint-Fargeau
did not prevent our princess from regretting with all her
heart that pompous Court of Versailles in which the young
Louis was giving such graceful ballets, brilliant carousals,

and piquant masquerades. The masquerades of 1657 carried the day over the political aims of 1652, and the fair exile experienced a vivid longing to be once more received into favour at the court of her royal cousin.

To take up sword or pen and fall foul of the government was almost always an easy thing to do in France; the difficulty lay in proposing peace after the war, to hit upon profitable reconciliations or lucrative treaties. Mademoiselle did her best; and at length, in that same year of 1657, she made her appearance in the royal camp near Sedan, having at her carriage-door the silly and complaisant Mazarin, who believed all she wished him to believe, and who presented the princess with a little Boulogne bitch, in token of good friendship; she made her excuses to the King for having been naughty, and promised to be wise in future. Louis behaved more graciously towards the fair rebel than did his mother, and said that everything should be buried in oblivion; but he did not forget the cannonade of the Bastille. After five years' seclusion, she again looked forward to resume her position at Court, to keep one of her own, to enthrone herself at the Luxembourg, and doubtless contract some sovereign alliance. Vain illusions! Conflicts of the heart were about to succeed to those political storms from whose effects she had just recovered. The most vainglorious of the daughters of France was destined to extinguish with the wet blanket of vile prose the brilliancy of a long and romantic career.

History, justly severe upon the Fronde, ought not, we think, to treat too harshly the Frondeuse of the blood-royal. Upon one delicate point of her private life the biographer cannot, unfortunately, show the same indulgence. The supreme criterion for the appreciation of certain women, and

the irresistible argument, is the man whom they have loved.
Assuredly we may pardon many things recorded of the
Grande Mademoiselle, even her shrewish relations with her
step-mother, even her haughty contempt for her half-sisters,
but we cannot pardon her M. de Lauzun. We are all well
acquainted with that individual, with his cunning and super-
cilious cast of countenance, servile or arrogant, according to
circumstances and interests, adroit in concealing a merciless
egotism, a revolting brutality, under the guise of a theatrical
liberality ; brave so far as was necessary to be insolent with
impunity, intelligent no further than to the extent at which
selfishness blinds the judgment, and delighting in mischief
when there was nothing to dread from it. To all this may
be added an incisive tone of voice, and language keenly sar-
castic or servilely obsequious, an insatiable and inordinate
sensuality, innumerable conquests among the fair sex, and
extraordinary adventures. At first sight, at a Court mas-
querade, in 1659, the bully made an impression upon the
précieuse, and she noticed him for his exquisite elegance
during the marriage fêtes of Louis XIV. When she met
him in the Queen's apartments, she remarked that he had
more wit than anyone else, and found a particular pleasure
in talking with him. The charm operated so effectually that
the princess of forty-three was at length fain to own that
she passionately loved the Gascon cadet, who was then in
his thirty-eighth year. Determined as she was naturally,
that discovery overwhelmed her. " I resolved," she says,
" never to speak to M. Lauzun again save in hearing of a
third person, and I was anxious to avoid opportunities of
seeing him in order to drive him out of my head. I entered
upon such a line of conduct ; I only exchanged a few trivial
words with him. I found that I did not know what I was

saying, that I could not put three words of good sense together; and the more I sought to shun him, the more desirous I was of seeing him." At her wits' end, the poor Princess cast herself at the foot of the altar, on one occasion when she took the sacrament, and ardently besought Heaven to enlighten her as to the course she ought to pursue. The inspiration is by no means difficult to anticipate. " Heaven's grace determined me not to struggle longer to drive out of my mind that which was so strongly established in it, but to marry M. de Lauzun."

Two things, however, were necessary to accomplish this : firstly, that M. de Lauzun should thoroughly understand that he was beloved, and that he would deign to espouse Mademoiselle's twenty-two millions ; and next that King Louis should consent to a marriage, the strangest certainly ever resolved upon. Strange, indeed, that she, the grand-daughter of Henry the Great, Mademoiselle d'Eu, Mademoiselle de Dombes, Mademoiselle d'Orléans, Mademoiselle the King's first cousin, the Mademoiselle destined to the throne, should ask the King's permission to marry a Gascon cadet. Louis, as the sequel to an overture made to him by several nobles collectively, friends of Lauzun, with M. de Montausier at their head, granted his permission. But when the question arose,. thanks to the blind vanity of Lauzun, of their union being celebrated at the Louvre and in the face of all France, like an alliance " of crown to crown ;" when a feeling which was shared by every member of the royal house was on the point of communicating itself to all the sovereign families of Europe, Louis, with great reason, began to take account of the political interests which this whim of the Princess brought into play, and retracted, as King, the authority which he had given as head of a family. Contemporary writers seem never tired of dwelling upon the manifestations of Mademoiselle's grief, at times as laughable as at others it was touching; receiving the condolence of all the Court as though she had been a lone widow, Madame de Sévigné tells us, and exclaiming excitedly in her despair to every fresh visitor, as she pointed to the vacant place in her bed, " He should be there! he should be there!"

This took place on the 18th of December, 1670. On the 25th of November, 1671, M. de Lauzun was arrested, thrown into the Bastille, and taken thence to Pignerol, where he was subjected to a captivity of ten years. What passed in that interval has proved a great subject of controversy amongst ingenious writers. The most probable explanation seems to be that, notwithstanding the King's refusal, the marriage between Lauzun and Mademoiselle had been accomplished. The evidence of twenty different persons might be cited in support of the fact, but one may suffice. An historian of the last century, M. Anquetil, relates that at the Château d'Eu, in 1774, an apartment was still pointed out which had been occupied by Lauzun, situated above that of the princess, and communicating by a secret staircase with her alcove. At the same period, Anquetil saw at Treport a tall person resembling Mademoiselle not only in her figure, but strikingly like her portraits. She seemed to be about seventy or seventy-five. She was called, throughout that part of the country, the Princess's daughter. She seemed to believe so herself, and was in receipt of a pension of fifteen hundred francs paid punctually, without knowing from what quarter they came. She occupied a handsome house for which she paid no rent, although for it she held no proprietary deed. All this, coupled with the age of the lady, who stated that she was born in 1671, would seem

decisive as to the clandestine marriage which probably occasioned the arrest of Lauzun.

Ten years of anguish and poignant regrets passed over
poor Mademoiselle's head—ten years employed in imploring
and bargaining for the restoration of her dearly beloved
captive. " Consider what you have it in your power to do
to please the King, in order that he may grant you that
which you have so much at heart," was the artful suggestion
daily repeated in her ear by Madame de Montespan. And
to render the discovery more easy, she took care to bring
with her, and to send to her very frequently, that charming
little Duke du Maine to whom the county of Eu, the duchy
of Aumale, and the principality of Dombes would have
been a fitting appanage. To despoil herself for the
deliverance of the man she loved with such an infatuated
affection, the Princess would not have hesitated a moment.
The difficulty was to despoil the man himself, already in
possession of a portion of what was required, and very keen-
witted indeed to keep what he had acquired. The negotiation, for a long while brought to a dead-lock by the resistance
of Lauzun, was at length concluded. M. de Lauzun, emerged
from Pignerol, but restricted at first to a residence in Touraine or Anjou, received at length permission to revisit Paris
and behold once more the benefactress who could still secure
to him the enjoyment of an income of forty thousand livres.
" I did not know him," exclaimed the woebegone Princess,
shortly after his release, " and my sole consolation is that
the King, who is more clear-sighted than I am, did not know
him either." Tardy clear-sightedness! M. de Lauzun had
then made himself known unmistakably—by beating her.
But, if the truth must be told, she had first scratched his
face.

Thus ended, in vulgar squabbles, more and more stormy, a connection so romantically begun. Lauzun, disappointed in his hope of a magnificent alliance, considered himself despoiled by the Princess's donation, and, finding himself after ten years' captivity the husband of a woman of fifty-four, showed her neither tenderness nor respect. It was, therefore, a relief to her when he took his departure for England in 1685. The ill-assorted couple never met again. Lauzun more than once endeavoured to obtain an interview with the Princess, but she would not forgive him, and died without consenting to his urgent appeals. It was in her latter years only, and under the perceptibly increasing sway of religious influences, that her miserably tormented mind recovered peace and repose. Mademoiselle, who had only given up dancing in 1674, withdrew gradually from Court when she found that she had become an object of pity, if not of mockery, therein. The *Grande Mademoiselle* expired on the 5th of April, 1693, in her palace of the Luxembourg, aged sixty-six. That singularity, which had so remarkably characterised her life, pursued her even beyond it. At her obsequies, celebrated with much magnificence, her entrails, imperfectly embalmed, fermented, and the urn which contained them burst with a loud explosion during the ceremonies. All present fled in the extremity of terror.

Was it from the singularity of her existence, from the essentially French tone of her character, from the grandeur of an epoch during which no one passed unnoticed, that the species of popularity half-indulgent, half-sportive, which attached to her name must be attributed? To all these doubtless, but likewise to another cause more decisive still. Mademoiselle does not take her place only in the sufficiently extensive catalogue of princely eccentricities; she holds a creditable position upon the list of French writers. Nor should it be forgotten that the gates of the Luxembourg were by her thrown open to all the *beaux esprits* of her time, "qui y trouvaient leur place comme chez Mécænas;" and that she fostered both by encouragement and example La Rochefoucauld and La Bruyère, and that it is no slight claim to remembrance that she led France to appreciate the *Maxims* of the one and the *Characters* of the other. May such considerations serve as extenuating circumstances when we bring her up for judgment for the flagrant crime of—M. de Lauzun.

CHAPTER VI.

AMONG so many heroines of beauty, glory, and gallantry, who achieved celebrity at this stirring epoch of French history, there is one whose name ought not to be effaced from, nor placed lowest on the list, although a humble—we were going to say, a humiliated, disdained, and sacrificed wife; a martyr to conjugal faith, but who, perhaps, can scarcely be called a " political " woman.

Mademoiselle de Brézé, as already intimated, had entered into the Condé family through the detestable influence of authority and politics. The Duke d'Enghien, therefore, unhappily held his wife in aversion; her mother-in-law, Charlotte de Montmorency, despised her; Madame de Longueville, her sister-in-law, did not esteem her; Mademoiselle de Montpensier declares that " she felt pity for her," and that was the gentlest phrase she could find to apply to a person who had so signally crossed her views and inclination.

Married at thirteen to the future hero of Rocroy and Lens, both before marriage and again more strongly after, the young Duke had protested by a formal act that he yielded only to compulsion and his respect for paternal authority in giving her his hand. Henry (II.), Prince de Condé, who thus exacted his son's compliance, merely followed his usual instincts as a greedy and ambitious courtier in seeking an alliance with Cardinal Richelieu, whose niece Mademoiselle de Brézé was, through her mother, Nicole du Plessis. Mademoiselle de Montpensier, who thought that she had more reason than any one else to be indignant at the match, tells us plainly that the Prince threw himself at the feet of his eminence to solicit from him both Mademoiselle de Brézé for the Duke d'Enghien, and M. de Brézé, her brother, for Mademoiselle de Bourbon, and that he only escaped from the disgrace of a double *mésalliance* through the Cardinal's clemency, who, in reply, told him that " he was quite willing to give untitled young ladies to princes, but not princesses to untitled young gentlemen."

Did the young Duchess personally merit that aversion and contempt ? Mademoiselle has told us, indeed, that she was awkward, and that, " on the score of wit and beauty, she had nothing above the common run." But Madame de Motteville, less passionate and more disinterested in her judgments, recognises certain advantages possessed by her. " She was not plain," she tells us, " but had fine eyes, a good complexion, and a pretty figure. She spoke well when she was in the humour to talk." The discerning court lady adds that, " if Madame de Condé did not always display a talent for pleasing in the ball-room or in conversation, the fidelity with which she clung to her husband during adversity, and the zeal she showed for his interests and for those of her son during the Guienne campaign, ought to compensate for the misfortune of not having been able to merit, by more eminent virtues, a more brilliant and widely celebrated reputation."

Here, then, it seems incumbent upon us to divine, from the *façon de parler* of that day, what were *the eminent virtues* which the Princess de Condé needed to deserve the esteem of her husband ; or to ask whether tried fidelity, courage, devotedness, were not then ranked among the eminent virtues. They were so, no doubt; and it is probable that what Madame de Motteville understands by those words, was the eminence of qualities peculiar to the women, who more than ever in her day derived from them a species of celebrity which closely resembled glory—the éclat of beauty, wit, grace, intrepidity, and power of charming; in a word, that which was possessed in so high a degree by a Madame de Longueville, a Madame de Chevreuse, a Marie de Hautefort, and a Mademoiselle du Vigean.

Whatever might have been the personal merit of the wife of the great Condé, did the little she had justify the wretchedness of her destiny? No: some beauty, wit, virtue, courage, a timid disposition perhaps, an unpretending virtue, a courage even mediocre, easily overthrown, and which needed the pressure of circumstances and danger for its development,—in all this there was nothing to invoke the ire of the implacable sisters.

In contemplating her truly deplorable existence, afflicted from its beginning to its end by every kind of grief and humiliation, one can scarcely resist the idea of the ascendency of an invincible fatality, making her a victim of the irresistible force of events and destiny. The woes of Claire de Brézé commenced in her earliest childhood. At the time of her marriage to the Duke d'Enghien she had lost her mother some six years, that parent having died in 1635. What befell her infancy, abandoned to the neglect of a fantastic and libertine father, ruled even before his widowhood by a mistress, the wife of one of his lacqueys, whom he killed one day during a hunting match in order to get him out of the way; of a father who, Tallemant tells us, carelessly remarked, when his daughter's marriage was agreed upon—as though she belonged to some one else—" They are going to make a princess of that little girl!"

She was destined, nevertheless, to have her hour of fame and distinction, and that hour dawned amidst disasters of every sort, and upon the captivity of her husband. At the moment of the arrest of the Prince, whilst the Princess-dowager was conferring with her adherents upon the best measures to be adopted for the deliverance of the Princes and for the safety of her little grandson, the young Princess, over-coming her timidity, interrupted Lenet, who was proposing a plan for their flight, and another for a campaign, and, after the humblest tokens of respect and deference for her mother-in-law, *entreated her not to separate her from her son, protesting that she would follow him everywhere joyfully, whatsoever might be the peril, and that she would expose herself to any risk to aid her husband.**

From that moment, we trace, almost from day to day as it were, in the *Mémoires* of Lenet proofs of the zeal and con-stancy of the Princess de Condé. She escapes from Chantilly on foot, with her son and a small band of faithful followers, traverses Paris, whence she reaches, in three days and by devious roads, Montrond, the place pointed out by Lenet as the safest retreat and the most advantageous to defend. Her letters to the Queen and ministers, to the magistrates, to her relatives, are stamped with nobility and firmness. Threatened in Montrond by La Meilleraye, who was advancing in force, she again made her escape under cover of a hunting party, after having provided for the safety of the place and others which depended on it, and went in search of, amid a host of difficulties, sometimes on horsback, at others in a litter or by boat, the Dukes de Bouillon and La Rochefoucauld, who

* Lenet.

escorted her to Bordeaux. One must turn to Lenet for all the details of that toilsome journey and of the insurrection at Bordeaux, which he has related with all the minutiæ and animation of an eye-witness and an actor who more than once figured in the front rank. No longer timid, no longer awkward, in presence of danger the daughter of Marshal de Brézé became the amazon and almost the heroine. She held reviews, councils of war, negotiated, and issued orders. Scarcely had she reached Bordeaux, her entry into which was quite an ovation, than she besieged the Parliament chamber to procure the registration of her requests and protestations against the unjust detention of her husband. " She solicited the judges on their way out of court, representing to them with tears in her eyes the unhappy condition of all her oppressed house. . . . The young Duke, whom a gentleman (Vialas) carried in his arms, caught the counsellors round the neck as they passed, and weepingly besought at their hands the liberation of his father, in so tender a manner that those gentlemen wept also as bitterly as he and his mother, and gave them both good hopes." She harangued the magistrates, supplicated them, urged them ; she even protected them, on one occasion that the populace of Bordeaux, finding them not so bold as they could have wished, endeavoured by clamour to obtain a decree contrary to the views of the party of the Princes. She repaired to the palace, and from the top of the steps conjured the furious rabble and made them lay down their arms. "And it must be owned," says Lenet, " that she had a particular talent for speaking in public, and that nothing could be better, more appropriate, nor more conformable to her position than what she said." On that day, the Princess de Condé, upon the steps of the Hôtel de Ville of Bordeaux, appeared no longer unworthy of being ranked with Madame de Longueville at the town-hall at Paris, or with Mademoiselle d'Orléans at the Porte St. Antoine. Brienne adds that she worked with her own hands, with the ladies of the city, at the fortifications, and that she was anxious herself to embroider, upon the banners of her army, the emblem and device of the revolt—a grenade exploding, with the word *coacta !*

We have already seen the result of that three months' resistance—the peace concluded at Bordeaux, the amnesty accorded to all those who had taken up arms in Guienne, in a word, all the conditions proposed by the Princess and the Dukes conceded, with the exception of one only—the principal, that which had been the prime cause of all that insurrection—the deliverance of the Prince de Condé, whom Mazarin persisted in retaining prisoner, whilst at the same time promising to do everything towards abridging his captivity.

The Princess was sent back to Montrond with her son, vexed no doubt at not having conquered, but proud of having dared so much, and satisfied at having deserved for that once to share his imprisonment. That day came, however,—the day of gratitude and justice. On one occasion already, whilst yet at Vincennes, the Prince, as he watered the tulips celebrated by Mademoiselle de Scudéry in song, remarked to some one, " *Who would have thought that I should be watering tulips whilst Madame la Princesse was making war in the south !*

But later, when the campaign at Bordeaux had ended, the Prince still a prisoner at Havre, forwarding a communication in cypher to Lenet, added thereto a short note for the Princess, couched in terms so tender that Lenet, fearing lest in the exuberance of her delight the Princess might betray

the secret of that correspondence, hesitated for some moments
to communicate it to her. That note, the first and sole recompense of her devotion, courage, and constancy, we must
here transcribe, as the tardy and begrudging compensation
for such long-continued ingratitude, such long-continued dis-
dain, for so many cruel and unmerited outrages.

" Il me tard, Madame, que je sois en état de vous embrasser mil fois pour
toute l'amitié que vous m'avez temoigné, qui m'est d'autant plus sensible
que ma conduite envers vous l'avoit peu méritée ; mais je sçauray si bien
vivre avec vous à l'advenir, que vous ne vous repentirés pas de tout ce que
vous avés faict pour moy, qui fera que je seray toute ma vie tout à vous et
de tout mon cœur."

Poor Clémence de Maillé! how, at that first testimony of
an affection which she had despaired of ever gaining, did her
heart, so long pent up, burst forth with ecstatic delight!
And how must Lenet, on witnessing that touching effusion of
irrepressible rapture, have congratulated himself at not
having persevered in his diplomatic prudence! She took the
letter, shed tears over it, kissed it, read it over and over
again, and tried to get it by heart—for she might lose it.
Then she selected from her toilette her finest ribbon (a bright
flame-coloured one), and sewed that precious missive to it,
in order to carry it always upon her person, beneath her
dress—upon her chemise, Lenet bluntly tells us, and who
adds that that gush of delirious delight lasted until the
morrow.

Alas! that warm ray was the only one that Condé, in his
glory, let fall upon her, and it was but evanescent. The
danger over, the prison opened, Condé restored to his
honours and his power, she became once more the despised,
alienated, humiliated wife. Mademoiselle, on meeting her
again, asked whether it were true that she had taken part *in*

that which was done in her name? On her return from Montrond (after the letter), she found her, it is true, *plus habile;*
but she was shocked at the delight manifested by the Princess
on seeing all the great world flock to visit her, so wholly forsaken as she had previously been, and she concluded that,
being carried out of her normal condition, she thought too
much of herself.

Then came humiliations the most cutting, and the deepest
grief. Twice was she attacked by dangerous illness, from
which it was asserted she could not recover. And each time
that report was welcomed at Court as the joyous announce‑
ment of a marriage or a succession. Everybody busied
themselves with finding another wife for the Prince; and
some thought once more of Mademoiselle: "that rumour
reached my ears," says she, "and I mused upon it." Unfortunately for her, the poor Princess recovered, and Mademoiselle had to wait for Lauzun. In another place she remarks
somewhat spitefully, "Madame la Princesse arrived in
better health than *could have been anticipated; no one could
have imagined that she would so soon recover.*"

At length a tragic event, the consequences of which exhibit
in a sinister light the perseverance of ill-feeling that had
always been shown towards her in the family of which she
had become a member, came to add itself to that almost un-
broken chain of tribulations, outrages, and troubles amid
which no sort of calamity seemed wanting. Two officers of
her household took it into their heads to quarrel and draw
swords upon each other. The Princess (she was then in her
forty-third year—1671) placed herself between the angry combatants with the intention of separating them, and by so
doing received a stab in her side. The individual who inflicted the wound was brought to trial. As for her,

" When she was cured, the Prince had her conducted to Châteauroux, one of his country-houses. She has been there kept for a long time imprisoned, and at present permission is only given her to walk in the court-yard, always strictly watched by the people whom the Prince always keeps about her. *The Duke is accused of having suggested to the Prince the treatment to which his mother is subjected* : *he was very glad,* it is said, to find a pretext for putting her in a place where she would *spend less* than in society."*

Was it the hereditary avarice of the house of Condé which thus revealed itself in the odious sentiment of that unworthy son ? Poor woman ! Her only crime was that of being too liberal. She had, it is true, foolishly placed her diamonds in pledge at Bordeaux to support the cost of the war. But had she not, as a set-off to her prodigality, brought to the Duke d'Enghien and his father her share of Richelieu's wealth ? That prudent advice of the excellent son was followed : the Princess was still a prisoner at Châteauroux, when the Prince her husband died, in 1686 ; and by way of a precaution— which cannot be thought of without a shudder, giving as it does the measure of an implacable hatred—he recommended that she should be so kept after his decease. This once, Mademoiselle did find a word of pity for the persecuted wife and mother. " I could have wished," says she, when speaking of the last moments of the Prince, "that he had not prayed the King to let his wife always be kept at Châteauroux, and I was very sorry for it. . . ."

And it was there, doubtless, that she died in 1694, at the age of sixty-six. The collections of funeral orations and sermons of celebrated preachers of that day will be searched in vain for any funeral tribute to her memory. And a feeling of disappointment arises that Bossuet, in his panegyric of the hero, could not find a word of praise, of consó-

* Mémoires of Mademoiselle de Montpensier, 4th part.

lation, or even of pity for the ill-fated shadow he left sorrowful and abandoned by all, to bear his name in pitiless obscurity to the grave.

Mysterious destiny! strange fatality! which neither personal demerits, wrongs, nor faults justified, which neither love, devotedness, nor unfailing virtue, approved and respected even by the calumnious, could avert.

PART II.

THE DUCHESS OF PORTSMOUTH.

Very little is known for certain concerning the antecedents of Louise Querouaille before she figured at the Court
of France as one of the maids of honour to the unfortunate
Henrietta, Duchess of Orleans, sister of Charles the Second
of England. The contemporaries of the merry monarch,
witnesses and censors of his political errors, in tracing them
to their source, have attributed them primarily to the foreign
favourite, who was, more than any other of the many mistresses of that Prince, odious in the eyes of the English people.

At the commencement of 1670, the splendour and corruption of the French Court had reached their acme. The
seraglio of the great King recalled to mind that of Solomon,
whilst his brother, enslaved by effeminacy and debauchery,
had only to hold up his finger and the most important personages of the state were suitably provided with mistresses
to such an extent that at length it became necessary to trans-
fer occasionally to foreign courts those attractive creatures
who, by antiphrasis doubtless, were always called "maids of
honour." It was in the household of his sister-in-law,
Henrietta of England, that Louis had first met the two
mistresses of his predilection ; and when he wished to assure
himself by a new tie of his royal vassal on the other side of
the channel, it was still the domestic circle of the Duchess
of Orleans which supplied him with the diplomatist in petti-
coats he wanted.

When Mademoiselle Querouaille's mission to the Court of

St. James's became thoroughly understood, and her position
as Duchess of Portsmouth assured in it, her previous history
was hunted up, the details of which no one knew—not even
the royal family of France, who had used her as an instrument without caring to trouble itself about her origin.
Madame de Sévigné, in her letters to her daughter, speaks
of the Duchess of Portsmouth in a very disrespectful fashion,
so much so as to reveal, if not the certainty, at least the
belief that the antecedents of the *maid of honour*, as she says,
were not the most honourable. In 1690, five years after
Charles's death, a pamphlet was published in London in
which the Duchess figures under the fictitious name of
Francelie; Louis XIV. designated as *Tirannides*, and our
English king as *Prince des Iles.* In the preface to the
French translation of this pamphlet, which bears the title of
Histoire secrète de la Duchesse de Portsmouth, it is stated
that the author desired to give, by these changes of name,
some additional piquancy to the revelations contained in his
book. According to such chronicle, the father of Louise
Querouaille was a wool merchant of Paris. After having
realised a moderate fortune in trade, he retired into Brittany,
his native country, with his two daughters ; the youngest,
Louise, being amiable and pretty ; the eldest, plain and un-
graceful. The dissimilarity of the two sisters, the one universally pleasing, the other displeasing everybody, created
such misunderstanding between them that their father was
obliged to separate them. He kept the plain daughter at
home, and placed the younger and pretty one as a boarder in
a neigbouring town to that in which he lived. Louise thereby
acquired accomplishments which enhanced her natural charms·
She was sharp, cunning, insinuating, and having gained the
confidence and goodwill of the lady to whose care her father

had entrusted her, the former introduced her amongst her relations and general society. In that circle Mademoiselle
Querouaille ere long inspired passions, rumours of which
reached the ears of the old wool-merchant. Fearing lest his
daughter might but too thoughtlessly respond to the attentions of which she was the object, he withdrew her from the
boarding-house, and took her to Paris, where he left her
under the care of his sister-in-law, then a widow. Her husband had been a dependent of the Duke de Beaufort, and
she herself lived, for the most part, upon the bounty of that
nobleman, who, on reconciling himself with the Court after
the Fronde, had obtained the post of high-admiral of France.
Shortly after the arrival of Louise in Paris, in 1669, the
Duke seeing her walking in the Tuileries gardens with her
relative, and being struck with the young girl's beauty, and
moreover it is said with the effect which she produced upon
the public, became suddenly enamoured of her. The author
of the *Histoire secrète* relates the manœuvres resorted to by
Beaufort and Louise to deceive the vigilance, more affected
than real, as it would seem, of her old aunt. In short, the
Duke's passion made rapid progress; and the young girl,
yielding to the wishes of a lover who adored her and heaped
magnificent presents upon her, allowed herself to be carried
off by him at the moment that he was about to enter upon
his naval command. That expedition had for its object the
succour of the Venetians, who for some twenty-four years
had been blockaded by the Turks in Candia. Mademoiselle
Querouaille, disguised as a page, embarked with the Duke,
who, shortly after landing, was cut to pieces in action. An
officer of the French force, whom the before-cited chronicle
merely designates as a marquis, and to whom Beaufort had

confided the secret of his love, offered to conduct Louise back to France. It appears that Mademoiselle Querouaille would have preferred to have been accompanied on her return by a certain smart page who had been in the Duke's service, but the marquis did not give her the option of such a choice. Yet, though Louise could not withdraw herself from the protection of the latter, there is no reason to believe that he forced his love upon her. The anonymous chronicler concedes that much; but, in his opinion, the Marquis might have hoped that Louise would have acknowledged his care and respect by the same favours which she had accorded to "Beaufort, and," he adds, "one may presume that a girl who previously, urged by love, had allowed the Duke to carry her off to Candia, could do no less for a man who showed her so much attention on the voyage back to France." More or less just as these inductions may be, it appears quite certain that this same prank of Mademoiselle Querouaille was the foundation of her fortunes. In giving his friends an account of the expedition in which he had taken part, the Marquis did not omit the episode of the Duke de Beaufort's pretended page. Henrietta of England, to whom this romantic tale was carried, became desirous of seeing the heroine of it, and Louise Querouaille was therefore duly introduced to the Duchess. The fictitious Cherubino was cunning enough to represent herself as being the victim of a forcible abduction. Henrietta listened to her story with the liveliest interest, took her into her household, and soon afterwards admitting her amongst the number of her maids of honour. Louise, at the age of nineteen, was thus at once introduced to all the pleasures and temptations of a magnificent and dissipated court. Her introduction took place at a critical moment (1669), and, in deciding her future, fate has made her destiny and character matter of history.

The conquest or the ruin of Holland had long been one of the favourite projects of Louis the Fourteenth. The Dutch, however, resisted. his overgrown power, as their ancestors had formerly defied that of Philip the Second of Spain. In order to carry his plans into execution, Louis found it necessary to detach England from the interests of Holland. This was matter of some difficulty, for an alliance with France against Holland was so odious to all parties in England, so contrary to the national prejudices and interests, that though Louis did not despair of cajoling or bribing Charles into such a treaty, the utmost caution and secresy were necessary in conducting it.

The only person who was at first trusted with this negotia- tion was the Duchess of Orleans. She was at this time about five-and-twenty, " a singular mixture of discretion, or rather dissimulation, with rashness and petulance ; of exceeding haughtiness, with a winning sweetness of manner and dispo- sition which gained all hearts." She was not, however, exactly pretty or well made, but had the dazzlingly fair com- plexion of an Englishwoman, "un teint de rose et de jasmin," a profusion of light hair, with eyes blue and bright as those of Pallas. She had inherited some of the nobler qualities of her grandfather, Henri Quatre, and all the graces and in- triguing spirit of her mother, Henrietta Maria. Early banished from England by the misfortunes of her family, she regarded the country of her birth with indifference, if not abhorrence, and was a Frenchwoman in education, manners, mind, and heart. She possessed unbounded power over the mind of Charles the Second, whose affection for her was said to exceed that of a brother for a sister; he had never been known to refuse her anything she had asked for herself or others, and Louis trusted that her fascinations would gain from the king of England what reason and principle and patriotism would have denied.

The shrewdness of mind and inclination for intrigue which characterised his sister-in-law's maid-of-honour did not escape the observation of Louis. In her he found an apt as well as willing instrument in the secret negotiation of which he had constituted her mistress the plenipotentiary. For such compliance the manners of the time may, to a certain extent, furnish La Querouaille with an excuse. At Versailles, ideas of honour and morality had lost their ordinary signification : the men envied generally the lot of Amphitryon, and the women lost every instinct of modesty when it became a question about satisfying a caprice of Jupiter. Breathing such a vitiated atmosphere, and having so many lamentable examples before her eyes, Mademoiselle Querouaille saw only the dazzling side of the proposition made to her— the hope of reigning despotically over the heart of a great prince, and of becoming the equal of that La Vallière whose *elevation* was the object of so much envy and feminine ambition.

It was arranged, therefore, that the piquant Bas-Bretonne should be brought under the notice of the amorous Charles II. during a visit to him, arranged to take place at Dover. In order to give the interview between the royal brother and sister the appearance of an accidental or family meeting, the pretext of a progress to his recently acquired Flemish territories was resorted to by Louis, who set out with his queen, his two mistresses De Montespan and La Vallière, the Duchess of Orleans and Mademoiselle de Montpensier, with their respective retinues, and attended by the most beautiful women of the Court. The splendour exhibited on this occasion exceeded all that had been witnessed, even during the reign of this pomp-loving monarch. Thirty thousand men marched in the van and rear of the royal party; some of them destined to reinforce the garrisons of the conquered country, others to work upon the fortifications, and others again to level the roads. It was a continued series of fêtes, banquets, and triumphs, the ostensible honours being chiefly for Madame de Montespan; the real object of this famous journey, well-nigh unparalleled for its lavish and luxurious ostentation, was known only to Henrietta of England, who enjoyed in secret her own importance, and this gave a new zest to the pleasures with which she was surrounded.

On reaching Dunkirk, the Duchess of Orleans embarked for England with her maid-of-honour and a small but chosen retinue, and met Charles at Dover, where this secret negotiation was initiated. The result anticipated came to pass, and proved that Louis had not miscalculated the power of his sister-in-law over her easy-going and unscrupulous brother. Charles fell into the snare laid for him, and Henrietta carried most of the points of that disgraceful treaty, which rendered the King of England the pensioned tool of France, and his reign the most abject in the annals of her native country.

Aiming rather to stimulate than gratify the languid desires of her brother for fresh feminine novelty, the Duchess of Orleans, with finished finesse, appeared not to perceive the attention which the piquant charms and almost childish grace of her young maid-of-honour won from the captivated King. Nor did she, at her departure, leave Louise in England, as some historians have erroneously supposed. In order to render the impression which her fair attendant had

made upon Charles more deep and lasting, it was sought by
her absence to incite the desire felt by her royal brother to
retain her in his Court.   The secret negotiation with which
Louis had entrusted his sister-in-law had not been, in fact, yet
completed.   To conduct it to a prosperous termination, to
preserve perfect harmony between France and England, it
was still needful to make use of another kind of female influence. It was necessary, moreover, that such influence should
become permanent—a thing hitherto very difficult at courts
wherein the fair sex disputed strenuously and shamelessly
for the royal favour.   But thus much seemed certain—that
the key to the will of the sovereign of Great Britain had
been found in Mademoiselle Louise Querouaille.

Charles had indeed written in reply to his sister, on the
8th July of the preceding year (1668), that "in every negotiation she shall have a share, which will prove how much I
love her."   In August he told the French ambassador—" The
Duchess of Orleans passionately desires an alliance between
me and France; and as I love her tenderly, I shall be happy
to let her see what power her entreaties have over me."
Henrietta, probably, did not consider that by thus bringing her
brother into alliance with France she was betraying her native
country.   She no doubt thought rather of augmenting the
greatness of Charles than of benefiting England.   The sea
should be given up to England; the territory of Continental
Europe to France.   Louis XIV. expressly declared, in
opposition to the views of Colbert, "that he would leave
commerce to the English—three-fourths of it at least—that
all he cared for was conquest."   But that would have
involved, as a first step, the conquest of England herself,
and have cost torrents of blood.   The fascinating Henrietta,
doubtless, did not perceive this when she trod so far in the

fatal footsteps of her ancestress, Mary Stuart. She had none of her rash violence, but not a little of her spirit of romantic intrigue, and that feminine delight of having in hand a tangled skein, of which she held securely the end of the thread.

The secret negotiation of the treaty, however, went on between the two kings. Louis had submitted to exorbitant conditions on the score of money, and to another, moreover, sufficiently weighty. It was that Charles, converted to the Romish faith, should share with him in the conquest of Holland, should send a considerable military force thither, and should keep for himself the Dutch islands opposite to England—an advantage so enormous to the latter power that it would have rendered national the odious alliance, and glorified the treason.

Two points still remained unsettled : first, to persuade Charles to commence the war before his conversion—a step considered easy to obtain ; but that conversion terrified him when the moment came for carrying it out. Secondly—and which proved the most difficult—was to induce him to despatch very few troops—too few to take and afterwards hold the territory promised him. Louis XIV. stipulated to send 120,000 men there ; Charles II. engaged to furnish 6000, which number his sister prevailed upon him to reduce to 4000.

Such was the sad, disgraceful, deplorable negotiation imposed by the great King upon his sister-in-law. She had always obeyed him (as she herself said), and she obeyed him in this matter, rendering her brother doubly a traitor by his abandonment of the latter condition, which lessened his treason.

Everybody had envied the Duchess her visit to England,

none knew the bitterness it entailed. The King confided in her, and yet distrusted her. Otherwise he would not have had her accompanied by the pretty doll, with her baby face, whose office it was to ensnare the licentious Charles. Henrietta was compelled to take her over to England, and, in fact, to chaperone her. For such self-abasement the King had hand-somely rewarded the compliant maid-of-honour, promising to give her an estate, and so much per head for each bastard she might have by Charles of England.

Henrietta endured all this shameful bargaining, hoping that her royal brother would obtain from the Pope the dis-solution of her marriage with the worthless, stupid, profligate Duke of Orleans, on whom her wit and charms were equally thrown away. She might then remain at his court and be the virtual Queen of England, by governing him through female influence. Her brilliant hopes, however, were destined to be speedily dissipated, and her career cut short by a painful and treacherous death.

On her return from England, two surprises awaited her: not only did she find the Duke, her husband, exasperated against her, but what she had least of all expected, the King very cold in his demeanour towards her. Louis had got from her all he desired. His changed attitude emboldened a cabal in her own household to effect her destruction. Those who formed it were creatures of her husband's de-testable favourite, the Chevalier de Lorraine, whom they believed had been banished by the King through her en-treaties. The poor Duchess wept bitterly on finding that she had now no support from any one about her. The Duke, in the exercise of his marital authority, took her from Court, not permitting her any longer to visit Versailles. The King might have insisted upon her attendance there but did not. In tears, she suffered herself to be carried off to St. Cloud. There she felt herself alone, with every hand against her.

The weather was excessively hot. On her arrival at St. Cloud, she took a bath, which made her ill, but she soon recovered from it, and during two days was tolerably well— eating and sleeping. On the 28th of June she asked for a cup of chicory, drank it, and at the same moment became red, then pale, and shrieked aloud. The poor Duchess, commonly so patient under pain, gave way under the excess of her anguish, her eyes filled with tears, and she exclaimed that she was dying.

Inquiries were made about the water the Duchess had drunk, and her waiting-woman said that she had not prepared it herself, but had ordered it to be made, and then asked that some of it might be given her, drank of it; but there is no evidence to show that the water had not been changed in the interval.

Was it an attack of cholera, as was said? The symptoms in no wise indicated that species of disorder. The Duchess's health was very much shattered, and she was doubtless liable to be rapidly carried off. But the event had very plainly been hastened (as in the case of Don Carlos); nature had been assisted. The Duke's valets—who were, as to fidelity, much more the servants of his banished favourite, the Chevalier de Lorraine—comprehended that, in the approaching alliance of the two kings, and the need they would have of each other's confidence, the Duchess might in some moment of tenderness recover her absolute power over the King, who would in such event sweep his brother's household clear of them all. They well knew the Court, and surmised that, if she were to die, the alliance would nevertheless be main-

tained, and the matter hushed up; that she would be
lamented, but not avenged; that facts accomplished would
be respected.

Good care was taken not to confide the secret to the
wretched Duke, her husband; it was even thought that it
might be possible to get him out of the way—to keep him
in Paris, where by chance, indeed, he was detained. Philip
of Orleans was really astonished when he beheld his agonised
wife, and ordered an antidote to be given her; but time was
lost in administering the *poudre de vipère*. The Duchess
asked only for an emetic, and the doctors obstinately refused
her one. Strange, too, the King, who, on his arrival, re-
monstrated with them, was equally unsuccessful in obtaining
for the sufferer that which she craved. The medicos held
steadily to their opinion: they had pronounced it to be
cholera, and they would not swallow their own words.

Were they in the plot? That did not follow. For,
besides the professional pride which forbade them to
belie themselves, they might fear to discover more than
they wished—to act in a very uncourtier-like manner by dis-
covering traces but too evident of poisoning. In such case
the alliance, perhaps, might have been broken off, and the
projects of both King and clergy for the Dutch and English
crusade have come to nothing. Such blundering fellows
would never have been forgiven. So the physicians were
.prudent and politic. It was altogether a grievous spectacle.
Here was a woman universally beloved, yet who inspired no
one with any strong feeling. Everybody was interested—
went and came; but no one would assume any responsibility,
no one obeyed her last and constant prayer. She wanted to
eject the poison by the aid of an emetic. No one dared to
give it her. " Look," she exclaimed, " my nose is gone—

shrunk to nothing." It was observed, in fact, that it was
already like that of an eight days' corpse. For all that,
they stuck to the doctors' opinion : " It is nothing." With
only one exception, nobody seemed uneasy about her ; some
even laughed. Mademoiselle de Montpensier alone showed
indignation at all this heartless indifference, and had the
courage to remark that " At any rate they should endeavour
to save her soul," and went in search of a confessor.

The people belonging to the household, one and all, recommended that the curé of St. Cloud should be sent for,
certain that, as he was unknown to the Duchess, their
mistress would confess nothing of moment to him. Mademoiselle, however, would not hear of him as confessor:
" Fetch Bossuet," she said, " and meanwhile call in the
Canon Feuillet."

Feuillet was a very wary ecclesiastic, and quite as prudent
as the physicians. He persuaded *Madame* to offer herself
up as a sacrifice to Heaven without accusing anyone. The
Duchess said, in fact, to Marshal de Grammont, " They have
poisoned me—but by mistake." She exhibited throughout
an admirable discretion and perfect gentleness. She embraced
the Duke, her husband, whispering to him—in allusion to
the outrageous arrest of the Chevalier de Lorraine—that
she had " never been unfaithful to him."

The English Ambassador having arrived, she spoke to
him in English, telling him to conceal from her brother
that she had been poisoned. The Abbé Feuillet, who had
not quitted her, overhearing the word "*poison*," stopped her,
saying, " *Madame*, think only of God now ! " Bossuet, who
next came in, continues Feuillet, confirmed her in those
thoughts of self-abnegation and discretion. For a long
time back, she had looked to Bossuet to console her in that

supreme moment. She desired that after her decease an emerald ring should be given to him which she had reserved for that purpose.

By degrees, however, the unfortunate Duchess found herself left almost alone. The King had taken his departure, after manifesting great emotion, and the Duke also in tears. All the Court had disappeared. Mademoiselle de Montpensier was too much affected to bid her farewell. She was sinking fast, felt an inclination to sleep, woke up suddenly, inquired for Bossuet, who placed a crucifix in her hand, and, whilst in the act of embracing it, she expired. The clock at that moment struck three, and the first faint light of dawn was visible (June 29th, 1670).

The English Ambassador expressed a desire to be present at the *post-mortem* examination, and the doctors did not fail to pronounce the cause of her death to be an attack of *cholera morbus* (so Mademoiselle de Montpensier states), and that mortification had for some time past set in. He was not the dupe of such opinion; neither was Charles II., who, at first, indignantly refused to receive the letter addressed to him by the Duke of Orleans. But to persevere in such a line of conduct would have been to bring about a rupture of the pending negotiation and the loss of the French subsidy. He calmed down, therefore, and pretended to believe the explanations that were offered him. It was, however, remembered that the Chevalier de Lorraine, the Duke's unworthy favourite, had openly accused *Madame* as the instigator of his banishment; and Saint-Simon asserts that the King, before consenting to his brother marrying again, was resolved to know whether he had really had the Duchess poisoned, and with that view summoned Furnon, Henrietta's master of the household. From him he learned that the poison had been sent from Italy by the Chevalier de Lorraine to Beauveau, equerry to the Duchess, and to D'Effiat, her captain of the guard, but without the knowledge of the Duke. "It was that *maître-d'hôtel* who himself related it," says Saint-Simon, "to M. Joly de Fleury, from whom I had it."

A story but too probable. But that which appears in-credible, and which nevertheless is quite certain, was that the poisoners were perfectly successful, that shortly after the crime the King permitted the Chevalier de Lorraine to serve in the army, appointed him marshal-de-camp, and allowed him to return to Court. What explanation, what palliation, can there be for such an enormous outrage to our common humanity? It has truly been said that "the intrigues which led to the murder of the unfortunate Henrietta of England present such a scene of accumulated horrors and iniquity, that, for the honour of human nature, one could wish that the curtain had never been raised which hid them from our knowledge."

The last political act of the Duchess of Orleans was one of decisive import, and calculated to secure for a long time the subjection of the English nation. Although seriously afflicted by the death of his sister, the thought-less Charles seemed especially occupied with the design of bringing over to England the attractive maid-of-honour who had made such a lively impression upon him, as had been intended, during the short visit to Dover already mentioned. On the melancholy tidings of Henrietta's death reaching England, the profligate Duke of Bucking-ham was despatched to Paris as envoy extraordinary, ostensibly to inquire into the particulars of that catastrophe

but in reality, as Burnet says, to conclude the treaty.
This he accomplished ; France agreeing to give two mil-
lions of livres (£150,000) for Charles's conversion to
popery, and three millions a year for the Dutch war.
Large sums of money were also distributed to Buckingham,
Arlington, and Clifford.

Buckingham, that complaisant companion of " the merry
monarch," who, " everything by turns and nothing long,"
having been the first to observe the impression the
mignonne maid-of-honour had made on the King's susceptible fancy, had little hesitation in attaching to his
diplomatic office the very undignified one of Sir Pandarus,
and therefore with a brave defiance of decorum bent all
his efforts to overcome the scruples, if any there might
be, lingering in the mind of Louise with regard to trans-
ferring herself to the service of the Queen of England,
poor Catherine of Braganza. As she was then placed
through the death of the Duchess of Orleans, a convent
was the only retreat Mademoiselle Querouaille could look
forward to in France ; and as religious seclusion was not
at all congenial to the lively nymph, she was not found
impracticable to Buckingham's overtures. Nor were the
latter's efforts entirely disinterested in the matter. He
had lately had a fierce quarrel with " old Rowley's " imperious mistress, the Duchess of Cleveland, and having
sworn hatred and revenge against that profligate beauty,
sought to turn the French maid-of-honour to his own
advantage by raising up a rival in the King's affections,
who should be wholly governed by himself. He therefore
represented seriously to Louis that the only way to secure
Charles to French interests was to give him a French
mistress ; and he told Charles jestingly that he ought to

take charge of his sister's favourite attendant, if only out of "decent tenderness for her memory."

The delicate affair, in short, was soon arranged; an invitation, so formally worded as to wear the semblance of propriety, was sent from the English Court, and Louise immediately departed for Dieppe, escorted by part of the Duke of Buckingham's suite, and his grace's promise to join her with all convenient speed. But, as usual with the man whose "ambition was frequently nothing more than a frolic, and whose best designs were for the foolishest ends," who "could keep no secret nor execute any design without spoiling it," he totally forgot both the lady and his promise, and, leaving the forsaken demoiselle at Dieppe to cross the Straits as she best might, sailed to England by way of Calais. Lord Montagu, then our Ambassador at Paris, hearing of the Duke's escapade, immediately sent over for a yacht, and ordered some of his own attendants to convey her, with all honour, to Whitehall, where she was received by Lord Arlington with all respect, and forthwith appointed maid-of-honour to the Queen.

The intoxication of Charles was complete, and the man who had supported patiently the furious outbreaks of Barbara Palmer * and the saucy petulence of Nell Gwynne, was the more able to appreciate "les grâces décentes" of the foreign maid-of-honour, who, in the profaned walls of Whitehall, diffused the delicate odour of Versailles.

The purpose of her receiving an appointment at the Court of St. James's was apparently foretold, for Madame de Sévigné thus writes to her daughter:—"Ne trouvez-vous pas bon de savoir que Querouaille dont l'étoile avait été

* Duchess of Cleveland.

devineé avant qu'elle partit, l'a suivie très-fidèlement?
Le roi d'Angleterre l'a aimée, elle s'est trouvée avec une
légère disposition à ne le pas haïr."*

It is doubtful, however, whether Charles did immediately
enjoy his conquest. If it be noted that the Duke of
Richmond only came into the world in 1672, we may be led
to suppose that Mademoiselle Querouaille did not yield without hesitation to the desires of her royal lover; and that sup-
position becomes almost a certitude, when one reads this
passage of a letter which Saint-Evremond addressed to his
fair countrywoman :—

> "Suffer yourself rather to follow the bent of your temptation, instead of
> listening to your pride. Your pride would soon cause you to be sent back
> to France, and France would fling you, as has been the lot of many others,
> into some convent. But allowing that you should choose of your own free
> will that dismal kind of retreat, still it would be necessary beforehand to
> render yourself worthy of entering therein. What a figure you would cut
> there, if you had not the character of a penitent ! True penitence is that
> which afflicts and mortifies us at the recollection of our faults. Of what
> has a good girl to be penitent who has done nothing wrong ? You would
> appear ridiculous in the eyes of the other nuns, who, repenting from just
> motives, should discover that your repentance was only grimace."

Louise committed the error of not only approving the
advice of that equivocal monitor, but the greater error of
following it. Experience came very soon to open her
eyes.

In 1672, as has been said, the Querouaille having presented the King with a son, her favour increased considerably. In 1673 she was created *Duchess of Portsmouth*, and
at the close of the same year Louis XIV., alike to flatter the
King of England, and to confirm him in his alliance with
himself against Holland, as to reward the good offices of

* Letter 190.

Louise Querouaille, conferred upon the latter the domain of D'Aubigny, in Berry. This domain given, in 1422, by Charles VII. to John Stuart, " as a token of the great services which he had rendered in war to that King," had reverted to the crown of France. In the letter of donation which Louis sent to Charles, it stated that " after the death of the Duchess of Portsmouth, the demesne of Aubigny shall pass to such of the natural children of the King of Great Britain as he shall nominate." Charles II. nominated Charles Lennox (his son by Querouaille), and created him Duke of Richmond on the 19th of August, 1675.

Although *maîtresse-en-titre,* and favourite mistress as she became, she could not, however, prevent the unworthy and frequent resort of the debauched prince to rivals of a lower grade, and Madame de Sévigné penned some amusing lines on the subject of those duplicate amours :—" Querouaille has been in no way deceived; she had a mind to be the King's mistress, she has her wish. He passes almost every evening in her company, in presence of the whole Court. She has a child which has just been acknowledged, and on whom two duchies have been bestowed. She amasses wealth, and makes herself feared and respected wherever she can ; but she could not foresee finding a young actress in her path by whom the King is bewitched. . . . He shares his attentions, his time, and his health between them both. The actress is quite as proud as the Duchess of Portsmouth : she spites her, makes wry faces at her, assails her, and often carries the King off from her. She boasts of those points in which she is preferable—that she is young, silly, bold, debauched, and agreeable ; that she can sing, dance, and play the part *de bonne foi.* She has a son by the King, and is determined that he shall be acknowledged.

Here are her reasons :—' This Duchess,' she says, ' acts
the person of quality; she pretends that she is related to
everybody in France. No sooner does any grandee die,
than she puts on mourning. Ah well! if she is such a
great lady, why did she condescend to become a *catin?*
She ought to expire with shame : for myself, it is my pro-
fession ; I don't pique myself on anything else. The King
keeps me ; I am at present his solely. I have brought him a
son, whom I intend he shall acknowledge, and I am assured
that he will, for he loves me quite as well as he does his
Portsmouth.' This creature takes the top of the walk, and
embarrasses and puts the Duchess out of countenance in a
most extraordinary manner."

In Mrs. Nelly, with all her good qualities, Charles had
not found exactly a rose without thorns to stick in his but-
ton-hole. In her too wild fun, or spirit of mockery, she was
apt, as most others, to give demonstration of all the variety
of her woman's nature and her woman's wit, and to make her
baffled and humbled sovereign wish in his inmost heart that
he had never had anything to do with her.

Such were the annoyances—doubtless unforeseen by Mademoiselle Querouaille on quitting France, and to which La
Vallière and Montespan were not exposed in the Court of
the *Grand Monarque,* where vice itself put on airs of
grandeur and majesty. It must be owned, however, that
Madame de Sévigné exaggerates when she pretends to
establish a sort of equilibrium between the position of the
actress and that of the Duchess. The triumphs of Nell
Gwynne were triumphs of the alcove ; whilst her Grace
of Portsmouth reigned without a rival over the realm of
diplomacy. Charles II. was in the habit of passing a great
portion of his time in her apartments, where often, in the

midst of a joyous circle, he met Barillon, the French Ambassador, who, from his agreeable manners, was freely admitted to all the amusements of the indolent monarch. It was by means of these frequent conversations that, seizing the favourable moment, the Duchess and the Ambassador succeeded in obtaining an order which suddenly changed the face of Europe, by bringing about the signature of the Treaty of Niméguen, and more than once it fell to her lot to obtain a success of the same kind, to which neither her arrogant Grace of Cleveland nor the piquant Nelly could ever pretend. In political affairs the Querouaille held her own triumphantly over all her rivals, and obtained a dominion that ended only with the life of Charles. Too sensible to exact a strict fidelity from the King, the Duchess of Portsmouth was content to sigh in silence so long as her womanly feelings alone were sported with ; but when it seemed likely that the influence which she strove to utilise to the profit of France might be trenched upon, her resentment broke forth in sudden and sweeping ebullitions which even the dread of a public scandal was impotent to repress. The correspondence of Bussy-Rabutin furnishes us with a scene of that description :—

" It is rumoured that Querouaille has been sermonising the King, crucifix in hand, as well both to wean him from other women as to bring him back to Christianity : in fact, it appears that she herself has been very near the point of death. However, three or four days afterwards, finding herself better, she rose from her bed, and dragged herself into the box where the King was seeing a play in company with Madame de Mazarin, and there she overwhelmed him with endless reproaches for his infidelity. Love and jealousy are strong passions."

Hortensia Mancini, Duchess de Mazarin, who was commonly thought to be the finest woman in Europe, and more than that—a very great lady, aunt of the Duchess of York, might have easily supplanted the "baby-faced" Querouaille in the inconstant heart of Charles Stuart, but that the haughty Italian paid small attention to the predilections of that prince, whom she cut to the quick by receiving before his face the advances of the Prince de Monaco, and so Charles returned "*à ses premières amours.*" That phrase, somewhat vague in so far as it applies to the sensual instincts of a man who did not even believe in friendship, describes at least accurately that passionate feeling with which the Duchess of Portsmouth had inspired him. Under certain circumstances—very rare, it is true—she went so far as to sacrifice to him entirely her political *rôle,* and when the question of the famous "bill of exclusion" arose, she was seen to throw herself at the King's feet, and implore her royal lover not to rush headlong to destruction ;* entreating him to abandon, if it must be so, the interests of his brother and those of Catholicism, rather than compromise his crown and life. Such proceeding appears still more generous, if we reflect that, in spite of the irregular position which she had accepted, the Duchess had remained deeply attached to her religion and her native country, and that at that juncture no one was ignorant that an era of persecution was about to commence for the reformed Churches of France. Two years later, on the eve of the Niméguen treaty, the decline of the great reign was already foreshadowed; the influence of incapable though *right-thinking* men became daily more marked, and the star of the austere Frances d'Aubigny (Maintenon) arose slowly above the horizon. Conversions at any price were clamoured for, and no extent of sacrifice deterred the proselytisers from bringing back within the fold souls of quality, save leaving one day

* Macaulay.

to Louvois' dragoons the charge of enlightening the Protestant vulgar. The Duchess of Portsmouth was, together with the Duchess of York, at the head of the English propagandists, and, curious enough, a regular exchange of edifying letters took place between the future foundress of Saint-Cyr and the joyous sinner of the Court of St. James's. Louis XIV., desirous of duly recompensing the services of the royal favourite, conferred upon her by letters-patent dated January, 1684, the French title of Duchess d'Aubigny.

Thus had Louise Querouaille reached the summit of her rapid prosperity; but a great turn of chance was at hand, and in a moment she was about to be hurled from that dizzy height.

Lord Macaulay has graphically sketched the memorable scene in which she figured so creditably when Charles was struck with his fatal seizure. On the 2nd of February, 1685, " scarcely had Charles risen from his bed when his attendants perceived that his utterance was indistinct, and that his thoughts seemed to be wandering. Several men of rank had, as usual, assembled to see their sovereign shaved and dressed. He made an effort to converse with them in his usual gay style ; but his ghastly look surprised and alarmed them. Soon his face grew black; his eyes turned in his head; he uttered a cry, staggered, and fell into the arms of one of his lords. A physician, who had charge of the royal retorts and crucibles, happened to be present. He had no lancet; but he opened a vein with a penknife. The blood flowed freely; but the King was still insensible.

" He was laid on his bed, where, during a short time, the Duchess of Portsmouth hung over him with the familiarity of a wife. But the alarm had been given. The Queen and the Duchess of York were hastening to the room. The favourite concubine was forced to retire to her own apartments. Those apartments had been thrice pulled down and thrice rebuilt by her lover to gratify her caprice. The very furniture of the chimney was massive silver. Several fine paintings, which properly belonged to the Queen, had been transferred to the dwelling of the mistress. The sideboards were piled with richly wrought plate. In the niches stood cabinets, masterpieces of Japanese art. On the hangings, fresh from the looms of Paris, were depicted, in tints which no English tapestry could rival, birds of gorgeous plumage, landscapes, hunting matches, the lordly terrace of Saint-Germain's, the statues and fountains of Versailles.* In the midst of this splendour, purchased by guilt and shame, the unhappy woman gave herself up to an agony of grief, which, to do her justice, was not wholly selfish."

On the morning on which the King was taken ill, the Duchess of York had, at the request of the Queen, suggested the propriety of procuring spiritual assistance. "For such assistance," continues Macaulay, "Charles was at last indebted to an agency very different from that of his pious wife and sister-in-law. A life of frivolity and vice had not extinguished in the Duchess of Portsmouth all sentiments of religion, or all that kindness which is the glory of her sex. The French Ambassador, Barillon, who had come to the palace to inquire after the King, paid her a visit. He found her in an agony of sorrow. She took him into a secret room, and poured out her whole heart to him. "I have," she said, "a thing of great moment to tell you. If it were known, my head would be in danger. The King is really and truly a Catholic; but he will die without

* Evelyn's Diary, Jan. 24, 1681-2. Oct. 4, 1683.

being reconciled to the Church. His bedchamber is full of Protestant clergymen. I cannot enter it without giving scandal. The Duke is thinking only of himself. Speak to him. Remind him that there is a soul at stake. He is master now. He can clear the room. Go this instant, or it will be too late."

Barillon hastened to the bedchamber, took the Duke aside, and delivered the message of the mistress. The conscience of James smote him. He started as if roused from sleep, and declared that nothing should prevent him discharging the sacred duty which had been so long delayed. Several schemes were discussed and rejected. At last the Duke commanded the crowd to stand aloof, went to the bed, stooped down, and whispered something which none of the spectators could hear, but which they supposed to be some question about affairs of state. Charles answered in an audible voice, " Yes, yes, with all my heart." None of the bystanders, except the French Ambassador, guessed that the King was declaring his wish to be admitted into the bosom of the Church of Rome.

The difficulty was to find a priest at a moment's notice; for, as the law then stood, the person who admitted a prose-lyte into the Roman Catholic Church was guilty of a capital crime. John Huddleston, a Benedictine monk, however, who had, with great risk to himself, saved the King's life after the battle of Worcester, readily consented to put his life a second time in peril for his prince. Father Huddle-ston was admitted by the back door. A cloak had been thrown over his sacred vestments; and his shaven crown was concealed by a flowing wig. " Sir," said the Duke, " this good man once saved your life. He now comes to save your soul." Charles faintly answered, " He is welcome."

Huddleston went through his part better than had been
expected, for he was so illiterate that he did not know what
he ought to say on an occasion of so much importance, and
had to be instructed on the spot by a Portuguese ecclesiastic, one Castel Melhor. The whole ceremony occupied
about three-quarters of an hour; and, during that time, the
courtiers who filled the outer room had communicated their
suspicions to each other by whispers and significant glances.
The door was at length thrown open, and the crowd again
filled the chamber of death.

It was now late in the evening. The King seemed much
relieved by what had passed. His natural children were
brought to his bedside—the Dukes of Grafton, Southampton,
and Northumberland, sons of the Duchess of Cleveland;
the Duke of St. Albans, son of Eleanor Gwynne; and the
Duke of Richmond, son of the Duchess of Portsmouth.
Charles blessed them all, but spoke with peculiar tenderness
to Richmond. One face, which should have been there, was
wanting. The eldest and best beloved child was an exile
and a wanderer. His name was not once mentioned by his
father.

During the night Charles earnestly recommended the
Duchess of Portsmouth and her boy to the care of James;
"And do not," he good-naturedly added, "let poor Nelly
starve." The Queen sent excuses for her absence by
Halifax. She said she was too much disordered to resume
her post by the couch, and implored pardon for any offence
which she might unwittingly have given. "She asks my
pardon, poor woman!" cried Charles; "I ask hers with all
my heart."

At noon of the next day (Friday, February 6th) he passed
away without a struggle.

As it commonly happens in the sequel of such sudden and mournful events, the most absurd rumours did not fail to be circulated on the subject of Charles's death. According to one, the Duchess of Portsmouth had poisoned the King with a cup of chocolate; another asserted that the Queen had poisoned him with a jar of preserved pears. Time has done justice to these ridiculous suspicions; but that which will probably never be discovered is the exact nature of the unfortunate monarch's malady, whom a deplorable fatality caused to fall into the hands of ignorant physicians who, not being able to agree amongst themselves, tortured the patient haphazard for many hours together.

Hume, at the end of his dissertation upon the hypothesis of the poisoning of Charles, relates the following anecdote :—
" Mr. Henley, of Hampshire, told me that the Duchess of Portsmouth having come to England in 1699, he learned that she had caused it to be understood that Charles II. had been poisoned, and that, being desirous of ascertaining the fact from the Duchess's own mouth, she told him that she continually urged the King to place himself at his ease as well as his people, and to live in perfect understanding with his Parliament; that he had taken the resolution of sending his brother out of the kingdom, and to convoke a Parliament, which was to have been put in execution on the day after that upon which he was seized with his first access; that, above everything, the King recommended her to keep it secret, and that she had only revealed it to her confessor; but she believed that her confessor had revealed the secret to persons who made use of that evil means of preventing the *coup d'état.*"

If such, indeed, was the political attitude of the Duchess during the last months of Charles's life, it may be conceived that the supreme recommendations of the dying monarch may have exercised little influence over the predetermined resolves of his ignoble successor, and it explains the sudden step she took to regain her native country. On her return to France she carried with her a large treasure in money and jewels. She had come to England poor, had lived there in splendour, but without much care for the future, and having proudly enjoyed a full-blown prosperity, was now about to endure adversity with courageous resolution. Having quarrelled with James II., the Duchess could not think of taking up her abode at Versailles, where her position would not have been tenable; she determined therefore to settle herself in Paris, where her house and surroundings became the object of a rigorous surveillance.

"It reached the King's ears," says Saint-Simon, "that great freedom of speech prevailed in her circle, and that she herself spoke very freely of him and Madame de Maintenon, upon which M. de Louvois was directed to prepare immediately a *lettre de cachet* to exile her far away. Courtin was an intimate friend of Louvois, who had a small house at Meudon, where the former was accustomed to enter his cabinet unceremoniously at all hours. On his entrance one evening, he found Louvois alone writing, and whilst the minister was absorbed in that occupation, Courtin perceived the *lettre de cachet* lying upon the bureau. When Louvois had finished writing, Courtin, with some emotion, asked him what that *lettre de cachet* was? Louvois told him its purpose. Courtin remarked that it was surely an ungracious act, for that, even if the report were true, the King might be content to go no further than advising her to be more circumspect. He begged and entreated him to tell the King so on his part before acting upon the *lettre de cachet;*

and that, if the King would not believe his words, he should get him, before going further, to look at the despatches of his negotiations with England, especially those relating to the important results he had obtained through the Duchess of Portsmouth at the time of the Dutch war, and during the whole of his embassy; and that after such services rendered by her, it would be dishonour to himself to forget them. Louvois, who remembered it all very well, after Courtin had reminded him of several important facts, suspended the execution of the *lettre de cachet*, and gave the King an account of the interview, and of what Courtin had said ; and upon such testimony, which recalled several facts to the King's mind, he ordered the *lettre de cachet* to be thrown into the fire, and had the Duchess of Portsmouth admonished to be more reserved in future. She defended herself stoutly from what had been imputed to her, and, true or false, she took heed in future of the nature of the conversation which was held at her house.

Louis XIV., become a bigot and a persecutor, suffered none but silent and submissive slaves to surround him. The Duchess showed herself docile to Courtin's advice, and passed in profound obscurity the many long years which remained to her of existence. Saint-Simon and Dangeau say nothing more about her, save to enregister the meagre favours which the Court measured out with an avaricious hand, and that woman, to whom was owing the signature of the Treaty of Niméguen, was reduced in 1689 to solicit a pension of 20,000 livres, which was considerably diminished when the disasters soon afterwards happened which impoverished the French nation.

Such was the parsimony exercised by the great Monarch towards a woman who had laboured strenuously for French interests so long as her sway over Charles of England lasted, and which sway only ceased with his life. " Therein she employed unceasingly all her talent for politics, all her fascinations, all her wit," says the English chronicler already cited, and whose object has been, according to his translator, anonymous like himself, to demonstrate that if Charles II. acted in a way so little conformable to the interests not only of several foreign states, but still more of his own kingdom, it was the Duchess of Portsmouth who urged him to it, through the passion with which she had inspired him, by her cunning, and the power she possessed over his mind. The same translator afterwards remarks, that " this lady obtained more easily from the King in a moment and with a *coup de langue* things the most unreasonable and the most contrary to true policy, than all the most judicious, the most voluble, the most insinuating persons could obtain from him in matters infinitely reasonable and just." Without attributing to the Duchess of Portsmouth a power of action so prejudicial to the interests of the British nation as her anonymous biographer has done, who wrote under the excitement of discontent caused, says Lyttleton, by " the strengthening of the alliance with France, the secret enemy of England and the Protestant religion, as well as by a costly war with Holland, her natural ally," Hume states that " during the rest of his life Charles II. was extremely attached to Querouaille, and that this favourite contributed greatly to the close alliance between her own country and England." Voltaire, without particularising the effects of the ascendancy of the Duchess of Portsmouth over Charles II., says that that monarch " was governed by her to the very last moment of his life." He adds that " her beauty equalled that of Madame de Montespan, and that she was in England what the other beauty had been in France, but with more influence." This assertion, accurate as it is so far as concerns political influence—for Madame de Montespan never exercised any over the government of Louis XIV.—is not equally so with regard to the question of beauty. On that head, indeed, the Duchess had her detractors. "I have seen that famous beauty, Mademoiselle Querouaille," wrote Evelyn in his *Diary*, about a month after her arrival in England; "but, in my opinion, she is of a childish, simple, and baby face."

PART III.

BOOK I.

CHAPTER I.

TWO LADIES OF THE BEDCHAMBER DURING THE WAR OF THE SPANISH SUCCESSION, LADY CHURCHILL AND THE PRINCESS DES URSINS—POLITICAL MOTIVES FOR THEIR ELEVATION IN ENGLAND AND SPAIN.

AT the outset of that historic period known as the *War of the Spanish Succession* a remarkable feature presents itself in the fact that two women were chosen to be, as it were, its advanced sentinels—the one of the Austrian party in England, the other of the French party in Spain. These were Lady Churchill (wife of the famous soldier, Marlborough), first lady of the bedchamber to our Queen Anne, and the Princess des Ursins, fulfilling, under the title of *Camerara-Mayor*, the same functions for the new Queen of Spain, Marie-Louise of Savoy, first wife of Philip V.

The perpetual struggle previously waged between France and Spain for two centuries constitutes a theme of no ordinary interest. True, that in modern times armed interventions and dynastic and family tendencies have attested the political predominance of the former power, but it was not so in the sixteenth and seventeenth centuries, when the bigoted Philip II. looked upon himself as the head of all Catholicism and the vicegerent of God on earth. The general character of the struggle, the events, the men, the results, are all worthy of consideration, and replete with illustrations of historical and political adventure. Every effort made by the two great adversaries shook Europe to its centre, and the ultimate result of each has always been in favour of the great cause of religious and political freedom. Two centuries of warfare between two absolute governments and two states so profoundly Catholic gave birth to the first European republic —Holland; and served to confirm the power of the great Protestant state—England; and to establish religious liberty in Germany.

A brief glance at the more immediate circumstances which brought about this *War of Succession* may here be necessary. The Treaty of the Pyrenees had terminated the long struggle above alluded to ; peace being cemented by the marriage of the Infanta Maria Theresa, daughter of Philip IV. of Spain, to the young Louis XIV. of France, on the 3rd of June, 1660. The royal husband renounced for himself and his heirs all right of succession to the Spanish throne, but was promised in return a moderate dowry, which, however, was only partially paid. Forty years after this marriage, Charles II. of Spain, widowed, childless, and broken in health, selected as his successor Prince Leopold of Bavaria, but he died when five years old. In this difficulty Charles consulted Pope Innocent XII., who decreed that the children of the Dauphin of France were the true, only, and legitimate heirs. But this negotiation was conducted with such profound secresy that it was only after the accession of Philip V., grandson of Louis XIV., that the Pope's interference became public.

The Holy Father's reply, however, was so positive, that all the scruples of Charles II. were removed. His previous will was immediately burnt in the presence of his confessor; and a new one drawn up wherein Philip d'Anjou was declared absolute heir to the crown and kingdom of Spain; which, in the event of his demise, were to devolve to the Duke de Berri, third son of the Dauphin; and, he failing, to the Archduke Charles; with the reservation, as regarded the two first, that they should not unite in their own persons the sovereignties of France and Spain; and in that of the third that he should renounce all claim to the empire of Germany if he ever became heir to the Spanish throne; while it was, moreover, finally decreed that, if by any extraordinary concatenation of events, neither of those three princes should be enabled to claim the bequest of Charles II., it should devolve upon the Duke of Savoy without any restriction whatever.

The precaution was well-timed; for shortly afterwards, Charles, losing the use of his faculties, descended into the vaults of the Escurial, where he had commanded the tombs of his father, mother, and first wife to be opened in order that he might consult their tenants upon the sacred obligations of the will he had just signed. Wildly interrogating the mouldering relics, upon which he imprinted impassioned kisses, the unfortunate monarch fell senseless upon an adjacent tomb, destined shortly to receive his own remains, and was carried from those gloomy sepulchres back to his couch only to be borne back again in a few short days a corpse.

The royal will—the subject of so much gloomy meditation, of discussions the most anxious in the councils of the Escurial, and of intrigues the most active on the part of the

foreigner, had been accepted by Louis XIV. in the name of
his grandson, the Duke d'Anjou. The cabinet of Versailles,
hoping to ally the Duke of Savoy to its policy, had brought
about a marriage between Philip V. and the daughter of
Victor Amadeus II., Marie Louise, sister of the young
Duchess of Burgundy. The House of Hapsburg, during a
period of almost hopeless anarchy, had exhausted its efforts
in the attempt to establish a political duality in Spain. " If
the government of that monarchy be closely scrutinised,"
wrote Count de Rébenac,* " it will be found that disorder
everywhere prevails to an excessive degree ; but that, in the
condition in which matters stand, scarcely any change can
be ventured upon without risk of incurring dangers more to
be dreaded than the existing evils, and a complete revolution
would be necessary before perfect order in the state could be
re-established." Rébenac added that it was not the elements
of strength that were wanting to Spain, but that they were
scattered as in a chaos, and that no master-mind existed
capable of reducing them to order and unity.   The dynasty, in fact, which reigned at Madrid at that juncture had
passed from incapacity to impotence, and henceforward there
only remained to Spain her *law of succession* to rescue her
from her abasement. The miserable Charles II. was then
making and unmaking his will continually—sometimes indi-
cating a prince of Bavaria as his successor, at others a
prince of the house of Austria. At last he chose, as has
been said, a grandson of Louis XIV., in the hope of interesting France in the preservation of the duality of the
monarchy. Two years afterwards one half of Europe was
in arms to hurl the youthful Philip from his throne.

* Memoirs of Count de Rébenac's Embassy to Spain in 1689, MS.
No. 63, fol. 224, Bibliothèque Nationale, Paris.

CHAPTER II.

THE PRINCESS DES URSINS.

THE MARRIED LIFE OF MARIE ANNE DE LA TRÉMOUILLE— SHE BECOMES THE CENTRE OF CONTEMPORARY POLITICS IN ROME.

AMONG the heroines of the Fronde there were certainly lofty minds and strongly tempered souls to be found ; but, when the French nation remitted to those Erminias and Hermengildas the care of its destiny upon some grave emergency or decisive occasion, those very women so conspicuous for their generous impulses, delicate tastes, and unsparing self-abnegation, only profited by their possession of power to inaugurate a policy the record of which has remained branded with opprobrium in history as a treason to their country. The bare remembrance, indeed, of those sterile agitations proves the first rock upon which the memory of the Princess des Ursins suffered shipwreck. In the brilliant daughter of the Duke de Noirmoutier, heiress of a name mixed up with all the struggles of that epoch, we behold a last survivor of the Regency, and the dramatic vicissitudes of a life devoted to the pursuit of political power, have blinded the mental vision of posterity to the grandeur of a work of which that eminent woman was the principal instrument. Proud and restless, as largely dominated as any other of her sex by the vivacity of her preferences and her dislikes, but full of sound sense in her views and in the firmness of her designs, the skilful adviser of a King and Queen of Spain has not received at the hands of posterity the merit due to an idea pursued with a wonderful perseverance amidst obstacles which would have daunted men even of the strongest resolution. Because her public career ended in a catastrophe, popular opinion, which readily follows success, considers as merely abortive that long career during which her hand sustained upon the brow of a French prince the tottering crown against which the arms of Europe, the distrust of Spain, and the discouragement of France vied in conspiring.

Yet in her girlhood, during the last days of the Fronde, Marie Anne de la Trémouille must early have observed how greatly beauty can aid ambition, and how, by tact, endowments the most frivolous may be brought to the service of interests the most serious and complicated. Married in 1650 to the Prince de Chalais, of the house of Talleyrand, she conceived for her young husband the sole passion to be noted throughout a life in which, especially during its later period, love figured only in the dullest of hues. This marriage took place during the wars of the second Fronde, and at an epoch when a rage for duelling, the anarchical and ruthless effect of Frenchmen's ideas touching the "point of honour," had infused a new element into the spirit of party, and had become a veritable mania. It chanced on the occasion of one of those duels in 1663—that of the two brothers Frette—wherein four fought on either side, and in which the Duke de Beauvilliers was slain, that the Prince de Chalais figured as one of the champions. The law against duelling, enforced by Henri Quatre, and revived with so much rigour by Richelieu against the father of the famous Marshal de Luxembourg, and from which practice the blood of Bouteville had not completely delivered France, was still in full vigour.

The consequences being so terrible, that the Prince de Chalais, to place himself beyond reach of them, was compelled to seek safety in flight. He succeeded in escaping to Spain, whither his wife followed him.

During this brief period of her union with the Prince de Chalais, whom she adored, Marie Anne de la Trémouille had shone as conspicuously by her wit as by her beauty in the famous circle of the Hôtel d'Albret, where she first met Madame Scarron, whose destiny it was later on in life— as Madame de Maintenon—to be so closely allied with the Princess. Thus united by ties of the tenderest affection, scarcely had the young couple quitted Madrid, after a three years' sojourn, to establish themselves at Rome, when the death of M. de Chalais left her a childless widow, without protection, and almost destitute—a prey to grief apparently the most profound, and to anxieties concerning the future readily conceivable.

Madame de Chalais was then in the plenitude of that attractive beauty so closely observed and described in all its most delicate shades by the graphic pen of the Duke de Saint-Simon when at a more advanced period of her life, but on which beauty, by a miracle of art and nature, the wasting hand of time had as yet scarcely brought a blemish.

The first years of her widowhood, passed in a convent, were marked by the liveliest sorrow. By degrees, however, love of society resumed its sway over her, and she reappeared therein with all her wonted attractiveness, markedly patronised in the highest circles of Roman society by Cardinal d'Estrées, the French ambassador — assuredly not without design, since at the same time that high functionary so distinguished her, he directed the attention of Louis XIV.

to the wit and capacity of the charming widow. It was,
therefore, in great measure with a political purpose, and by
the diplomatic tact of the two brothers d'Estrées, that the
second marriage of the Princess de Chalais with Flavio
Orsini, Duke di Bracciano, himself a widower, was arranged
(1675). Thenceforward the Palazzo Orsini became the focus
of French influence, which was further increased by a marriage promoted between her sister Louise Angélique de la
Trémouille and her brother-in-law, the Duke de Lanti.

She thus, therefore, became definitively an inhabitant of
Rome and *quasi* Roman. What did she do there ? How did
she consort with an Italian husband ? With what ambition
was she soon inspired in the more elevated position in which
her second marriage placed her at Rome ? What talents,. what
political aptitude were manifested by her, and developed at
a court which at that time bore the highest repute for skill
in politics and diplomacy ? How did Italian finesse and
cunning blend and harmonize with the quick penetration
and delicate tact of the Frenchwoman ? What advantage
did the French government, which, after the death of the
Prince de Chalais, could no longer treat her as a proscribed
subject, seek to draw immediately from her position and disposition ? What were her relations with the first personages
at the court of France, with the Roman cardinals, with the
French ambassadors at Rome, with the representatives or
the principal personages of other nations, and what splendour
did her palace display, whether through the influence of
natural taste or a calculating ambition ? In a word, what
was the mode of life, and what was the career of the Duchess
di Bracciano, at Rome, before she proceeded to make application of the science she must there have acquired upon
another and a wider stage ? These are the curious and in-

teresting points, upon which the recent discovery in the public library at Stockholm, of copies of nearly one hundred inedited letters addressed by the Princess des Ursins to Madame la Maréchale de Noailles and Madame de Maintenon, in addition to five long letters published by the Abbé Millot,* enable us to furnish very nearly complete details, ranging from 1675 to 1701.

Owning as its mistress a woman so abundantly charming, the Palazzo Orsini became more than ever the rendezvous of the best society. The Duchess di Bracciano held therein an actual Court, as numerous also as it was distinguished. Each visitor delighted to frequent it, in order to witness with his own eyes to what a degree of perfection and gracefulness a French lady could attain. The men especially sought her society; for although womanly, and more so than many around her, the habitual subject of their conversations pleased her better than those of persons of her own sex, and she therein exhibited a solidity of understanding, a correctness of view, together with a perfect lucidity of expression which captivated the Roman nobles, and made them feel it a satisfaction to submit their ideas to her, and hear her discuss them. The Duke di Bracciano was not mentally up to her mark, nevertheless in the first season which followed their union, a season of complaisant affection, when susceptibility was held in check by a more spontaneous admiration, he felt himself flattered by the homage she received, and which wore the semblance of an eulogium upon his choice and good taste. But, eventually, too mediocre, or too much kept in the background, not having wit enough himself to appreciate that of his brilliant partner without blushing at

---

* Among the *pièces justificatives* appended to the Mémoires du Maréchal de Noailles.

his own defect, or, it might be, sufficient consideration not
being given to the inevitable arousing of his masculine
amour propre, he sought to attribute to himself the popularity which she obtained, and that which might have constituted his pride became his torment. It would have been
wanting in dignity to himself, he felt, ever to have owned or
even in the least degree betrayed the secret motive of his
wounded self-love ; but the excessive extravagance of his
wife, and the enormous expenses in which she involved him
afforded ample pretext for his complaints : such was the
ground, therefore, upon which he fell back. The Princess
unhappily comprehended all this, and went to greater lengths
than ever : hence untoward misunderstandings ere long arose
between them.

Nevertheless, through the effect of her irresistible attractions, the Duchess di Bracciano became the centre of a
cosmopolitan society which, in the midst of the noisiest
diversions, debated daily in the capital of the papal dominions the weightiest problems of contemporary politics.
Whilst externally her palace on the Piazza Navone blazed
broadly with illuminated devices and coloured fires, and
made all the echoes of Rome resound in pealing harmonies
with the name of Louis the Great, in the interior of her
magnificent saloons the vicissitudes of the long struggle
waged between that monarch and the Holy Father were
watched with inquietude, whether as concerning regal claims
or the question of religious freedom—a portentous strife
which seemed to increase in energy at each fresh act of
violence on the part of Louis XIV. against his Protestant
subjects. To the arduous questions in which theology ran
so closely parallel with State interests, to the burning rivalries of doctrines and persons which then set by the ears the

most illustrious among Christian prelates, were added the
daily accidents of a policy to which fell the burden of main-
taining in all corners of the universe a constant equilibrium
between the Houses of France and Austria—a permanent
problem which soon helped to complicate the perspective
opened by the next succession to the Crown of Spain.

In such a school—borne along the brimming tide of
pleasure by the soft breeze of homage—did Madame di
Bracciano's political intelligence rapidly ripen : and if by
a glittering gaiety, ease of manner, and a species of
decorous gallantry, her life appeared to continue the traditions of Anne of Austria's time, the restrained firmness
of her opinions, her reverence for absolute authority, her
settled resolve to owe nothing to any one save to her own
Great King, combined to link her fast to the new school of
power and respect founded by Louis XIV. in the plenitude
of his sway. Thus the passion for politics and power was
not slow to obtain the mastery over the mind of a woman
constituted like Marie Anne de la Trémouille, who had failed
to find in her second marriage any community of taste or
intellect.

The disputes between Louis and Innocent XI. proved, perhaps, another source of disunion between the ducal pair. The
Orsini were in some sort a sacerdotal family, at the same
time that they stood at the head of the Roman aristocracy : it
had always furnished Pontiffs and Cardinals to the Church.
It was not, therefore, probable that the Duke di Bracciano,
who was its chief, should hold, in those famous quarrels, an
opinion contrary to that of the Holy Father, more especially
if, as it was rumoured, having no child, he had by an adoption
long kept secret, sought for a son in the family of Innocent XI. himself. The same induction cannot be drawn

from acts which were comprised in the life of the Duchess di
Bracciano. Whether at Rome or at Madrid, the ideas held
by the Court of Versailles upon dogmatic questions, or upon
the relations of the Church with the State, were hers also;
and in Italy, in the halls of the Vatican, she openly evinced
her detestation of the Jesuits, in whom the Ultramontane
doctrines were personified. Therein, in all probability, lay
a new stumbling block against which the conjugal harmony
jarred, already shaken as it was by all the dissemblances of
habit, appreciation, and of taste, which difference of nationality engendered. " *Ce ménage ne fut pas concordant,*"
says Saint-Simon; " *quoique sans brouillerie ouverte, et les
époux furent quelquefois bien aises de se séparer.*"

To escape from these different causes of domestic ennui,
the Duchess di Bracciano varied her sojourn in Italy by long
and frequent visits to France, going thither to present, by
clever and well-timed calculation, the spectacle of a Roman
princess whom no one even within the grandiose precincts
of Versailles surpassed either in true French *esprit* or steady
devotion to the Sovereign. The Duchess formed a close
intimacy with the Maréchale de Noailles, to whom she was
related; she made the acquaintance of the minister Torcy,
who was capable of appreciating all the varied resources of
her woman's nature and her woman's wit; and she was presented to Madame de Maintenon, who had become the god-
dess of the Court. Her second visit took place shortly after
the period of the Treaty of Ryswick—that is to say, near
upon that fatal conjuncture at which Louis XIV. saw England escape him for ever, supported as she was by the Dutch
alliance, and had hope only from the Court of Spain to counterbalance the formidable union of his enemies. This was
the reason that each of those personages, at Versailles or

Paris, had for retaining the Duchess di Bracciano in the interests of France in the future succession of Spain, and recommended them to her at the Papal Court, to the Spanish Ambassador at Rome, the Duke d'Uzeda, or indeed to any other Spaniard of distinction whom she might meet with in that capital.

The letters addressed to the Duchess Lanti, her sister, which are, as it were, a last echo of the conversations of the Hôtel d'Albret,* were for the most part written from Paris between the years 1685 and 1698, the latter being the date of the demise of the Duke di Bracciano. The advanced age and failing health of her second husband had, in that year, summoned her back to Rome, and a kind of reconciliation, brought about chiefly through the good offices of Cardinal Porto-Carrero—soon afterwards destined to play a great part in the political affairs of his native country—had preceded that demise, which placed the Duchess in possession of estates and property reputed to be considerable, but upon which heavy incumbrances, increased by lawsuits, brought down upon her endless anxiety and almost ruin.

The obligation of discharging an immense amount of debt compelled Madame di Bracciano to part with the property of the duchy bearing that name. She was, therefore, forced to relinquish that title and adopt that of Princess des Ursins (Orsini), under which she has taken her place in history. The beneficence of the French King was assured beforehand to a noble widow married under his auspices, ruined, so to speak, in his service, and whose palace had become the residence of his ambassador from the moment that the Prince de Monaco had superseded the disgraced Cardinal de Bouillon in that high post. The Princess obtained, therefore, one of

* Collection of M. Geffroy, pp. 1—25.

those Court pensions, the ordinary patrimony of all great
families, and of which the good offices of the Maréchale de
Noailles, the staunch patroness of her kinswoman, had ere
long succeeded in doubling the amount, when the death of
Cardinal Maidalchini had left the considerable subsidy dis-
posable by which that member of the Sacred College was
secretly secured to the policy of Louis XIV. She had,
indeed, herself solicited an increase of her pension in a
charmingly witty letter, in which she undertook to prove how
useful it would be for the King's service that she should be
richer. " My house," says she, " is the only French abode
open to the public. It is in my assemblages there that one
can speak to people whom it would be difficult to meet with
elsewhere." And thus she rose sufficiently high in the
esteem of the cabinet of Versailles to obtain even the recall
of the French Ambassador from Rome.

CHAPTER III.

AT the moment when the Court of Versailles very earnestly sought the support of the Princess des Ursins, the important business of the Spanish succession engrossed the attention of all the politicians of Europe. The question, however, still presented that undecided aspect which left the field open to every species of ambition and manœuvre. The influence of the Court of Rome and that of the Spaniards there located was necessary to the success of the House of Bourbon. Among these latter was to be numbered the Cardinal Porto-Carrero, Archbishop of Toledo, who dreamed of being, in his own day, it is said, the Ximenes of Spain. Madame des Ursins, as already stated, had formed a close friendship with that prelate, who, as a member of the Council of Castille, exercised a powerful influence alike over the mind of Pope Innocent XI. and of King Charles II. of Spain. She led him to perceive in the choice of the Duke d'Anjou a sure means of reaching the goal of his ambition. She dazzled his mental vision with " the advantages which he might derive from the just gratitude of Louis XIV." Porto-Carrero allowed himself to be seduced. At the same moment, Charles II., disquieted, tormented, and worn out with an endless train of doubts, consulted Pope Innocent XI. The latter, whom the management of Madame des Ursins and the credit of Porto-Carrero had brought to look with favour upon the pretensions of France, sent a friendly communication to the Duke d'Anjou. These counsels determined the irresolution of the Spanish King, and the Bourbons reaped the benefit of the succession of Charles V.

Thus matters stood between France and the Princess when it became necessary to choose a *Camerara-Mayor* for the young Queen. Madame des Ursins had given Louis XIV. ample proof of her devotion; she had in some sort enchained him : she could, therefore, with so much the more security invoke the gratitude of his court, which feeling, under existing circumstances, it was advisable for the cabinet of Versailles to make manifest. Thoroughly secure in that quarter, she wrote direct to the Duke of Savoy,—Philip V. making his father-in-law comprehend that it was the wish of France to see her installed in such post—and the Duke of Savoy referred the matter to Louis XIV. From that moment her elevation was certain. Such choice was the consummation of French policy.

There is something very striking indeed in that indomitable resolution one day to govern Spain, conceived and adopted so far from the theatre of events—to exercise the functions of *Camerara-mayor* to a queen of thirteen years of age, when to obtain that exalted guardianship in Court and State, every ambitious heart was throbbing from the Alps to the Pyrenees. Yet Madame des Ursins importuned no one, for no one had thought of her, Louis XIV. no more than his ministers, the Duke of Savoy no more than the King of Spain ; but that remarkable woman had mentally aimed at that as the supreme object and end of her aspirations. For its realisation she combined her measures, therefore, with an activity so ardent, with an accuracy of perception so marvellous through the mesh of intrigues which spread from Versailles to Turin and to Madrid, that she succeeded in getting herself accepted simultaneously by the three courts, through letting them think that the choice of her individuality had been for each of them the effect of a spontaneous inspiration.

The principal instrument in this affair ought to have been, and was in fact, the Maréchale de Noailles. No woman had a better footing at court or exercised a more incessant activity among the ministers. The young Count d'Ayen, her son, a personal friend of the Duke d'Anjou, and who derived a precocious importance from the gravity of his life, was, moreover, disposed to second at Madrid the secret negotiation first broached in the cabinet of Madame de Maintenon, the barriers of which *sanctum* scarcely gave way even before the Maréchale. The progress of the negotiation may be followed from day to day in the letters addressed to Madame de Noailles, conducted by that lady as her indefatigable correspondent pointed out. The first idea of Madame des Ursins may be therein detected, developed as it is with equal art and caution, and strengthened by addressing itself to the mother of a numerous family in arguments which could not fail of their effect. "I conjecture from all this," wrote the Princess, "that the Duchess of Burgundy will have the satisfaction of seeing her sister queen of that great monarchy, and as there must be some lady of rank to direct that young princess, I entreat of you, madame, that you will offer my services, before the King can cast his eyes upon some one else. I venture to say that I am better fitted than any other person whomsoever for such office from the numerous friends I have in that country, and the advantage I have in being a grandee of Spain, which would lighten the difficulties another might encounter in the matter of ceremonial customs. I speak, moreover, Spanish, and further, I am certain that such choice would be agreeable to the whole nation, by whom I can boast of having always been loved and esteemed. My design, madame, would be to go to Madrid, to remain there so long as it should please the King, and afterwards to return to Court and render an account to his Majesty of my sojourn. If it were only a question of accompanying the Queen as far as the frontier, I would not think further of the matter, for that which makes me chiefly desire it, after the King's service, which with me goes before everything, is the wish that I have to prosecute personally at the Court of Madrid certain business of importance connected with the kingdom of Naples. I should be very glad also to see my friends there, and amongst others the Cardinal Porto-Carrero, with whose aid I would find means of marrying a round dozen of your daughters in that country. You must know, madame, that I reckon upon him almost as firmly in Spain as I do upon you in France. Judge after this whether I could not bring rain or sunshine upon that Court, and whether it is with too much vanity that I offer you my services therein. I did not believe that I could persuade you to enter into this matter, madame, save in making you take a weighty interest in it, for I apprehend that you may be very weary of employing longer the Cardinal de Noailles in my behalf, to whom I have communicated my views, but you can rouse him up again, if necessary. Thus you will be the only person upon whom I shall rely for the entire conduct of this affair." Rome, 27th December, 1700.*

* Collection of M. Geffroy, p. 88.

Each difficulty is seen to vanish, one after another, under the combined efforts of secret influence and patient and persistent suppleness. Then when the moment had arrived at which it was necessary for the Duke of Savoy to decide upon a matter that affected so closely the personal expedience of his daughter, and to set M. de Torcy in motion, promptly rallied to the support of the candidate favoured by Madame de Maintenon, we find the Princess des Ursins tracing for the use of that minister a programme which a diplomatist already grown grey under the toils and anxieties of office would not have disowned.

"ROME, January, 1701.

" I dare not, Madame, allow two couriers to depart one after another, without writing to you about my business, but as I have nothing new to tell you, I shall only do myself the honour to communicate to you some reflections I have made. It is certain that the success of all this depends upon His Highness the Duke of Savoy; you have written to me clearly enough upon the subject to enable me to see that, and besides the thing speaks for itself. I am seeking, therefore, the means of gaining the confidence of that Prince, who, *au fond*, ought not to feel the slightest repugnance in preferring me to anybody else. However, as I can promise myself nothing certain from his letter, which I have the honour to forward to you, I wish to propose one thing to you which would in no way commit the King, and which not the less would assuredly determine His Royal Highness. That is, Madame, that M. de Torcy, acting for himself, and without mixing up the King's name in any way, should in course of conversation, ask the ambassador, who is at Paris, the name of the lady whom his master destines for this post, and that he would be good enough to mention me as thoroughly adapted for it, in his estimation. Ambassadors keep journals of everything that goes on, and inform their sovereigns of the most trifling matters they hear discussed in ministerial circles. What I have suggested might be taken as an insinuation which would certainly determine the Duke of Savoy to do what we desire, whilst leaving him nevertheless at full liberty to act agreeably to his fancy. I submit this idea to your prudent judgment, and should it appear to you right, you can turn it to what account you like, for you are more clever than I am."*

The trenches thus cleverly opened, the fair besiegers were not likely to fail of ultimate success. The Princess's letters to the Maréchale, so nicely calculating in the force of every phrase throughout the course of the siege, are, after her victory, the natural and almost naïve expression of delight at a success which both sides promised themselves to render fruitful. It is an instance of poor naked human nature caught in the fact. But, as in other instances, she cannot play the woman with impunity. Madame des Ursins dwells with complacency upon her description of the fabulous *cortége* which he has in preparation. Lackeys innumerable, a legion of pages and gentlemen, *fiocches* and carriages, emblazoned with gold, a suite with which in the present day a sovereign would not encumber himself, and which ate up the remainder of her fortune, all these marvels by means of which it was proposed to win over the admiration of the Spaniards to the new dynasty, were not unserviceable also in gaining over the young Duchess of Burgundy, and the details of them were welcomed by an approving smile in the sanctuary of Madame de Maintenon. The Princess des Ursins being,

---

* Collection of M. Geffroy, p. 90.

moreover, too knowing to exact anything in the shape of money from the King in addition to the high favour and all-powerful protection she had just received at his hands ; she showed herself, to use her own words, *aussi fière que gueuse.*[*] But there is a time for all things ; when we have gained possession of the tree itself, we need not be in such a hurry to strip it of its fruits.

[*] Letter to the Maréchale de Noailles of 21st June, 1701.

CHAPTER IV.

MADAME DES URSINS ASSUMES THE FUNCTIONS OF CAMERARA-
MAYOR TO THE YOUNG QUEEN OF SPAIN—AN UNPROPITIOUS
ROYAL WEDDING.

IT was, therefore, with a paraphernalia almost regal that
Madame des Ursins set forth to conduct the Princess of
Savoy to her husband. Our heroine was then in her fifty-
ninth year (1701), according to most authorities, in her sixty-
second, according to others; and either age would have been
for any one else the period for retreat. But by the rare
privilege of a singular energy, physical and moral, still
beautiful, and having as yet only prepared herself for playing
the grand part of her life's drama, she was about to make
that advanced age a point of departure in her militant career,
the outset of a new existence. She had not committed the
error of remaining attached to old customs or old styles of
dress, she had, as the present phrase runs, advanced with
the age. She had sympathised with it with a juvenile
ardour, she had noted, at a distance, its deviations. She
was desirous, by opposing it on many points, to take
advantage of its decreptitude. She could not shut her
eyes to the dazzling aspect of Madame de Maintenon's
laurels.

We have shown what the Princess was as a young woman,
and also at the mature age of forty; but it is during the
twenty-four years of her green old age (1698—1722) when

having become a great political personage, we have to behold
her exercising a powerful influence over the destinies of two
great kingdoms, and aspiring to soar to a greater height
than ever her painstaking ambition enabled her to attain.
It was then that ambition began to take entire possession of
her soul, and displaced in her heart every other sentiment
that her previous sixty-two years had not extinguished.
There can be no doubt of that fact when we discover in
her letters such a glow of youthful feeling, such scarcely
repressible delight, and finally that air of triumph with
which she proposes to welcome and profit by her first
elevation.

Her ambition, moreover, could not have had a more
brilliant and legitimate aim than that of associating herself
in the glorious task of France become the instructress of
Spain; and Madame des Ursins, who joined to her own
the aspirations of the other sex, entered upon her new
mission with a zeal, an ardour, and an activity more than
virile.

Into what profound decadence Spain had then fallen is
well known to any reader of modern history, and the history
of modern Europe contains no more terrible lesson. The
Austrian dynasty, insatiable and jealous, had sought to
impose at once upon Spain, Europe, and the world, her
political and religious despotism. Charles V. had con-
fiscated Spanish liberties and conquered the Commons.
Philip II., his son, constituting himself the representative
of Catholicism, had persecuted on all sides, whether by open
violence or intrigue, by the aid of corruption or torture,
the new principle of Protestantism. He had failed in every
quarter. The sanguinary executions of the Duke of Alva
had been answered by the creation of a new free State—

Protestant and Republican Holland. With the *Invincible Armada* was engulfed the last menace of the Spanish navy, which had been answered by the triumph of Protestant England under the glorious reign of Elizabeth. The Spanish nation itself had conspired, it must be confessed, to that decadence. It had shown no reaction either against the enervating despotism of royalty, or even the nature of the climate and soil, unequal and excessive in every way. The epoch of heroic deeds once elapsed upon the glowing arena of the Middle Ages, the Spanish people had despised labour, commerce, and industry. The soil, neglected, had returned to its primitive sterility, and almost entire provinces had become solitary deserts. Indolence and poverty are evil counsellors. The Spanish people, the nation of the Cid, had transformed her noble and fervent religion of the Middle Ages into a degrading, and too often cruel superstition. It was unhappily the popular sentiment of which Philip III. was the exponent when he expelled the Moors in 1603, thus depriving Spain—poor and already depopulated —of one hundred thousand rich and industrious families; and it was national opinion also which had accepted and maintained the domination of the monks and the hateful empire of the Inquisition.

France, on the contrary, had proceeded rapidly along the path of an admirable progress. After having put an end to the sanguinary period of the religious wars, after having repressed the formidable ambition of the House of Austria, she had proclaimed the principles of tolerance and justice, destined to become common to all modern communities, and she had afforded the example of a centralisation which it was thought would prove an element of prosperity and power. Would the establishment of such a centralisation

consort with the native energy of Spain, which the peculiar
genius of her great provinces still retained ? Was it necessary, in order to rouse that generous country from its languor, merely to appeal to its recollections of the past, to the
sentiment of its dignity, to what remained of its antique
virtues, or was it indeed necessary to inoculate it with an
infusion of some better blood ? Finally, had it not become
a question whether Spain should be governed for itself, or
rather as an annexation of France, by considering it as a
simple instrument of the policy of Louis XIV.

Such were the grave questions which the accession of
Philip V. had raised. Louis XIV. had solved them in the
sense most favourable to his ambition, and if he recommended his grandson not to surround himself with Frenchmen and to respect the national feeling, it was only to bend
the more gently the genius of Spain to his own designs. The
correspondence of Madame de Maintenon—eloquent echoes
from Marly and Versailles—openly reveals that policy. No
wonder that it should do so. The interests involved in the
preservation of the balance of power in Europe were not
those which affected the great King : those of the cabinet of
Versailles, he considered ought to be the sole rule, not only
for France, but for Europe entire. So thought everybody
also who surrounded the pompous Louis. Those even who
pretended to hold themselves aloof from his moral domination—the Duke de Beauvilliers, the Duke de Chevreuse, and
the Archbishop of Cambrai—divided their hopes between
the Duke of Burgundy and the new King of Spain, the
brother of their well-beloved disciple ; and, surrounding
Philip V. with creatures of their own, would not admit that
they could govern otherwise than by Frenchmen and French
ideas. Even for that party which arrogated to itself the

title of "honest folks," animated by noble sentiments and generous illusions, it was difficult sufficiently to enlarge the narrow patriotism of the time, and to admit within it a sympathetic alliance with the ideas of any foreign nationality.

Madame des Ursins was less exclusively and more truly devoted to Spain, without failing in her devotion to France. She was a Frenchwoman at Madrid in sustaining the alliance between the two countries in view of their common interests, and in attacking by reforms the deep-seated abuses which had prepared the complete ruin of Spain ; she was so especially likewise in waging a determined fight against an institution the most repugnant to the character and intelligence of France—the Inquisition. But she became Spanish also when needful, whether she had to humour warily the national susceptibilities, or to confide the principal posts to Spaniards rather than to Frenchmen, or, finally, whether in 1709, when the guardianship of Philip V. had become a very heavy burden to the declining Louis, she manifested her indignation at the very idea, too readily accepted at Versailles, of abandoning Spain, and was stubbornly resolved, on her own part, to struggle by the side of Louis XIV.'s grandson to the last extremity.

The whole period which extends up to the moment of her first disgrace was solely employed by her in establishing her power by masking it. She still remained without a very precise mission ; the indirect encouragement of Torcy and Madame de Maintenon, it is true, soon came to sustain her, and her entire study centered in meriting at their hands, and especially at those of Louis XIV., a more effective confidence.

She had first to make herself acceptable to the Queen

of Spain. Marie-Louise of Savoy, whom her *Camerara-mayor* met for the first time on board her galley in the harbour of Villefranche, at the moment when the tearful eyes of the young princess were casting a last glance at the lovely Italian land, was that admirable queen whose life in default of mental courage became worn out by the corroding of adversity, and whose popular name has remained as a symbol in Spain of every royal and domestic virtue. Not quite fourteen at the period of that meeting, the princess was already as tall as the Duchess of Burgundy, whose perfect shape she also possessed, with a more regular cast of features and an incomparable charm in her graceful and affable manners. Smiling through her tears, and in the midst of her grief ever displaying gentleness blended with majesty, she played the queen on all occasions in a marvellous way for one so youthful, that everybody who had the honour of approaching her during the journey was struck with astonishment. Marie-Louise was a gentle and affectionate girl, of an intelligence and will in advance of her years, and which happily did not injure her natural gracefulness. For this young creature, for this child, suddenly become a wife and a queen, the presence of Madame des Ursins, still handsome even at sixty-six, sprightly and as skilful as she was eager to please, was the sole refuge beside the indolent love of a boy-king of eighteen, who gave her no protection. These two women, whom nature had created so dissimilar, were about to be united for ever in one common destiny. The young Queen appeared to be immediately struck with the value of the support which a mind so supple and vigorous offered her, and when the departure of her Piedmontese waiting-maids had torn from the poor girl-queen the last trace of family and country, she clung to her grand *camerara* as the ivy to the tree which supports it. On the other hand, Madame des Ursins did not fail to hold herself out as representing the respected authority of Louis XIV. and Madame de Maintenon ; on the other, she knew well how to initiate herself, by means of the domestic duties, of which she designedly exaggerated the importance, into the innermost prejudices of the royal wife. She made herself useful to Marie-Louise, became indispensable amidst an intercourse so privileged and private; at the same time she afforded pleasure in so doing, and that proved during the whole period of her sojourn in Spain the most solid foundation of her favour and power.

Through the Queen the *camerara-mayor* was certain of governing the King. Proportionately as the absolute monarchy, in spite of the severest warnings, set up pretensions even more and more excessive and insensate, it became also more manifest that its old traditions had rendered the princes degenerate, and that the blood was equally menaced with impoverishment in the family of Louis XIV. as in that of Charles V. The new King of Spain was deficient in moral force and determination. He had generous proclivities, without the least doubt. He was gloriously born, as the phrase then ran. Like all his race, he showed bravery on the field of battle ; but energetic persistence in long-continued designs firmly conceived, he was ever wanting in. Wearied to excess by the weight of a crown, he ended by resigning its functions ; compelled to resume them, he succumbed beneath their weight, conceived scruples touching the legitimacy of his royalty, and sunk into a crazy melancholy, which degenerated later into downright insanity.*

* The singing of Farinelli had at first the effect of charming away his dark moods, but he speedily gave way to such hallucinations that he quite

The Princess des Ursins in directing her steps towards Villefranche, the little Piedmontese port, which had been fixed upon as the place of Marie-Louise's embarkation, had merely wished to present herself to the Queen, her mistress, at the moment when the latter would be ready to enter her galley and set sail for Spain. By that means, she would avoid the necessity of putting all the royal train in mourning. For, as she had already suggested with remarkable foresight to the Maréchale de Noailles—the Court of Turin was then in mourning, and there would have been a necessity to conform to the French custom, followed by the Dukes of Savoy: on the contrary, by stopping at Villefranche and meeting the Queen at the moment of her embarkation, she would merely have to observe the usage of Spain, which only enjoined mourning upon the master and mistress of a house.

Authorised to do what seemed fit to her on that score, she had awaited therefore the arrival of the young princess at Villefranche, and with so much the more satisfaction, that at Turin she would have been exposed to a thousand annoyances. There she would have encountered the Princess de Carignan—the great lady who had taken care of her niece, Marie-Louise of Savoy, and like many other Piedmontese ladies, she wished very much to follow her into Spain, and perhaps remain there. There were many little projects, it appears, formed at Turin with the view of governing the young Queen.* For a long while it was

neglected his personal appearance, pretended to go fishing in the middle of the night, and to mount the horses which figured on the tapestry of his chamber.

* Memoirs of Louville, tom. i., and those of De Noailles, tom. ii., pp. 164, 165.

thought that they would be realised, because the report
ran that the Princess de Carignan would in fact accompany
her niece to Madrid. But Louis XIV., foreseeing that
source of embarrassment, had given an order to dismiss
all the Piedmontese ladies at the frontier, so soon as the
Queen should meet her Spanish household. Those ladies
were aware of this; but their discontent was only the
greater, and it was much to be feared lest if Madame des
Ursins should herself repair to Turin, to present herself
to the young Queen, she might be exposed to some insult
on their part. Who could tell whether, at that court,
before the departure of Marie-Louise had removed all
hope, her "position might not be menaced"? In that,
then, there arose an additional motive, and the principal
one, to stop at Villefranche, in order not to see the Queen
before the moment of embarking with her, and of entering
immediately and irrevocably upon the exercise of her
duties.

When Marie-Louise arrived there in the month of
October, 1701, the anchor of her galley was instantly
weighed and sail set for Nice, where a last farewell was
taken of Piedmont and the soil of Italy; and next, her
foot touched the French shore to make slight halts at
Toulon, at Marseilles, and at Montpellier, and despatch
thence, by way of thanks for the splendid fêtes given by
the local authorities, a salvo of homage to the Great
King at Versailles. Madame des Ursins was seated in
the royal litter, at the Queen's side, and everywhere had
her share of the honours rendered to that princess in
the various cities of France and Italy. At length the
Spanish frontier was reached, and there the Piedmontese
ladies, to the great regret of Marie-Louise and their own,

were compelled to stop and retrace their steps to Turin. The Spanish dames, appointed by Philip V., replaced them. The young Queen thereupon lost much of her characteristic amenity, and Madame des Ursins gained nothing on the score of benevolence of intention; but the jealousy of the Spanish ladies was less formidable to her.

The marriage by procuration had been performed at Turin. The definitive espousals, it was settled, should be accomplished at Figuieras, on Spanish soil, in order that Marie-Louise might not enter into the country, where she was destined to reign, save with the irrevocable titles of wife and queen. Thither was to come, on an appointed day, King Philip V. He did not keep his bride waiting for him, for, impatient to behold her to whom, by procuration, he had already given his hand, and whose charms had been highly extolled to him, he passed beyond the place fixed upon for the official reception, and went forwards disguised, without pomp or noise, to meet her. He was followed by a very small number of cavaliers, and so soon as he perceived the queen's retinue approaching the town of Hostalnovo, he quitted his attendants, and " pricked forward like a courier " towards the royal litter. Desirous of preserving his incognito, he presented himself as a king's messenger, sent to get the earliest tidings of the Queen, and he addressed himself in Spanish to the Princess des Ursins, to receive the information which he asserted he was ordered to obtain. The Queen immediately guessed that the messenger was no other than the King himself. She was, therefore, anxious to answer him herself, and so their conversation commenced, touching her health and that of

King Philip V., the incidents of her journey, and it was continued for about a quarter of an hour. For some time the Queen pretended not to recognise him; but, at last, her emotion getting the better of her, she broke through the assumed incognito in which the King had shrouded himself, and was anxious to alight from her litter. Philip, without further revealing himself, stayed her with his hand. Whereupon, she grasped hold instantly of that royal hand, which by an attention, divined by her heart, was rendered so dear to her; "she took it in both of her own, kissed it, and held it for some moments, after which the king rode off to rejoin his suite, and returned satisfied to Figueiras."*

There was celebrated the marriage of Philip V. with Marie-Louise of Savoy. But oh, unforeseen mischance! Several days were destined to elapse ere he could really possess her the sight of whom had only had the effect of redoubling the ardour of his desires. His happiness was retarded by an incident of a very extraordinary nature, one which caused him personally much unpleasantness, and moreover, gave his young bride a bad impression of the character of a nation she was about to rule over. For the supper, which was prepared for her after the marriage ceremony, the viands had been cooked partly in the Spanish, partly in the French fashion, because at Turin the art of the celebrated *Chef* Vatel had been adopted. But the Spanish ladies whose duty it was, under the direction of Madame des Ursins, to serve the dishes, did not expect such a strange commencement of their functions. All their national susceptibilities were aroused at the sight, and determined to wean abruptly their new Queen from the

* MS. Hist. de l'élévation de Philip V., p. 372.

customs of her own country, and to impose upon her, from the moment of her very first repast, the diet of Spain, they did not hesitate to upset all the French dishes, without a single exception, in order to serve up nothing but Spanish cookery. The King said nothing; and the Princess des Ursins, notwithstanding her stupefaction and secret wrath, was unwilling to commence her career in Spain by scenes of reproach and severity. The Queen also, whose natural vivacity and tender age could not be expected to observe the same restraint, had, nevertheless, sufficient control over herself at first to keep silence. But when she found herself with the King and Madame des Ursins in the apartment allotted to their privacy, her displeasure burst forth, and with so much the greater force that it had been so long restrained and that no foreign eye hindered its manifestation. She shed tears plentifully, sobbed, regretted the absence of her Piedmontese ladies, waxed indignant at the audacity and rudeness of the Spanish dames, and even declared that she would proceed no further, but would return to Piedmont. Night came on, the king left her to undress, and waited to be summoned to his bride's apartment; but the young Queen, " *entêtée, comme une enfant qu'elle était,*" says Saint Simon, "for she was scarcely fourteen," appeared disposed to attribute to the King himself, the rude conduct of his subjects; and in spite of all reasoning on the subject, and the remonstrances of Madame des Ursins, replied that she would sleep alone and go back as quickly as possible to Turin. It may easily be guessed how untoward and disagreeable such an affair proved to Philip V.; he was greatly discomfited by it, and when the second night came, as the Queen had not recovered her good humour, it was he,

who acting upon the advice of the Duke of Medina Sidonia
and Count San Estevan de Gormas, anticipated a fresh
refusal, by causing her to be told that he would not now
share her couch. That spontaneous determination was
adroit, and produced its effect. Marie-Louise was exceed-
ingly piqued at it in the depth of her girlish *amour-propre*,
and ended by making an honourable *amende* to the King,
blaming and condemning her own childishness. She promised to conduct herself for the future like a woman and a
queen, and on the arrival of the third night, the nuptial bed
at length reunited the hitherto dissevered husband and wife.
The next day they left Figuieras, touched at Barcelona, and
thence hastened on to Madrid, wherein they made their
triumphal entry by the Alcala Gate, towards the end of
October, 1701, amidst a great concourse of nobles and
populace. There also the Princess des Ursins was installed
definitively in her functions of *camerara-mayor*. These she
was destined to fulfil during a period of thirteen years, from
1701 to 1714, and by favour of that influential position, to
exercise a virtual sovereignty, the acts of which it will now
be our task to duly appreciate.

CHAPTER V.

ONEROUS AND INCONGRUOUS DUTIES OF THE *CAMERARA MAYOR*
—SHE RENDERS THE YOUNG QUEEN POPULAR WITH THE
SPANIARDS—POLICY ADOPTED BY THE PRINCESS FOR THE
REGENERATION OF SPAIN—CHARACTER OF PHILIP V. AND
MARIE-LOUISE—TWO POLITICAL SYSTEMS COMBATED BY
MÁDAME DES URSINS—SHE EFFECTS THE RUIN OF HER
POLITICAL RIVALS, AND REIGNS ABSOLUTELY IN THE
COUNCILS OF THE CROWN.

THE sudden departure of all her Italian waiting-women
had, as we have seen, on first setting her foot in Spain, for
a moment thrown the young Queen into a condition border-
ing on despair. By advice, however, the respectful devotedness of which served to soften its austerity, and by an
absolute abnegation of herself, Madame des Ursins drew
closely towards her the broken-hearted princess by discreetly
assuaging all her first girlish sorrows. She became a friend,
a sister, almost a mother to the exiled-one, and her influence
profited no less by the first embarrassments of the conjugal
union than by the unbridled passion which ere long placed
under the yoke of his wife a husband of eighteen, chaste as
St. Louis, with the amorous temperament of Henry IV.
In order to strengthen that ascendency and to remain exclusive mistress of a confidence of which power was the price,
the Princess des Ursins flinched neither under fatigue
calculated to exhaust the sturdiest frame, nor before services

the nature of which would have outraged her pride, had it
not been to her, as Saint-Simon says, *une même chose d'être
et de gouverner.* That gilded servitude is described with a
charmingly punctilious complaisance in her letters to the
Maréchale de Noailles and the Marquis de Torcy, and notwithstanding the commiseration which she claims for it, it
may be clearly seen that Madame des Ursins enters into the
details of her domestic service far less for the purpose of
carrying a complaint to Versailles, than to have it there set
down to her credit.

"Gracious Heaven! to what sort of occupation, madame,
have you destined me? I have not a moment's repose, and
cannot find time even to speak to my secretary. There is
no longer any question about resting after dinner, nor of
eating when I am hungry. I am but too glad to be able to
make a bad dinner standing, and moreover it is very rare
that I am not summoned away before swallowing the first
mouthful. In truth, Madame de Maintenon would laugh
heartily if she knew all the details of my office. Tell her,
I beseech you, that it is I who have the honour of receiving
the King of Spain's dressing-gown when he gets into bed,
and of handing it to him along with his slippers when he
rises. So far as that goes I don't lose my patience; but
every night when the King enters the Queen's chamber to go
to bed, the Count de Benavente confides to my care the
King's sword, a certain utensil, and a lamp, the contents of
which I generally manage to spill over my dress,—rather
too good a joke. The King would never rise were I not to
go and draw aside the bed-curtains, and it would be a sacrilege if anybody but myself were to enter the Queen's
chamber whilst they were abed. Very lately, the lamp went
out because I had spilled half the oil. I could not find

where the windows were, and thought that I should have broken my neck against the wall, and we were—the King of Spain and I—near a quarter of an hour stumbling against each other in trying to find them. Her Majesty has got so used to me that sometimes she is good enough to call me up two hours earlier than I should otherwise care to rise. . . . The Queen delights in this sort of pleasantry; still, however, she has not yet regained the confidence she placed in her Piedmontese women. I am astonished at this, for I serve her better than they did, and I am certain that they would not wash her feet or pull off her shoes as readily as I do." *

How unlike a contemporary mistress of the robes in England, the haughty Duchess of Marlborough!

Such a state of slavery weighed very lightly upon the Princess, for, although it was conformable to the custom of a palace, in which a solitary royalty seemed to exist without keeping up any relations with the human race, nothing could have been more easy than for the *camerara mayor* to have provided substitutes for the performance of her unbecoming duties. One of the recommendations of Louis XIV. to his grandson had been, in fact, that whilst scrupulously respecting all popular customs, to wage an implacable war in his court against the monstrous etiquette which, under the last Austrian princes, had palsied Spanish royalty. This was one of the labours to which the *camerara mayor* devoted herself; but she took good care not to reform anything appertaining to her own functions, comprehending clearly enough the policy of keeping to herself sole access to the royal personages, and sacrificing without grudge her dignity to her power and influence. A contrary policy, as will be seen, caused the downfall of Queen Anne's potent favourite.

* Letter to the Maréchale de Noailles, Dec. 1701. Recueil de M. Geffroy.

But we must pass over these domestic duties to speak of
state affairs and the gradual initiation therein by the
Princess of this young couple. During the campaign of
Italy in which Philip V. was anxious to take part, Madame
des Ursins, suitably to the duties and prerogatives of her
charge, did not quit the Queen for a single moment. She
was present with her on every occasion at the sittings of the
Junta, and, under pretext of familiarising her with politics,
she herself penetrated every state secret. The Princess
well knew how to make etiquette subserve her purpose, to
maintain it to the utmost, modify or slacken it according to
her interests. She understood what kind of concessions
the genius of the Spanish nation demanded, and also what
reforms it permitted. She judged at a glance of the disposition of the grandees, and yielded to no illusion relative to
the degree of support she might expect from them. "With
these sort of folks," she wrote to the Marquis de Torcy,
"the surest way is to show firmness. The closer I observe
them, the less do I find that they merit the esteem which I
thought it would have been impossible not to accord
them." According to the Princess, the Spanish nation in
the persons of its grandees, had yielded obedience to a
son of France only, under the idea that France alone
could defend and protect it. France remaining powerful
and victorious, Spain would be safe : but, at each defeat
that occurred in Flanders or Germany from the irresistible
sword of Marlborough, the eyes of the grandees were
turned towards the Archduke, and their fidelity was shaken.
The skill and merit of Madame des Ursins was to perceive
how, in so short a time, to derive so much advantage from
the grace and affability of the Queen, whom she made really
popular among the faithful people of central Spain, and it

was wonderful to see the roots of that new royalty strike so quickly in the hearts of the old Castilians, as to render it able later during the stormy times to weather every rude attack. With an intuitive foresightedness not a little remarkable, the Princess des Ursins had from the first proposed to herself a twofold object. She sought to become the intermedium of the close alliance formed between the grandsire and the grandson, in order to regenerate Spain by causing French measures to prevail in the government of that misruled country; but to the extent only that their application should appear possible without wounding the national sentiment. That policy was the wisest and assuredly the most useful for the Peninsula in the extremity to which the inept power it had just escaped from had brought it. Among the princes who were neither vicious nor cruel, there are none who had done more harm to mankind than the last descendants of Charles V. At the end of the seventeenth century, the immense empire of Philip IV. and Charles II., reduced to a feebleness which the Ottoman empire in our own days has scarcely felt, was nothing more than the phantom of a nation. The House of Austria had triumphed over feudality and municipal resistance as completely as the House of Bourbon; but the successes of monarchical power had been as sterile on one side of the Pyrenees as they had been profitable to it on the other, for in Spain the impotence of the vanquisher had still surpassed that of the vanquished.

So much blood shed by axe and sword, so many lives sacrificed under torture, had scarcely tended further to strengthen royal authority or cement the union of the Spanish kingdoms; and those princes whose domains still spread widely across the globe, had no longer to oppose to Europe, during the long agony in which their race was perishing, either an army, a fleet, a general, or even a statesman.

The first of the sovereigns summoned to assist in restoring this unhappy country to its ancient grandeur was assuredly the least fitting to accomplish such a task. But seventeen years old, when Charles II. chose him for his successor, the Duke d'Anjou was indebted both to nature and education for a mind rather constituted to serve than reign. Brother of the heir to the French throne, he had been reared in studied subordination towards the latter, and the discipline of Beauvilliers and Fénelon, which had curbed the violence of character in the Duke of Burgundy, had produced less beneficial effects in the melancholy temperament of his younger brother. With a natural rectitude of thought and a pride which at times revealed the hereditary haughtiness of his race, Philip V. had in the same degree as his nephew Louis XV., whom he resembled in many ways, that morbid weariness of life, that contempt for mankind and distaste for business. He was afflicted, moreover, with that fatal impotence of will which makes a libertine king the slave of his mistresses, and, a faithful husband the passive instrument of a charming queen who may happen to be prompted by the most skilful of councillors.

But nothing had as yet indicated the melancholy condition of mind which later drove the young King to the confines of despair and insanity. On his first entrance into his kingdom, escorted by a crowd of brilliant nobles, Philip was radiant with youth and hope. He strode forwards sustained by the strong arm of a people who thought to escape, by the intervention of the most powerful sovereign in Europe, from the evils of war, and more especially from that severance of the Spanish monarchy more dreaded by the nation than all its other woes together. In a capital which he was forced to quit on two several occasions, in a court soon afterwards prostrated before his rival, and even in those provinces of Arragon and Catalonia, the burning centres of civil war, nothing at first was heard save shouts of joy and protestations of fidelity. Nevertheless it did not need great sagacity to foresee the perils reserved for the new establishment. The French regime disquieted interests too numerous and prejudices too powerful throughout the Peninsula not to explode at the first difficulty which it might encounter on its path.

Thunderstruck by the unforeseen will of Charles II., Europe, which at the first moment had seemed indisposed to contest its dispositions, had not long deferred their reconsideration. Persuaded that the aggrandisement of his family was equivalent in the eyes of Louis XIV. to an aggrandisement of territory, England, Holland, and Portugal, taking in hand the successorial pretentions of the house of Austria, out of which those cabinets had made such a good bargain in two treaties of partition, sent fleets into every sea, whilst awaiting the moment to carry into the heart of Spain, hostilities which the emperor had already commenced in Italy. An implacable coalition, of which the Peace of Ryswick had suspended the effects without modifying the causes of it, was formed to snatch the two peninsulas from the domination of France. The latter power resolutely accepted the struggle this time for a just and honest cause; but the war was scarcely begun ere the certitude was acquired that in doubling the dangers of France, Spain would add nothing to its resources. With what contemptuous bitterness did Spain, in fact, watch the long train of disasters which from the pinnacle of power brought Louis XIV. to the brink of an abyss by one of those vicissitudes the effect of which is never more rapid upon the popular mind than when fortune deserts men who have been long powerful and flourishing!

Such was the theatre upon which Providence had placed a timid and ailing prince, but which event threatened to endanger even the very existence of the French monarchy itself. Louis XIV. seemed to have attained his object in the guidance of his grandson, who followed the great monarch's injunctions with filial docility. The Queen governed Philip V., and Madame des Ursins governed the Queen. Saint Simon thus explains this ascendancy:—" She guided the Queen," says he, " who had placed in her all the affec- tion and all the confidence of a young person who knew no other adviser, who depended wholly upon her for her particular daily conduct, and for her amusements, and who found in her graciousness, gentleness, and complaisance, combined with every possible resource. For the rest, such empire was not that which weakness and incapacity yields to genius and strength." Marie-Louise had not been less carefully brought up than her sister, the Duchess of Bur- gundy, nor less well instructed. She had innate talent and, in her early youth showed intelligence, good sense, firmness, and was capable of being advised and restrained, and who later, when her character became more developed and formed, manifested a constancy and courage which the natural graces of that same intelligence infinitely enhanced. A lively sympathy between the two women alone deter- mined the authority of the older over the younger, and if the King's confidence in the *camerara-mayor* was a homage rendered to the real superiority of her intelligence, it might be said that a happy conformity of tastes, views, and dispositions, attached his Queen to the Princess des Ursins.

Two political systems confronted each other at Madrid. The one ultra-French, the other purely Spanish, represented by the grandees and inclining towards the Archduke of Austria, the competitor of Philip V. The first-named had for champions, Cardinal Porto-Carrero, " virtually the actual prime minister," the Archbishop of Seville, Arias, the provisional president of the Council of Castille, the Marquis de Louville, and all the King's French household ; subsequently it was directed by the Cardinal and the Abbé d'Estrées, Ambassadors of France. The second party re-united the most illustrious names of the monarchy. It had for its chiefs, successively, the Count de Melgar, Admiral of Castile, the Marquis de Léganez, and the Duke de Medina-Cœli. The first-named policy tended to destroy, by its exclusive ideas, the popularity of Philip V., the second prepared to betray him. They were both reduced to impotence, and became fatal to those who ventured to defend them. Madame des Ursins combated the one and the other, and aimed at inaugurating in Spain a mixed policy, heeding the cabinet of Versailles without annihilating the cabinet of Madrid, satisfying the just desires of Spain and the susceptibilities of the nation, without disdaining the sometimes useful advice and the ever requisite resources of France. Such was, therefore, the plan adopted by the young Queen. But, in order to realise it, it was necessary to have the field open, it was necessary that Madame des Ursins should be delivered from her rivals, and should reign as absolutely in the councils of the Crown as in the minds of the King and Queen.

The principal chief of the Austrian party, the Admiral of Castile, was the first to become dangerous. "He loved the house of Austria, for which he had fought, under the preceding reign, by sea and land, and from which he had received the highest honours." On the contrary he detested the house of Bourbon, against which he had strongly "pronounced" at the time when the last will of Charles II. was in preparation.* But he had confronting him the vigilance of Madame des Ursins. She fathomed his intrigues and baffled his early manœuvres; though she had not always to struggle openly against him. He rendered himself justice; he comprehended his own impotence, and had recourse to treason. He had frequent conferences with a Dutch spy, plotted with him the downfall of Philip V., and the elevation of the Archduke, and finally handed him a correct topographic plan of Andalusia and Estremadura. The cabinets of Vienna and London assured of such an aid, declared war against Philip V. Nevertheless, although the Spanish government was duly apprised of these proceedings, it still wanted that boldness which the continuous use of power and long-indulged prosperity give. It only determined upon dispatching the admiral abroad, and appointed him ambassador to the French Court; a dubious favour which at once revealed its fears and its weakness, but which at least postponed a peril it dared not yet face. The admiral saw plainly that he was suspected in Spain, and that in France he would be a cipher; nevertheless, he pretended to take his departure thither; but halted when half-way, and went to join the Portuguese troops banded with those of the allies. The cabinet of Madrid had from that time forward acquired

* Combes, p. 109.

the right of punishing him. The Count de Melgar was condemned *par contumace;* his friends were forced to blame his conduct openly; and his melancholy death which happened shortly afterwards, the result of an insult reserved sooner or later for all traitors, deprived a formidable faction of its leader.

The ultra-French party did not find a less rude adversary in Madame des Ursins. Of this, Louville, even before the arrival of the Princess, had a presentiment. " I would much rather have Madame de Ventadour," he wrote Torcy. So early as the month of January, 1703, he saw his influence destroyed, foresaw his coming defeat and meditated a *coup d'éclat*—the getting rid of the *camerara-mayor.* He declares to the Duke de Beauvilliers,—" If prompt measures are not taken to extricate the Catholic King from his slavery, he is lost. In the first place, Madame des Ursins must be got rid of, there need be no hesitation about that." In the month following, he insists that they should " keep firm, and get rid of her;" and, in July, 1703, to bring Torcy to a decision, he adds,—" She is now detested by the Spaniards." Madame des Ursins repaid him hate for hate, and never spoke of him save with a lofty contempt befitting an offended great lady. " He has cut a greater figure," she wrote to Cardinal de Noailles, " by the insolent things he has written about me, than by any merit of his own. I think that I can never forgive him if he does not first retract everything which he has advanced against me. In truth, it ought not to be permitted that so insignificant a person should outrage a woman of my rank." Matters having reached this pass, it was clear that one or the other must succumb. It was the lot of the Marquis de

Louville. Two couriers reaching Versailles from Spain,
determined his fall. On the 22nd of October, a despatch
from the Duke de Beauvilliers announced it to him. " It
is done," wrote the duke, " we are lost. The step is
taken. You are to be instantly recalled."*

The Archbishop of Seville, Arias, who was of the same
politics, was shortly afterwards sent back to his diocese.
The Duke de Montellano replaced him in the presidency
of Castile, and a Papal brief, obtained some months
after his disgrace, enjoined him not to quit Seville again.
There remained Porto-Carrero and the Cardinal d'Estrées,
recently nominated ambassador of France. They were
the firmest supporters of their cause and the most formidable adversaries of the Princess : Porto-Carrero, by his
high position, by the recollection of services rendered at
the period of the will ; Cardinal d'Estrées, by his influence
at the Court of Versailles, by the protection of Noailles,
by the energetic support of the entire French party. The
strife was fierce ; but the resources of Madame des Ursins
were equal to the emergency. The Duke de Montellano,
president of the Council of Castille, counterbalanced the
authority, until then unlimited, of Porto-Carrero ; the
auditorship of finance, which had always appertained to
the prime minister, being taken from him. Weakened by
this check and rivalry, the Cardinal abruptly changed his
policy and placed himself at the head of the anti-French
party ; he refused to act with Cardinal d'Estrées, and
tendered his resignation. Had he remained firm in that
course, probably he might have re-enacted his political
part in the ranks of his new friends, and have caused the
government great embarrassment. On receiving a letter

---

* Collection of M. Geffroy, p. 457.

from Louis XIV., he had the weakness to give way, withdrew his resignation, and resumed his seat at the council board. But factions hate and despise more intensely those who abandon their ranks than those who fight against them: that manœuvre irritated alike the French and the Spaniards; both, in their turn, abjured. Porto-Carrero was the turn-coat from every cause: as a politician he was annihilated.

In this affair, Cardinal d'Estrées had been, without knowing it, the tool of Madame des Ursins. "He was," according to Saint Simon, "a hot, hasty, impetuous, high-handed man, who could tolerate neither superior nor equal." It will readily be imagined that the *camerara-mayor* could not brook the ascendency which he aimed at ursurping. She resolutely resisted him in all things and on every occasion. She opposed, with might and main, the success of his policy; she set her face against his imperious manners and tedious formalities. Philip and his Queen grew tired of the strife. They took part with Madame des Ursins and wrote to Louis XIV. After that letter "the Cardinal d'Estrées was looked upon as the great stirrer-up of strife. His arrival at the Court of Madrid had interrupted the perfect harmony about to be re-established. Not a day passed without some one suffering from his intractable and arrogant temper." Madame des Ursins worked in the same groove with Torcy. The Cardinal's cabal, by way of revenge, "raked into the private life of the *camerara-mayor,*" hoping to destroy by scandalous tales her reputation in the eyes of Louis XIV. and Madame de Maintenon. Those tactics failed of success; Louis XIV., it is true, recalled Madame des Ursins; but the Queen of Spain defended her favourite with such earnest importunity, that the severity of the Court of Versailles was disarmed. An endeavour was made to reconcile the two adversaries; but that reconciliation, if sincere, was not lasting. Supreme authority admits of no equal partition : difficulties multiplied themselves. Philip V. at length declared to Louis XIV., "that if, to keep his crown, he must resign himself to have Cardinal Porto-Carrero always as his minister, he knew what he should prefer to choose." In the month of September, 1704, therefore, all the French household, with Cardinal Porto-Carrero, quitted Madrid.

CHAPTER VI.

To recall Madame des Ursins at the earliest possible
moment and inflict upon her a well-merited disgrace was
the earnest desire of Louis XIV.; but, omnipotent as that
Prince was, he found his hand arrested by a very serious
difficulty, the *camerara-mayor*, in fact, screened herself
behind the Queen, and the King of France was well aware
that in recalling her he would deal a blow alike against the
affection and self-love of his grand-daughter which she
would never forgive—an extremity which was not less
repugnant to his policy than to his good feeling. Moreover the departure of Madame des Ursins would not
render the Cardinal d'Estrées' position less insupportable
in a court, all the approaches to which were barred to
him, and in which his isolation was a constant insult to
France. There was nothing left, therefore, but to grant
the latter a recall which, smarting with a humiliation so
unforeseen to his overweening arrogance, he demanded in
accents of rage and despair. However, in order to salve
his *amour-propre*, the Abbé d'Estrées continued to discharge
the functions of the embassy, as though his uncle's absence
were only temporary; but that state of things did not suit
either of the two factions which for more than twelve
months past divided the French household of the King of

Spain, surpassing each other in vituperation and calumny.
Despite a sort of truce stipulated between the embassy
and the palace, the Abbé d'Estrées soon found himself in
the same position in which the Cardinal had been placed;
for Madame des Ursins did not like the arrangement of
the Abbé being left behind, but as Madame de Maintenon
insisted upon it, she was obliged to accept it with as good a
grace as possible.* The Abbé, vain of his family and his
position, was not a man much to be feared as it seemed.
Madame des Ursins accordingly laughed at and despised him.
He was admitted to the council, but was quite without influence there, and when he attempted to make any representations
to Madame des Ursins or Orry, they listened to him without
attending in the least to what he said. The Princess
reigned supreme, and thought of nothing but getting rid of all
who attempted to divide her authority. At last she obtained
such a command over the poor Abbé d'Estrées, so teased
and hampered him, that he consented to the hitherto
unheard-of arrangement, that the Ambassador of France
should not write to the King without first concerting his
letter with her, and afterwards show her its contents before
he despatched it. But such restraint as this became, in a
short time, so fettering, that the Abbé determined to break
away from it. He wrote a letter to the King without showing
it to Madame des Ursins. She soon had scent of what he
had done; seized the letter as it passed through the post,
opened it, and, as she expected, found its contents were not
of a kind to give her much satisfaction. In fact, in her
emotion of anger and indignation she made a false step in
her state-craft of a nature one can hardly imagine a person

* Saint Simon.

so astute as the Princess making. This blunder led to a great *imbroglio.*

The question has been raised—Did Madame des Ursins always use the intimate and uncontrolled influence she had obtained over the young Queen of fourteen in a purely devoted and disinterested way ? It would be difficult, certainly, to answer in the affirmative. Louville, her rival and enemy, a man of talent and ardour, but passionate, represents her as the wickedest woman on earth, to be got rid of at the earliest possible moment and at any cost, "sordid and thievish to a marvellous degree." He raises the same accusation against Orry, a clever man whom Louis XIV. had sent to Spain to put some order into her finances. These accusations seem to have been unjustifiable. The Marshal Duke of Berwick, who kept himself aloof from all these odious bickerings, does more justice to Orry, and everything leads the impartial student to think that Madame des Ursins on that score comes out of the scrutiny with still cleaner hands. " *Je suis gueuse, il est vrai,*" she writes to Madame de Noailles on first going to Spain, " *mais je suis encore plus fière.*" Detailing to Madame de Maintenon somewhat later the indignities they both had to put up with from accusations of a like nature, she speaks of them in a tone of lofty irony and sovereign contempt which appears to exclude anything like falsehood.

But what seems more certain—if the truth must be told—is, although a little singular at first sight, that at the age of sixty and upwards, Madame des Ursins still had lovers. "She is hair-brained in her conduct," * wrote Louville to the Duke and Duchess de Beauvilliers. One Sieur d'Aubigny, a kind of household steward whom she had

---

* " Elle a des mœurs *à l'escarpolette.*"

promoted to be her equerry, was lodged in the *Retiro* palace near the apartments of her women, where he was seen one day brushing his teeth very unconcernedly at the window. *C'était un beau et grand drôle très-bien fait et très-découplé de corps et d'esprit,** and not a *bête brute,* as Louville calls him. But he was bold and somewhat insolent, as one who conceived that he had a right to be so. On another occasion, Louville and the Duke de Medina-Cœli entering the apartments of Madame des Ursins, into which she ushered them in order that they might talk more unrestrainedly, D'Aubigny who was installed at the other end, seeing only the Princess and believing her to be alone, began to apostrophise her in terms of very rude and coarse familiarity, which threw all present into confusion. The feminine failing of Madame des Ursins, was, we are told, this; " gallantry and *l'entêtement de sa personne* was in her the dominant and overweening weakness above all else, even to the latest period of her life." So Saint Simon says, and he renders her full justice moreover for her spirited and elevated qualities.

But to return to the matter of the intercepted despatch. What piqued the Princess most was, to find details in it exaggerating the authority of D'Aubigny, and a statement to the effect that it was generally believed that she had married him. On reading this passage the pride of the great lady was more outraged even than her modesty. Beside herself with rage and vexation, she wrote with her own hand upon the margin of the letter, " *Pour mariée, non* ("At any rate, not married "), showed it in this state to the King and Queen of Spain, to a number of other people, always with strange clamouring, and finally crowned her

* Saint Simon.

folly by sending it to Louis XIV., with furious complaints against the Abbé for writing it without her knowledge, and for inflicting upon her such an atrocious injury as to mention such a thing as this pretended marriage. Her letter and its enclosure reached the King at a very inopportune moment. Just before he had received a letter, which, taken in connection with this of the Princess des Ursins, struck a blow at her power of the most decisive kind. At the same time that the original thus annotated was despatched to the Marquis de Torcy, a copy of it was addressed by the Princess to the Duke de Noirmoutier, her brother, and the latter caused it to be circulated throughout Paris, to the great scandal of a society which had still some little respect left for morals and royal power.

Louis XIV. owed it to himself not to allow such excessive audacity to go unpunished. At the same time the affairs of Spain were then in such a state of confusion, the danger of exasperating the young Queen appeared so great, that it was necessary to defer severe measures, however justifiable they might be. It was only some months afterwards, when Philip V. had quitted Madrid for the frontiers of Portugal, to take command of his army, reinforced by a French corps under the command of the Duke of Berwick, that Louis thought it possible to make himself obeyed and to strike what he himself called a decisive blow.

" The complaints against the Princess des Ursins," wrote the King to the Abbé d'Estrées,* " have reached such a point that at length it is necessary to take notice of them. I should have used less delay if I had only consulted the welfare of the State ; but I was compelled to wait until the King quitted Madrid. I had reason to foresee that he would

* 19th March, 1704. Memoirs of Noailles, tom. ii., p. 297.

be only too much influenced by the Queen's tears, that they might hinder him from deferring with sufficient promptitude to my advice. . . . If the King offers resistance, let him see how onerous is the war which I am waging for his interests. Do not tell him that I will abandon him, for he would not believe you; but let him understand that whatever may be my affection for him, I can, if he does not respond thereto, make peace at the expense of Spain, and grow tired of supporting a monarchy wherein I only see disorders and contradictions in matters the most reasonable that I may urge in his own interest. In fine, after such an *éclat*, nothing short of success will do; my honour, the interest of the King, my grandson, and that of the monarchy are concerned therein. . . . The directions that I give you are absolutely necessary for my service, but the consequences will be disagreeable for you. They have not ceased to make mischief between my grandson and yourself; matters have made such an impression that he has already on several occasions requested me to recall you."

Louis XIV. gave the Abbé, therefore, an order to leave forthwith, adding to the expression of his lively regret the assurance that this disgrace, wholly involuntary as it was, should not damage his future fortunes. Such was the extremity to which a subject had brought the most absolute prince in Europe. It may thus be seen what extensive roots the woman had already thrown out in Spain who balanced so nicely the power of the French King in his grandson's court. It will shortly afterwards be more clearly apparent; but if the *éclat* of such a part enhances the importance of Madame des Ursins, her character remains singularly compromised by it. However indulgently we may be disposed to look upon it, we cannot dissever from a system of policy the unworthy hostility waged by a French-woman against two ambassadors of her sovereign with so cruel a perseverance. The Cardinal d'Estrées was desirous of carrying the same measures in Spain as Madame des Ursins; he there represented their common master with a loftier title and a more legitimate authority. His errors of conduct, which were numerous, had in some sort been forced upon him, and if he had the misfortune to fall into ambushes, to another person must be attributed the fault of preparing them. In that period of two years, the least honourable of her political life, the Princess had solely as a stimulant her egotistic and impatient ambition. In subor-dinating to her interests those of two monarchies, in alleging as an excuse for the violence of her attacks the right of her own superiority, she confirmed in the minds of her adversaries by her example the truth, that for ardent natures it is less perilous to exercise than to pursue power.

Philip, reduced by the Queen's absence to his natural indolence, opposed no resistance to the injunctions of his grandfather. Assailed in her tenderest affections, wounded in her dignity as a sovereign, and resenting at fifteen years of age that twofold outrage in as lively a degree as in the maturity of life, Marie-Louise restricted herself at first to a disdainful silence which, nevertheless, revealed the hope either of a terrible vengeance or a speedy retaliation. Madame des Ursins submitted to the commands of her sovereign with the stately haughtiness, the expression of which is conveyed in one of her very best letters to Madame de Noailles. The consciousness of the great services ren-dered by her to both monarchies with an inviolable fidelity, the bitter astonishment at finding her relative, until then so devoted, "prefer to herself persons who were merely her allies, and whose wickedness ought to have inspired her with horror," her adroit flattery of Madame de Maintenon, " to whom Providence had reserved, as by an assured privilege for her virtue, the sacred mission of causing truth and justice in the end to triumph ; " " Heaven wishing to avail itself of her services for that purpose in spite of herself;" such are the chief features of that clever defence, in which calculation tempers rage and resentment, and which ought to be read in its entirety in the interesting letters of the Princess.*

But the letters likewise of the great King which have come down to us, show that there was no need of the foolish insult conveyed by her own epistle, to make him angry with Madame des Ursins. The complaints raised against her were then universal, at least at Versailles, and at a distance it was difficult to separate those which were founded on false reports. With the well-known temper which characterised Louis XIV., it must have seemed a thing inconceivable that such importance should be conceded to a woman whom he had placed there to do his bidding. Finding that his grandson and the young queen were disposed to resist his recall of the *camerara-mayor*, he addressed them as a father and as a king:—

" You ask for my advice," he says to Philip V. (20th August, 1704), " and I write you what I think ; but the best advice becomes useless when it is only asked for and followed after the mischief has happened. . . . You have hitherto given your confidence to incapable or interested persons. . . . (And speaking of the recall of Orry and of another agent) it seems, however, that the interest of those particular persons wholly engages your attention, and at a time when you ought only to have

* Letter of May, 23rd, 1704. Geffroy's Recueil, p. 169.

elevated views *you dwarf them down to the cabals of the Princess des Ursins, with which I am unceasingly wearied.*"

And to the Queen, Louis XIV. writes still more explicitly (20th September, 1704,):—

"You know how much I have desired that you should give your confidence to the Princess des Ursins, and that I forgot nothing that might induce you to do so. However, unmindful of our common interest, she has given herself up to an enmity which I do not comprehend, and has only thought of baffling those who have been charged with our affairs. If she had had a sincere attachment for you, she would have sacrificed all her resentments, well or ill-founded, against the Cardinal d'Estrées, instead of dragging you into them. *Persons of your rank ought to keep themselves aloof from private quarrels and conduct themselves with regard to their own interests and those of their subjects, which are always identical.* I must therefore recall my ambassador, abandon you to the Princess des Ursins, and leave her solely to govern your realms, or recall that lady herself. That is what I think I ought to do."

In these truthful and kingly words, the true cause of Louis' dissatisfaction may be seen, and the marginal note, true or false, in the despatch, appears nothing more than a secondary accident.*

The politic monarch, moreover, thought it well to take extreme precaution in timing his blow aright. The moment of the young King being with the army and separated from the Queen was expressly chosen, for fear lest the latter in her despair, might oppose some obstacle to its execution.

* The affirmation of Madame des Ursins was no doubt true, since in a letter of hers to Orry, dated in 1718, she begs him to present her friendly remembrances to M. d'Aubigny's *wife.*

CHAPTER VII.

MADAME DES URSINS had received Louis XIV.'s command to withdraw into Italy. Quitting Madrid as a State criminal (*en criminelle d'état*), the Princess directed her steps towards the land indicated for her exile. We must refer, however, to "The Memoirs of Saint Simon" those of our readers who are desirous of admiring the presence of mind with which Madame des Ursins, recalled thus unexpectedly and struck by the Olympian bolt, suffered herself to be in nowise disconcerted, but skilfully managed to retreat slowly and in good order, yielding ground only step by step,* without appearing to disobey, she found time to arouse her friends at Versailles into action, " who representing the severity of such a fall for a dictatress of her quality, urged that the King, having been obeyed, and having glutted his vengeance, a feeling of commiseration ought to be shown thereafter, and that it was not advisable to push the Queen to extremity." These reasons commented upon by the Duke d'Harcourt, a man of great weight in the affairs of the Peninsula, by Marshal de Villeroy and the Noailles, prevailed with Louis XIV., who granted the Princess his permission, ardently solicited, to stop at Toulouse and there take up her abode. That was but the

---

* " *A lents tours de roue.*" St. Simon, tom. vii.

first step to a rehabilitation towards which laboured with equal ardour, though by very different ways, the youthful spouse of Philip V. and the grave companion of Louis XIV. Madame de Maintenon, accepting willingly the part of missionary of Divine justice, held it as a point of honour not to deceive the hope of the illustrious accused, who had attributed those functions to her at a juncture so *à propos*. And whether that she felt a real affection for Madame des Ursins, whether that she wished to mitigate the Duchess of Burgundy's regret for her sister's vexation, whether, in short, she feared to see Louis XIV. lose by so abrupt a change all authority over the affairs of Spain, she was disposed in every event to serve the exile. The Princess, to give time for the storm to expend its fury, well knowing that acts hastily determined upon are ordinarily the least durable, did not seek to hurry matters herself with the French King, but wrote to Madame de Noailles, hoping that her letter might be shown: "You are not ignorant of my attachment and respect for Madame de Maintenon; the obligations that I owe her are ever present to me, and the reliance that I place in the generosity of her heart."* All the correspondence from Toulouse is in that vein, and, still further, she adroitly represents herself as a victim, as a woman disabused of worldly grandeur, and afflicted solely at having displeased Louis XIV.

This conduct allayed the mutterings of the spent tempest. The court grew accustomed to behold in her an unfortunate noblewoman resigned to her exile with an antique patience.

At the end of four months passed in the capital of Languedoc, in the depth of a retreat enlivened by an assiduous correspondence with the two courts, Madame des Ursins

* Recueil of M. Geffroy, Letter lvi.

received permission to appear at Versailles and there to
justify herself. The intervention of Madame de Maintenon
had nothing more in it than was perfectly natural under the
circumstances ; not that she had the desire to govern Spain,
as Saint Simon affirms, nor even France, however entirely
she might govern Louis XIV. What she desired to establish
on either side of the Pyrenees was a species of moral control
of the house of Bourbon. And, by keeping her informed of
the most minute particulars touching the King and Queen,
by inspiring the Duchess of Burgundy's sister with the
duteous affection of the elder for her *aunt*, Madame des
Ursins rendered the Marquise de Maintenon the only service
the latter cared for, and the only one, to speak the truth,
which could add anything to her importance.

The motives of Louis XIV. were of a very different kind,
and his politic mind did not hesitate to sacrifice to them his
grievances, however legitimate they might be. Far from
pacifying the Court of Spain, the departure of the Princess
des Ursins had been the signal for an outburst of the most
complete anarchy. To the rule exercised by the Queen had
succeeded an entire absence of direction, and matters were
conducted with an incoherence so shocking, that M. de
Torcy having exhausted both his advice and his patience,
opened with perfect terror the despatches drawn from that
Pandora's box. The accord—at least apparent, which the
preponderance of Madame des Ursins had maintained among
the members of the *despacho* by the intervention of the
Duke de Montellano, her creature, was abruptly broken up,
and the Austrian party gathered strength from the effect of
that disorder and that universal dissolution. The Archduke,
proclaimed King of Spain by the Emperor under the name
of Charles III. and recognised in that quality by England

and Holland, had just landed at Lisbon; the campaign opened against the Portuguese had ended, after some ephemeral successes, by a sort of disbanding of the Spanish army, through want of clothing, pay, and provisions, in the supply of which nothing was done after Orry's departure, recalled to France from the same motives as the Princess. Gibraltar, the defence of which had been confided by an inexplicable negligence to fifty men, was torn away for ever by a handful of British seamen from the crown of the Catholic kings; Catalonia, Arragon, the kingdom of Valentia, made ripe for insurrection by the Prince of Darmstadt, were on the eve of escaping from their allegiance. At the beginning of 1705, the armies of Philip V. were composed of five or six thousand men in rags, their tottering fidelity daily tampered with, and the little band of French auxiliaries exhausted itself in fruitless efforts to retake Gibraltar, which, covered as it was by the English fleet, remained mistress of the Straits, after the first disaster inflicted on the French marine in that war which was destined to cost it its last vessel.

To the government of prime ministers, and still more that of women, Louis XIV. had an insuperable antipathy, It must therefore have cost him much to renounce the flattering hope of seeing his grandson make practical application of the lofty instructions in which his personal royalty reflected itself with so much splendour; but such a prince as he knew but too well that a political idea is valueless when it remains inapplicable. Impressed with the sorrowful conviction, he was compelled to recognise that Philip's ailing temperament rendered all equilibrium between intelligence and will impossible, so far so that that unhappy Prince could not elude his fate save by escaping from himself. In

the approaching perils which the disasters of the French
armies foreboded, the hope of preserving Spain even under
the dictation of Madame des Ursins was better, after all,
than the certainty of losing that crown by estrangiug the
camarera-mayor. After the battle of Blenheim, the defec-
tion of the Duke of Savoy and the disastrous Italian campaign, the restoration of the Princess to her charge was, on
the part of Louis XIV., a first concession to evil fortune, a
determination for which his sagacity triumphed over his
repugnance. And so Saint Simon ought to have seen, instead of representing the triumph obtained by Madame des
Ursins at Versailles as the inexplicable effect of a species of
sudden fascination.

That victory suddenly transformed her who was but a
short time previously an accused person into "a court
divinity." The Spanish ambassador, followed by a swarm of
courtiers, went forth to meet her outside the gates of Paris,
and offered her his mansion during her stay in the capital.
There she received "all France" we are told.* Her every
look was interpreted, and the words she addressed to ladies
of the highest consideration impressed them with a rap-
turous sense of her condescension. Nothing could exceed
the King's attentions in every way that could contribute to
her honour and distinction, and from the majestic fashion
with which it was all received, with such a rare admixture of
grace and politeness it reminded the beholders of the early
days of the Queen-Mother. Whether the particular determination of the King shone through this marked graciousness, or that the well-known dexterity of the Princess did
not allow of any doubt of her success, she was welcomed on
all hands, not with those timid precautions and that am-

* Saint Simon.

biguous reserve which characterise the incertitude of courts, but with that lively, prompt and decided enthusiasm which only greets unclouded favour and assured fortune. At the balls which were given at the royal residences, Louis XIV., the Duchess of Burgundy, and all the princes treated her with the most affable condescension. If Louis XIV. showed great tact in appearing to attribute to his conversations with Madame des Ursins a preconceived resolution which had really been the simple result of events, and if the easy grace of the gentleman covered in some sort the retreat of the politician, it will be readily imagined that the Princess did not suffer herself to be beaten in address. When the desire to see her return to the side of the young Queen of Spain was intimated to her, she spoke of the disgust with which the condition of that miserable country filled her, and which made it impossible to do any good there. To the King's impatience she opposed the impaired state of her health, and placed herself under medical treatment, having at that identical moment a real interest in being pronounced out of health. She delayed from day to day a departure that was more and more pressed for, cautiously making it understood that in order to avoid the mishaps and the mistakes of the past, the safety of Spain must be sought in a complete unity of direction, and that the inevitable preponderance of the Queen would constrain the placing of that political direction, not in the embassy, but in the Palace. This was to demand nothing less than a *carte blanche* to govern the kingdom; but however audacious in itself such exigence might be, it offended no one, so glad were all concerned, after so many mistakes, to find one head which could courageously confront the responsibility of a situation that had become so perilous. She was the only Frenchwoman who could govern Spain, and the cabinet of Versailles, satisfied with having shown its strength, exhibited henceforth that majestic condescendence towards her which is the flattery made use of by monarchs in their relations with indispensable agents.

She was not in a hurry, therefore, to return to Madrid. Probably she was anxious to enjoy her triumph, and by it to crush for a long while the trembling jealousy of her enemies; perhaps, sure of setting out when she chose, it was her aim to make her presence in Spain felt. Be that as it may, we do not believe, as it has been supposed, that she herself was tired of her political *rôle* whatever may have been the mask with which her prudence sought to cover her ambition during her disgrace, the existence of that ambition is clear enough as a matter of history. We admit nothing more, in answer to the insinuations of Saint Simon, that dazzled with the royal favour she had dreamed of supplanting Madame de Maintenon in the great King's confidence. Of a judgment eminently sound and precise, she had too much of the practical in her character to cradle her imagination with such chimæras. Madame des Ursins' quick-sightedness fathomed all the advantages she might derive from the general discouragement, and promised herself to let nothing be lost by it either for herself or her dependents, however equivocal their position might be towards her. She procured the admission of D'Aubigny into the cabinet of Louis XIV., and, a thing more difficult still, into that of Madame de Maintenon. She caused Orry to be reinstated in his former functions, at the same time that one of her most dangerous enemies, the father Daubenton, received an order to quit Madrid, where his restless nullity had lost itself in a maze of intrigues. Authorised in a manner to form her ministry, she nominated the President Amelot as Ambassador for Spain, a diplomatist although very high minded, yet of somewhat subaltern ability, one of the lights of that magistracy from which Louis XIV. loved to recruit the staff of his government, and whence Madame des Ursins herself sprung on her mother's side. The Marshal de Tessé was appointed to the command of the army, and Orry, a pupil of Colbert and a distinguished financier, was one of those clever and hard-working citizens who were amongst the best of French ministers of that epoch. This selection, equally excellent for both monarchs, was better still for the Princess, to whom it guaranteed a valuable concurrence without leaving her to apprehend any resistance. Those three men, from the very moment of their arrival in Madrid, found themselves face to face with two grave difficulties. The first was the opposition of the grandees; the second, a foreign invasion. Aristocratic conspiracies were hatching in the capital. The Archduke Charles had landed in Catalonia, and several noblemen were endeavouring to clear the road for him as far as Madrid. The Marquis de Leganez was the soul of this plot. Ever since the accession of Philip V. he had eluded taking the oath of allegiance: and later, summoned to take up arms against the Archduke, he had refused. From that moment he became a suspected person. His sole refuge was a conspiracy: and that was his destruction. Arrested by order of the new administration, he was conducted to the fortress of Pampeluna, afterwards to Bordeaux, whence his vain and tardy protestations in favour of Philip V. failed to extricate him. This energetic blow struck terror into the hearts of the grandees and prepared the triumphal return of the Princess.

CHAPTER VIII.

IN the balls given at Marly, she appeared loftily self-possessed, easy and familiar by turns, ogling people one after another with her eye-glass; and at one of these balls she made her appearance with a tiny spaniel under her arm, as though she had been in her own house, and (which was more remarked than anything else) the King caressed the little dog on several different occasions, when he went up to converse with her, and he did so nearly throughout the evening. " She had never before been seen to take so grand a flight."

Madame des Ursins, who, though a woman of imagination, was, as we have said, but little liable to be dazzled, might still have been pardoned giving way during these months of royal favour to an excess of intoxication; but above all, and at the same time that she displayed the treasures of her continual and inexhaustible conversation, she evinced a lively appreciation of the King's mental qualities. She returns to the subject afterwards too frequently, and enters too minutely into detail of what she discovered in him, not to show on her part a truthfulness stronger than flattery. She never speaks of the King otherwise than as *l'homme du monde le plus aimable,* as the *meilleur ami,* and *le plus honnête homme du monde.*

" If I had further, Madam, as you observe to me (she writes to Madam de Maintenon) the happiness of his being more accustomed to me, I ingenuously confess to you that it only depends upon his Majesty to perceive that I find him *very good company.* Really, although I can boast of having, in my time, entertained in France, Italy, and Spain, all the wittiest and most agreeable persons therein, I have never been so much pleased with them as with his Majesty. You must own that this is a very frank avowal."

There were not wanting those who even went so far as to suppose that the views of Madame des Ursins went much further—"the age and health of Madame de Maintenon tempting her." The question must have occurred to the Princess, it was hinted, whether the prospect of replacing her in France was not more alluring than any she was likely to meet with in Spain. Such conjectures, however, touching the inmost secrets of a woman's heart, are more easily formed than verified.

That which appears far more certain is, that independently even of politics there was a mental triumph achieved by her in this close contact with the great King. Madame de Maintenon, Madame des Ursins, and Louis XIV. were all three for some time under the same spell: " I often recall to mind your ideas and that amiable countenance which so charmed me at Marly," Madame de Maintenon writes to her a year later; " do you still preserve that equanimity which allowed you to pass from the most important topics of conversation with the King to indulge in *badinage* with Madame d'Heudicourt in my cabinet? " Madame des Ursins, who was only at that moment a bird of passage, was of those in whom the delight of pleasing and the feeling of success doubly enhanced every innate grace. That slight fascination which she probably underwent, she repaid with a shower of sparkling phrases.

Louis XIV. himself was seduced both by her grace and her talent. He had expected, according to all accounts, to find in Madame des Ursins a woman of the Fronde, some-

what post-dated : instead of that he discovered a person.
whom it cost little to be naturally a person of authority,
with a capacity for governing, and whose social powers never
failed of their charm, so elevated were their characteristics.
She, even as a third party, from her intercourse with
Madame de Maintenon, felt herself grow quite young again.
Of these three potential persons, the assertion may, be
hazarded that Madame des Ursins was still that one who
best maintained her position, possessed the happy knack of
turning all things to advantage through her lucid common
sense : of the three she played her part the most unrestrictedly, and therefore so much the better, through an
energetic will in carrying out what an acute judgment told
her was best.

Her brow encircled with the halo of victory, Madame des
Ursins, after a year's absence, re-entered that Spain which
she had quitted humiliated : she returned to it amid the
acclamations of its populace, welcomed in all its cities as a
sovereign. The citadels fired salutes as she passed ; the
Spanish Court went out to meet her as far as Burgos ; the
King and Queen received her at some two leagues from
Madrid. She returned strengthened by disgrace, so much
the stronger that her absence had proved injurious, treating
henceforward as between Power and Power with the Court of
Versailles, which, yielding to a political necessity, recognized
and graciously accepted, had restored her with its own hand
to the summit of power, and seemed, by that signal preference, to menace beforehand all those who should pretend to
struggle against her sovereign mission.

Once re-established in Spain, Madame des Ursins, thus
acting in harmony once more with Louis XIV., set herself
to pursue a more measured course, more regular and

thoroughly irreproachable with relation to those whose envoy she was. She took no step save in concert with the sagacious ambassador M. Amelot. If the letters she addressed to Madame de Maintenon, and which commence immediately after her departure from Paris, do not reveal her genius in all its vigour and brilliancy, they at any rate allow us to divine it in certain passages, and give us clearly the chief outlines of her character. The natural tone of her mind was serious, positive, somewhat dry at bottom, but frank, deliberate, and bold. Unlike Madame de Maintenon, she had political ideas which she dared not only avow, but put into execution. Before all else she decided upon the complete restoration of the King's authority. With reference to a claim advanced by the grandees against the captain of the guards, she was anxious to break up effectually that cabal of the grandees who profited by the weakness of the new régime in order to create titles and prerogatives for themselves : otherwise it would be the means of throwing Spain again into the same embarrassments as those in which France found herself during the Fronde, " when Frenchmen only busied themselves with provoking one another." She was of opinion that the chiefs of that party should feel the effects of the King's displeasure before there was time to receive replies from France, in order that it might clearly appear that it was a determination taken by the King of Spain himself, and not a suggestion of others :

" Do not be frightened, Madame, I entreat you, at these resolutions. It is fortunate that the grandees have given us such a lucky opportunity of mortifying them. Lacking strength and courage, these haughty nobles are ceaseless in their attempts to overthrow the authority of their king, and against whom I am incensed beyond measure for all which they did so long as they had the uppermost in the *Despacho* (Privy Council)."

The virile tone of that paragraph carries us far beyond Madame de Maintenon. There was one thing, however, of more importance to Madame des Ursins than appeasing the grandees, and that was to procure troops and find the means of paying them. That done, she might laugh at every other difficulty. " Would to heaven," she exclaimed, " that it were as easy to get the uppermost over the priests and monks, who are the cause of all the revolts you hear of! "

The first portion of the Princess's labours was accomplished. Her most dangerous enemies had fallen : she reigned. But there yet remained a few hostile nobles, and she resolved to strike at them. One of them, formerly her ally, the Duke de Montellano, president of Castile, excited the suspicion of this mistrustful woman. She manifested towards him, from the moment of her return, a haughty coldness. She dreaded to see in a post of such eminence a man placed by his birth amongst her worst enemies. Montellano, offended at her attitude towards him, tendered his resignation. The King hesitated, but the Princess made him accept it, and the corregidor of Madrid, Ronquillo, a man of obscure origin, was nominated to the presidentship. Amelot was equally mistrustful of certain grandees in the Privy Council, as was the Princess ; and, whether they tendered their resignation or that it was required of them, the Duke de Montalto and the Count de Monterei were replaced by devoted partisans of the Princess. The high aristocracy, indignant at this manœuvre, worked against her in an underhanded opposition, in which the double character of the Duke de Medina-Cœli was more and more developed. Their plans were foiled in the very outset, but we shall see them again make their appearance upon the political arena at a moment when it required nothing less than all the power and skill of Madame des Ursins to triumph over them.

The Princess was, in fact, triumphing on the very brink of a volcano. Spain was in a blaze, and every day seemed to call in question the existence of that throne under the shadow of which she had come to reign. Lord Peterborough had torn Barcelona from Philip V., and the greater part of its garrison had recognised the Archduke, who, acting henceforward as King of Spain, had just made his entrance into that city amidst the acclamations of the Catalan people. The principal fortresses of the province had shared the fate of the chief city; and on one side the insurrection spread to Saragossa, whilst on the other, the important city of Valencia proclaimed Charles III. The situation was little better in the west of the kingdom, for an Anglo-Portuguese army had penetrated into Estramadura, commanded by a French refugee who had been made an English peer,* and whose hatred pursued Louis XIV. on every field of battle. Constrained to carry on the struggle simultaneously in Flanders, Italy, and beyond the Pyrenees, in order to defend the integrity of a monarchy which more and more hesitated in its obedience, the French King had just sent to Spain thirty battalions and twenty squadrons, which it became necessary to supplement by despatching a new army. Unhappily, the time was approaching when the French soldiery had more cause to dread their own generals than those of the enemy; and these forces, besides being insufficient, were placed under the command of Marshal de Tessé, a cunning courtier but mediocre general, incapable of any

---

* The Duke of Berwick.

initiative strategy, and whose sole study was to carry out to
the letter the personal instructions of Louis XIV. and
Chamillard. However, either from want of sufficient re-
ources or want of skill, Tessé failed this once in the execution of his master's formal orders, which directed him to
suspend all his operations in order to retake Barcelona at
any cost. A siege languidly conducted in presence of a
fleet mistress of the seas, on which the French flag dared
no longer show itself, was followed by a disaster aggravated
by the presence of the King of Spain and by bitter recri-
minations between the two nations together engaged in
that fatal enterprise. Alike indifferent to misfortune and
success, still it might be seen in Philip, since the presence
of his rival in Spain, that there was an indomitable resolution to die sword in hand in defence of the sole right which
touched his pride and his conscience. Before Barcelona he
had displayed a useless courage, and when de Tessé rendered
it necessary to raise the siege by his refusal to continue it,
the insurrection had closed to the King every road which
gave access to his capital. To rejoin the Queen Regent in
the heart of the two Castiles, Philip was compelled to take,
in mortal agony, the road to France, in order to direct his
steps by way of Rousillon towards Navarre, thus giving his
enemies a plausible pretext for turning his going out of the
kingdom into a desertion of the crown.

Trials not less formidable awaited the young Queen at the
hands of fortune. Excited by the greatness of the danger,
but finding a succour in the *sang-froid* of Madame des
Ursins, which her youth and ardour denied her, adored by
the inhabitants of Madrid, to whom in the hour of crisis she
confided herself with a touching helplessness, the *Savoiana*,
by the spell of her gentle and steady virtues, alone maintained

the royal authority in a country where "it was necessary to have almost an army in each province." *

At length the day came when despair reigned everywhere save at the *Retiro* Palace. The square d'Alcantara, defended by ten battalions, the last remains of the Spanish army, had surrendered without fighting. Whether through folly or treason, Salamanca had also just fallen into the enemy's hands, and the Anglo-Portuguese troops advanced by forced marches upon Madrid, in order there to proclaim Charles III. There was nothing left but flight—but to quit a city of proved devotion and confide in others of doubtful fidelity. The King had rejoined the French army; the Queen, accompanied by her *camerara mayor* and a few female attendants, was compelled to repair to Burgos, in order there to keep up at least some shadow of legitimate government. The little party was without resources, money, almost without victuals. The silver plate belonging to the palace was hastily flung into the melting-pot; the sovereign of so many realms, after having borrowed by pawning so many thousand pistoles, packed up with her own hands those jewels which were a tribute to her from the new world, the pride and recreation of her sorrowful youth, previous to pledging them to the Jew brokers. Her court, lately so numerous, had been dispersed by the wind of adversity, not with the intent of influencing events, but, shameful to record, only to await them; and Marie Louise *enceinte* with the first child of her marriage, shaped her course towards the land of the Cid, resolved to go thither and defend the monarchy even among those rugged mountains which had been its cradle. Destitution prevailed throughout the solitudes of Castile as

---

* Despatch of Marshal de Tessé to Chamillard, 4th Feb., 1706.—*Mémoires de Noailles*, tom. ii., p. 380.

well as in those poor *posadas*, bare as an Asiatic caravanserai. If in the central provinces the populace showed itself faithful, it was not without extreme suffering and the most cruel perplexity that the journey could be accomplished by almost impracticable ways, through detachments of the enemy, launched in pursuit of the royal retinue. Nothing certainly is more honourable to the memory of the Princess des Ursins than the letters in which she relates with charming naturalness the daily accidents of that adventurous life, which she supported at the age of sixty-five with all the gaiety of a youthful tourist.*

In the midst of these disasters, therefore, Philip V. found a firm support in the devotion of the people and in the indefatigable zeal of Madame des Ursins. At Madrid and in all the provinces, except Catalonia, the allies were received with that repugnance which presages a disastrous future and belies the most brilliant promises of victory. Madame des Ursins multiplied herself: speeches, letters, overtures—she spared nothing to obtain from the people the money indispensable for carrying on the war. She thus arrested desertion, consolidated in Old Castile, and even in Andalusia the King's authority ; she propagated, in short (if we may so express it) the feeling of devotedness. She knew how to surround Philip V. with the austere majesty of royal misfortune endured with courage and consoled by the watchful love of the nation. At the same time her cheerful and confident spirit restored to its serenity the little court of Burgos. She locked within her own bosom her discouragements and inquietudes : she clung to hope, and that successfully. She sought and found in her own firm will consolation

* Letters of the Princess to Mad. de Maintenon, from the 24th of June to 26th October, 1706.—Tom. iii., pp. 305 to 367.

justified by events. All her correspondence at this epoch, at times amiable, witty, affectionate, at others grave, precise, and altogether politic, full of facts, plans, exact details, worthy of a minister, and of a great minister too, shows the extraordinary genius of the woman. It was not she alone, certainly, who saved the dynasty, for it was necessary to fight and conquer to do that, but she was unquestionably one of the most vigorous instruments ever made use of by Providence to work out its own purposes in defence of a nation.

She had some ideas about war too—we do not say they were of the best, but she had some—and about plans of defence and the choice of generals. She anticipated coming dangers, which she laid bare and exposed without allowing herself to be discouraged by them. She described the native troops in their true colours, the places of importance entirely unprovided for, according to Spanish custom ; she energetically claimed help from France, and after asking for strong battalions in the body of her letter, adds in a postscript that she has advised the King of Spain to have prayers offered up. She did not forget to send appropriate flatteries also to Madame de Maintenon.

A few days after the arrival of the Duke of Berwick, in order to thank Madame de Maintenon for such aid, she spoke to her about Saint-Cyr, well aware that nothing could be more agreeable, and knowing *the weakness of mothers.*

"The Queen has highly approved of all your Saint-Cyr rules ; our ladies are anxious to have them, and I am working hard at translating them into Spanish to afford them that satisfaction. If her Majesty were not under engagements very different to those of the young ladies of Saint-Cyr, I really believe that she would like to be one of your pupils."

Her flattery knew well in what language to couch itself; but there were moments at which, discontented at feeling Spain abandoned and lost sight of by Versailles, she became plain spoken even to rudeness. Great allowance, however, ought to be made for the Princess's occasional bluntness when it is remembered that she was then in her sixty-fourth year, suffering from rheumatism and a painful affection of one of her eyes, a condition altogether very unpropitious in which to commence the career of arms in the capacity of field-marshal to a youthful Queen. Notwithstanding all this, however, she exerted herself to enliven everybody, to console, to inspire fortitude and a spirit of joyousness around her, never to see things on their darkest side or through her ailing eye, but to obey rather the buoyant spirit and an inclination to hope for the best, which was natural to her.

" It often happens, Madame," she writes to Madame de Maintenon, "that when one thinks all is lost some fortunate circumstance occurs unexpectedly which entirely changes the face of things." "I think," she says in another letter, " that fortune may again become favourable to us ; that it is with its favours as with too much health ; I mean that one is never so near falling sick as when one feels oneself so remarkably well, nor so near being unfortunate as when our measure of happiness is full to the brim. I reverse the medal, and I await some consolation which may effectually alleviate my sorrows. I wish, Madame, that you would do the same, and that your temperament were your best friend, as mine is that on which I can surest reckon ; for I think, to speak frankly, that I have more obligation to it than to my reason, and that there is no great merit in possessing that tranquillity of mind, of which you are disposed, in your extreme kindness, to think me possessed, and on which you bestow so much praise."

Madame de Maintenon, in fact, who, strong-minded as she might be, was nevertheless perpetually tormenting herself and wailing about something or other, continually eulogised that natural equanimity which she envied, that courage allied with good temper, that amiability, and that *beau sang qui ne laissait rien d'âpre et de chagrin en elle.*

Her letters to Madame de Maintenon from Burgos, admirably paint this characteristic tranquillity of mind. " To enliven you," she writes, " I must give you a description of my quarters. They consist of a single room, which may measure twelve or thirteen feet at most. One large window which will not shut, facing the south, occupies almost entirely one side. A somewhat low door gives me admittance to the Queen's chamber, and another still smaller opens into a winding passage, into which I dare not go, although it always has two or three lamps lighted in it, because it is so badly *paved* that I should break my neck there. I cannot say that the walls are whitewashed, for they are so dirty. My travelling bedstead is the sole piece of furniture I have in it, besides a folding stool and a deal table, which latter serves me alternately for a toilette, to write upon, or to hold the Queen's dessert—there being no receptacle in the kitchen or elsewhere wherein to put it. I laugh at all this. . . . and amidst all the sombre occurrences which have befallen us, I console myself with my own reflections. I imagine that fortune may take a good turn, and I calmly and trustfully wait for those consolations which are powerful to assuage all my trouble."* " Action becomes you," Madame de Maintenon might remark with great truth. It was, in fact, an original and most distinctive feature in the Princess des Ursins' character, that of having been known to be a person so thoroughly calm in the main during a career so active and a destiny so agitated ; and it was to this very characteristic equanimity that she was indebted, after so

---

* Mém. de Noailles, tom. iii., p. 375, and Letters to Mad. de Maintenon, tom. iv., p. 163.

abrupt a downfall at sixty-two, for the lot reserved for her of dying in peace and of old age at eighty. But there are many other traits worthy of study in her composition, and which place her in perfect contrast with her friend Madame de Maintenon.

BOOK II.

CHAPTER I.

THE succession of the Duke d'Anjou to the Spanish crown had, in fact, destroyed the balance of power in Europe; and our William the Third, then recently dead, but even beyond the grave the most resolute enemy of Louis the Fourteenth, had bequeathed to him the new league which bore the name of the Great Alliance, and which had for its aim to place the Spanish crown upon the head of the Archduke Charles, the son of the Emperor of Germany; or in default of dispossessing Philip the Fifth of his kingdom, to trace round the two nations of France and Spain a limit which should never be overpassed by the ambition of either. All hope of success for the Archduke Charles—the legitimate successor to the last four effete kings of Spain—all the means which he might have of preserving in Europe two houses of Austria, and of continuing that grand Austrian duality which the sceptre of Charles the Fifth had produced, but which was then broken in twain, rested chiefly upon the English alliance. There, for the adversaries of Louis the Fourteenth, was the knot of the question. With the treasures of England, with her navy, with her troops also, together with the advantage of her situation, which allowed of her doing so much mischief to France, the Imperialists might effect much; without her they could scarcely do anything. Hence with them the necessity of keeping in power a party favourable to them—the Whigs, a party which preferred that ancient duality to the new duality—in other words, the ambition of Louis the Fourteenth to therewith augment the House of Bourbon, and in effect more dangerous than the other to the English nation. But that necessity created another: it was requisite to have near Queen Anne some one who, at Court, should be, as it were, the advanced sentinel of the Whigs, attached to the interests of Austria, and who would hinder from penetrating, or at any rate prevailing therein any other interest than theirs. This precaution was so much the more indispensable that Queen Anne's feeling towards the Whigs was purely official, and not a genuine sympathy. To these zealous partizans of Parliament and liberty, to these avowed heirs of those who had made the revolution of 1640, she secretly preferred the Tories. Amongst them she found admirers of the absolute order of government that Louis XIV., lord of France instead of being legislator of it, had for too long a time substituted for the too much contemned troubles of the Fronde. And the rather as they might be termed, under that relation, a veritable French party, did she lean towards them, because they were the defenders of the royal prerogative. The exactions, the delays, the innumerable formalities of constitutional monarchy, wearied her to such an extent, that more than once the rumour ran that she was willing to treat for the recall of her brother, the ex-King James the Third. These reports were not without foundation, as the Duke of Berwick tells us in his " Memoirs "; the desire alone of preventing civil war, to which fresh endeavours on the part of that prince would give rise, was alleged as the generous motive for relinquishing a design which the disgust of a too-limited power had inspired. The Whigs well knew how to conjure that peril. But they had always to dread that whilst continuing to wear the crown, Anne might not so much consider the welfare of England as that of her own pleasure, where such welfare interfered with her peculiar sympathies ; and lest in turning to the side of the Tories she might carry away from the Archduke Charles the support of England, in other words his chief reliance. The question was how to guarantee themselves from that untoward eventuality ? One means devised—and it was not the less available in this case of royalty exercised by a woman —was to secure to Queen Anne the adhesion of the Mistress of the Robes, Lady Churchill, the clever wife of the brilliant soldier, afterwards Duke of Marlborough.

This remarkable woman, who, without possessing great talents, and with the disadvantage of an imperious and capricious temper, exercised for so long a period such exceptional influence over public affairs, was the second of the three daughters of Richard Jennings, a country gentleman of good family but moderate fortune, her mother being Frances Thornhurst, daughter of Sir Gifford Thornhurst, of Agnes Court, in Kent, and his heiress. She was born at Holywell, near St. Alban's, 29th May, 1660, the very day of the restoration of Charles the Second. In recompense for the services rendered by their father during the civil wars, the two elder sisters were received when very young into the household of the Duchess of York.

When only twelve years old, Sarah Jennings had the good fortune to become the inseparable companion of the Princess Anne, who was about the same age. Her beauty was not characterised by regularity of feature, but she possessed an animated countenance, with eyes full of fire. She was small of stature, more piquante than imposing, and her chief charms were centered in her magnificent tresses, the delicacy of her features, and certain peculiar graces of mind and person. These attractions were enhanced by a conversation full of vivacity and intelligence. Prudent and virtuous—for even Swift, who was otherwise the remorseless enemy of the Duke and Duchess of Marlborough, renders homage to the virtue of the latter—in the midst of a corrupt Court, and enjoying the highest favour of the Royal Family, she had for admirers some men of the highest rank in England. Amongst those who aspired to her hand may be cited the admired Earl of Lindsay, afterwards Marquis of Ancaster, "the star and ornament of the Court," whose suit she rejected for that of the young and handsome Colonel Churchill. A single trait suffices to prove the lady's attractiveness—the avaricious John Churchill wooed and wedded her although all along he knew Sarah to be altogether portionless.

This successful wooer—afterwards Lord Churchill and Duke of Marlborough—who had entered the army at sixteen, was the son of a poor cavalier knight who had come to London after the Restoration. Love, not War, was the first stepping-stone to his subsequent high fortune. The Duke of York, heir to the Crown, "young and ardent in the pursuit of pleasure," became enamoured of Arabella Churchill one of the maids-of-honour to his first wife, and afterwards his avowed mistress. Through this lady's interest, her elder brother John obtained a pair of colours in the Guards. In his twenty-third year he made his first campaign in the Low Countries when Charles and Louis united their forces against Holland. Distinguished by his commanding stature and handsome face, he was known to the French soldiery as the "handsome Englishman." Turenne complimented him on his gallantry and " serene intrepidity " before the allied armies. The Marshal had been attracted to him by his courage, and is said to have laid a wager, which he won, on the subject of Churchill's gallantry, on the occasion of a post of importance having been abandoned by one of his own officers. " I will bet a supper and a dozen of claret," said he,. " that my handsome Englishman will recover the post with half the number of men commanded by the officer who lost it." The event justified the Marshal's opinion. Emboldened by the praise of such a general, Churchill solicited but did not obtain the command of a regiment from Louis XIV.,* the great King refusing his services, as he declined those of Prince Eugene a few years later. He was esteemed one of the handsomest and most attractive gentlemen of the day. Lord Chesterfield, the *arbiter elegantiarum*, declared that the grace and fascination of young Churchill was such, that he was "irresistible either by man or woman."

On his return to London at the close of the war, the young soldier became attached to the household of the Duke of York, and rose rapidly in that witty, gallant, and corrupt Court, where shone the Grammonts, Rochesters, and Hamiltons, and where Churchill sought the society of the sultanas who shared with Charles the government of England. The handsome Churchill became, for a short time, the object of the violent but fickle fondness of the head sultana, the Duchess of Cleveland. On one occasion the audacious gallant was very nearly caught in the frail beauty's apartments

---

* This curious fact was lately ascertained by M. Moret, through the discovery of an inedited, but authentic document, in the *Archives de la Guerre* in Paris. It appears in a letter of Lord Lockhart, the English Ambassador at Paris, who asks that the colonelcy of a regiment might be given to Churchill. It is dated 27th of May, 1674.—*Archives de la Guerre*, vol. 411, No. 193.

by "old Rowley," and only escaped by leaping from the
window at the risk of his life. For this exploit the grateful
Duchess presented her daring lover with five thousand
pounds. Churchill made no scruple of receiving the money,
so early had the sordid propensity for gain taken hold of
him, and with it he at once bought an annuity of five
hundred a year, well secured on the estate of Lord Chesterfield's grandfather, Halifax.*

After some disputes and obstacles on the part of the
Churchill family, which the Duchess of York herself took
the trouble to obviate, the two lovers were united in the
month of April, 1678: and whilst the husband advanced in
the confidence and favour of James, his wife made still more
rapid progress in the affections of the young Princess, his
daughter.

During many years of married happiness, Churchill testified the greatest affection for his wife, and always kept her
minutely informed—even amidst councils and battle-fields—
upon the state of public affairs, and showed the most entire
deference and the liveliest affection for her. Most of his
letters end with these words: "I am yours, heart and soul."
Lady Churchill governed this great man, in fact, like a
child—who himself governed kings. Like the Princess des
Ursins, she possessed incontestably certain qualities, a
liking and capacity for public business, a knowledge of men,
the shrewdness of her sex, the obstinacy of her race, an
inconceivable love of domination; but she was hard, vin-
dictive, insatiable of honours and wealth, and united to the
pride of a queen the rage of a fury.

Aided by his sister, by the King's imperious mistress and
his own incontestable merit, Churchill climbed fast up the

* Chesterfield's Letters, November 18th, 1748.

ladder of preferment. He obtained successively the command of the only dragoon regiment in the service, a Scotch peerage, and the post of Ambassador to the Court of France. Lord Churchill, however, was destined to be advanced still higher in court favour through the influence of his wife and his own genius as a general.

At the Revolution of 1688, he coldly foorsook James II., his benefactor, and carried over his formidable sword to the House of Orange. The Revolution augmented his fortune. Created Earl and General by William III.; Duke, Knight of the Garter and Commander of the British Armies by Queen Anne. Marlborough was one of those men whom conviction astonishes, devotedness confounds ; who acknowledge no other law than that of their own interest, no other deity than success, and which the uncontrollable current of human affairs not unfrequently brings rapidly to the surface. Cradled in revolutions, he had seen the Commonwealth pass away, the Stuarts fall, the House of Orange proclaimed. He had taken part in intrigues, plots, apostacies, defections : doubt alone survived every other political instinct of his heart. Faithful to the very brink of misfortune, he ever adhered unswervingly until the dawning of the evil days. Well aware how quickly dynasties expire in a country convulsed by revolutions, he had learnt to anticipate approaching catastrophes, and to secure to himself beforehand an *appui* amongst the victorious survivors. Whilst he was defending the cause of the House of Orange in Europe, he corresponded secretly with the Stuarts, kept up assiduous relations with the little Court of St. Germains, and made underhand preparations for marrying one of his daughters with the Pretender, then ex-King (James III.), at St. Germains, and, perhaps, on the morrow *de facto* King of

England.   But if Marlborough's soul was mean and sordid,
his genius was vast and powerful.   In parliament, at St.
James's, in foreign councils, in foreign courts, on the field of
battle, everywhere he dominated men.   His education had
been so very much neglected that he could scarcely write
correctly his native English, and yet, when he rose to speak
in the House of Lords, the entire assembly hung upon his
words, and the most consummate orators, the heads of the
British forum, were envious of that natural eloquence which
without effort went straight to the heart; and he exercised that
charm even upon his foes, to such a degree that Bolingbroke
once remarked to Voltaire, when speaking of him : " He was
such a great man that I have forgotten his vices."*

At the period of which we are now treating, Marlborough
was the most powerful personage in England : by his wife,
the Queen's favourite, he ruled the household; by the
Whigs, become his friends, parliament and the ministry;
by his rank and his military popularity, the army; by Prince
Eugene, his comrade in arms, the councils of Austria; by
his old friend Heinsius, the States-General; by the weight
of his name, his conduct and address, the suppleness of his
character, Prussia and the princes of the Empire.   It was
he who raised their regiments, who regulated their sub-
ventions, who appeased their quarrels.   He was the head
and arm of the coalition.   As potent as Cromwell, more of
a king than William III.; without affection or hatred, he
justified the saying of Machiavelli : " The universe belongs
to the phlegmatic."

We will now revert to his no less celebrated wife, who, as
Lady Churchill and Duchess of Marlborough, so long and
wholly swayed the mind and ruled the court of Queen Anne.

* Voltaire, Beuchot's edition, tom. xxxvii.   Lettre xii., p. 172.

Brought up in such close intimacy with the Princess, Lady Churchill had assumed from childhood an absolute ascendancy over her mind. Anne was indolent and taciturn; she delighted in the lively talk of her companion and bosom friend, and loved her in spite of her haughty temperament, to which her own easy disposition yielded without offering the slightest resistance. Married to a sullen and insignificant husband, whose sole delight was centred in a crapulous love of the bottle; she had lost her only son during his minority—had seen her father, James II. dethroned, her brother, the Chevalier St. George, proscribed, and, to the exclusion of that well-beloved brother, she was compelled to leave her crown to a stranger—the Elector George of Hanover, for whom she felt an invincible aversion. Anne confided all her griefs to her favourite Mistress of the Robes, and by degrees an ardent affection for her inseparable companion, which had in it all the delicate tenderness of feminine friendship, sprung up in the Princess's bosom. Such was the strength of the attachment that it was the desire of the Princess that all distinction prescribed by etiquette should be waived. She required that in their epistolary correspondence they should treat each other as equals, under the assumed names of Mrs. Morley and Mrs. Freeman. Lady Churchill chose the latter, which would be, she said, the emblem of her "frank, open temper." Under these assumed names they wrote frequently to each other to communicate their sentiments of joy, anguish, hope or fear, according to the events of the day, and gave themselves up unrestrictedly to the momentary impulse of their hearts.

"I both obtained and held the place in her service," the favourite goes on to relate, "without the assistance of flattery —a charm which, in truth, her (the Princess's) inclination for me, together with my unwearied application to serve and amuse her rendered needless ; but which, had it been otherwise, my temper and turn of mind would never have suffered me to employ. Young as I was when I first became this high favourite, I laid it down as a maxim, that flattery was falsehood to my trust, and ingratitude to my dearest friend. . . . . From this rule I never swerved : and though my temper and my notions in most things were widely different from those of the Princess, yet, during a long course of years, she was so far from being displeased with me for openly speaking my sentiments, that she sometimes professed a desire, and even added her command, that it should be always continued, promising never to be offended at it, but to love me the better for my frankness."

CHAPTER II.

STATE OF PARTIES IN ACTION ON THE ACCESSION OF ANNE
—HARLEY AND BOLINGBROKE AIM AT OVERTHROWING
THE SWAY OF THE DUCHESS—ABIGAIL HILL BECOMES
THE INSTRUMENT OF THE DUCHESS'S DOWNFALL.

THE year following that in which the Duke d'Anjou succeeded to the throne of Spain saw Anne Queen of England.

On her accession Queen Anne had found three parties in
action—the Tories, the Whigs, and the Jacobites. The
first asserting the sovereignty of the royal prerogative; the
second the extension of public liberty; the last demanding
the exclusion of the Protestant George of Hanover, designated by the Commons as the Queen's heir, and the recall of
the Chevalier St. George, the Romanist son of James II.,
then an exile in France, where Louis XIV. had welcomed
him under the title of James III.

Of these three parties, the last, who were desirous of a revolution with a change of dynasty, naturally found themselves excluded from public affairs; the Queen, facile and
conciliating, divided the power of the State between the two
others, and chose a ministry comprising the most eminent
men among both Whigs and Tories.

Those statesmen jointly carried on the government for
four years, after which the opposition of their sentiments
and interests became so violent that it divided them. The
Tories, representing the landed interest, which had suffered
during the war, clamoured for peace with all their might;

the Whigs, on the contrary, representing the monied interest, had lent their funds to the State, and desired the continuance of hostilities, as it enhanced the value of their capital. The Whigs triumphed in this first struggle. They ejected, in the first instance, three Tories from the Ministry, and afterwards obtained the dismissal of all the rest— Mansel, Harley, and Bolingbroke, and then ruled without division. They reckoned amongst their ranks the most illustrious men of the day : Marlborough, the great soldier; the skilful financier, Godolphin ; the formidable speaker, Robert Walpole ; the army, public opinion, parliament, and even the very heart of the Queen, through the Duchess of Marlborough, who, intoxicated with her almost unlimited sway, no longer deigned to ask, but commanded.

The influence of the Duchess of Marlborough at the court of Queen Anne was now well understood by the continental powers of Europe. When England, in 1703, received a foreign potentate as her guest, the Duchess, was, of all her subjects, the object peculiarly selected for distinction. Charles, the second son of the Emperor of Austria, having recently been proclaimed, at Vienna, King of Spain, in opposition to the Duke of Anjou, completed his visits to sundry courts in Germany, whither he had repaired to seek a wife, by paying his respects to Anne of England. Anne received her royal ally with great courtesy at Windsor, whither he was conducted by Marlborough, and there entertained with a truly royal magnificence. All ranks of people crowded to see the young monarch dine with the Queen in public, and his deportment and appearance were greatly admired by the multitude, more especially by the fair sex, whose national beauty was, on the other hand, highly extolled by Charles. The Duchess of Marlborough, though no longer young, still graced the court which she controlled. It was her office to hold the basin of water after dinner to the Queen, for the royal hands to be dipped, after the ancient fashion of the laver and ewer. Charles took the basin from the fair Duchess's hand, and, with the gallantry of a young and well-bred man, held it to the Queen; and in returning it to the Duchess, he drew from his own finger a valuable ring and placed it on that of the stately Sarah.

It was two years after this visit that Charles sent a letter of thanks for the assistance granted him by the Queen against the French, which he addressed to the Duchess of Marlborough, " as the person most agreeable to her Majesty." The King might have added, as a partisan most favourable to the aid afforded him, and most inimical to the sway of France, which, by the will of the late King of Spain, Charles the Second, had been unjustly extended over the Spanish monarchy.

At the time of the overthrow of the Tories, she had pushed obsession of her royal mistress even as far as constraint. To the Whigs, who had proscribed her brother, Anne preferred the Tories; but, in spite of these sympathies, the favourite had demanded the dismissal of the Ministry, and the Queen had yielded, though not without the deepest grief, to her imperious Mistress of the Robes.

Thus got rid of by an intrigue, the Tories, and at their head the two celebrated statesmen, Harley and Bolingbroke, worked steadfastly in the dark to regain power. Harley was a skilful and eloquent orator. He had quitted the bar to enter parliament, and his suppleness as well as his talents had rapidly carried him on to the Speakership and the Ministry. He had specially directed his attention to finance, and passed for the most skilful financier of his day. A man of wit and taste, he loved books and manuscripts, and patro-nised the most illustrious writers of the reign : Swift, the English Rabelais, Pope, Boileau, and Prior, the Regnier of Great Britain. But he was not unjustly reproached for his obstinacy of character, the changeableness of his opinions, his proneness to descend to little means, and an unfortunate passion for drink.*

The other chief of the Tory party was Henry St. John, so well-known under the name of Bolingbroke.† He descended from an old Norman family allied to the royal house of Tudor. His grandfather, as though he had foreseen the future, had bequeathed him the greater part of his property, and Bolingbroke began the world under the happiest auspices of birth and fortune. At twenty-six, after a career of youth-ful licentiousness, he married and entered parliament. He had all the necessary qualifications for playing a distinguished part therein : a noble countenance, ready eloquence, an in-credible capacity for work, a mind which later astonished Voltaire, a memory so retentive that he avoided reading mediocre books from the fear of retaining their contents. At thirty, his lofty and copious oratory, unceasingly fed by study of the ancient models, captivated both Lords and Commons. His powerful and versatile genius embraced at once poetry and jurisprudence, history and the *belles lettres.* He was associated, like Harley, with the first writers in England—Pope, Prior, Swift, Dryden, even with Addison himself, the Whig poet and essayist. He was one of those

* This habit of drinking had then invaded even the highest ranks of English society, the Queen herself not being exempt. Walpole, Harley's enemy, has traced a curious and tolerably accurate portrait of him in his " Letters."

† He was only created Viscount Bolingbroke in 1712, but we give him the name by which he is best known in history.

consummate orators who, joining grace to eloquence, was the foremost alike in pleasure or business. He was in the habit of saying that only fools were unable to find or enjoy leisure. He possessed, in short, the peculiar talents and vices which were destined later to immortalise as well as disgrace Mirabeau.

Uniting their talents and their rancour against the imperious and uncompromising woman who had compassed their disgrace, Harley and Bolingbroke, in their turn, had set about overthrowing the sway of the Duchess. They craftily endeavoured to undermine, therefore, that friendship which constituted her strength, and sought for a rival who might supplant her in the Queen's heart. There was then at court a young lady named Abigail Hill, the daughter of a bankrupt merchant of London, who, when in poverty, had been taken by the hand by the Duchess of Marlborough, to whom she was cousin, and through her influence appointed bedchamber-woman to the Queen. By a singular chance, Abigail Hill was also a cousin of Harley, who during his administration married her to Masham, a dangling official of the royal household, who had been indebted for his post rather to his birth and connections than any personal merit.

Up to the period of Marlborough's brilliant victory of Ramilies (May, 1706), the influence of the Duchess over the mind of her sovereign was not visibly lessened by her own indiscretion, or by the arts of her opponents. From the moment of Anne's accession, she had flung herself with ardour into politics. To dominate was her favourite passion. And she imagined that she could decide affairs of State as easily as she directed a petty intrigue, or suppressed a squabble within the interior of the royal household. Instead

of using the absolute sway she had over the Queen with tact
and moderation, she exercised it with an imprudent audacity.
Her party predilections were diametrically opposed to those
of Anne, who was sincerely attached to the principles of the
Tories, and who ardently desired to bring them into power.
The Duchess did not allow her a moment's repose until she
had, by concession after concession, surrounded herself by
the chiefs of the Whig party, whom she at heart detested.
Hence an endless succession of piques, misunderstandings,
and jars between the royal Lady and her imperious Mistress
of the Robes.   The glory and the important services of the
Duke had, however, long deferred the explosion of these
secret resentments; but it was when Harley found it impossible by any means to establish himself in the favour of the
Duchess, and gain her over to his interest, that he hit upon
a plan which succeeded to the utmost, as trifles often do
when more important engines fail.   The one he used was
ready to his hand in the person of the bedchamber-woman,
who had been placed about the Queen by the Duchess herself.   In a letter, supposed to have been addressed to
Bishop Burnet, the Duchess gives a brief account of this
person, who was her kinswoman, in explanation to his
inquiry as to the first cause of her disagreement with the
Queen.

Abigail Hill—a name rendered famous from the momen-
tous changes which succeeded its introduction to the political
world—was the appropriate designation of the lowly, supple,
and artful being on whose secret offices Harley relied for the
accomplishment of his plans.   Mistress Hill at this time
held the post of dresser and chamber-woman to her Majesty.
The world assigned certain causes for the pains which the
proud favourite (the Duchess) had manifested to place her

cousin in a post where she might have easy access to the Queen's ear, and obtain her confidence. The Duchess, it was said, was weary of her arduous attendance upon a mistress whom she secretly despised. She had become too proud to perform the subordinate duties of her office, and proposed to relieve herself of some of them, by placing one on whom she could entirely depend, as an occasional substitute in the performance of those duties which even habit had not taught her to endure with patience. Since after the elevation of the Duke, in consequence of the battle of Blenheim, she had become a princess of the empire,[*] she was supposed to consider herself too elevated to continue those services to which she had been enured, first in the court of the amiable Anne Hyde, then in that of the unhappy Mary of Modena, and since, near her too gracious sovereign, the meek, but dissembling Anne.

The ungrateful kinswoman had been early acquainted with adversity, which was the remote cause of her ultimate greatness. "Mrs. Masham," the Duchess tells us, in her succinct narrative, "was the daughter of one Hill, a merchant in the city, by a sister of my father. Our grandfather, Sir John Jenyns, had two-and-twenty children, by which means the estate of the family, which was reputed to be about four thousand pounds a year, came to be divided into small parcels. Mrs. Hill had only £500 to her fortune. Her husband lived very well for many years, as I have been told, until turning projector, he brought ruin on himself and family. But as this was long before I was born, I never knew there were such people in the world till after the Princess Anne was married, and when she lived at the Cockpit; at which time an acquaintance of mine came to

* Lediard, vol. ii., p. 2.

me and said, *she believed I did not know that I had relations who were in want,* and she gave me an account of them. When she had finished her story, I answered, *that indeed I had never heard before of any such relations,* and immediately gave her out of my purse ten guineas for their present relief, saying I would do what I could for them."

Not contented with conferring important benefits on Abigail's brothers and sister, the Duchess tells us that even the *husband* of Mrs. Masham had several obligations to her. "It was at my instance," says the indignant benefactress, "that he was first made a page, then an equerry, and afterwards groom of the bedchamber to the Prince; for all which he himself thanked me, as for favours procured by my means.'

Towards the Queen, Mrs. Hill displayed a servile, humble, gentle, and pliant manner, in singular contrast with that of the commanding and haughty Duchess. Anne, accustomed to opposition and remonstrance, nay, sometimes rebukes, upon certain points she had at heart, was delighted to find that as regarded both religious opinions and politics, her lowly attendant coincided with her. Mrs. Hill was, or pretended to be to serve her purpose, an enemy to the Hanoverian succession, if not a partizan of the exiled Stuarts—subjects on which the Queen and the Duchess were known to have frequent controversies, which sometimes degenerated into angry disputes. Such was the woman whom the Tories set up to oppose and undermine the influence of the redoubtable Sarah. Mrs. Masham was able to give them, by means of her court-appointment, continual access to the Queen. She had neither the wit nor the intelligence of her rival, but she pleased Anne by the simplicity of her manners

and the amenity of her temper. Moreover, two powerfu
ties, political and religious, though strangely contradictory
in their sympathies, attached her to her royal mistress. An
ardent Jacobite, she, equally with the Queen, desired the
return of the Pretender; like her, too, she was a zealous
Protestant.

Carrying out Harley's injunctions, Mrs. Masham strove
secretly to sap the power and credit of the Whigs at Court,
by daily representing to Queen Anne the disquieting influence of their chief, Marlborough—master, as he was, of
the parliament, the army, the ministry, the court,—more
sovereign, in fact, than the Queen herself; and she recalled
to mind that last dismissal of the Tories, so rudely and im-
periously dictated by the Duchess. The Queen, moved even
to terror by such advice, drew closer by degrees to her new
confidante, and shortly manifested towards her a favour
which the Duchess of Marlborough was the first to perceive.
But instead of seeking to revive a friendship still endeared
to the Queen, the Duchess complained sharply of it being
shared. At the same time she heaped every species of contempt, sarcasm, and insult upon Mrs. Masham, spread the
vilest calumnies about her, and then, perceiving the inutility
of her efforts, directed the current of her wrath against the
throne. In the month of August, 1708, during a thanks-
giving service at St. Paul's on the occasion of the battle
of Oudenarde, Anne found that she had not put on her
diamonds, and blamed the Duchess for the omission, it
belonging to her duty as Mistress of the Robes. The
quondam favourite made her Majesty a haughty reply ; and
Anne, hurt at it, repeated her reproaches with greater
warmth. The Duchess, furious, imposed silence upon her
royal mistress. " I don't ask you for an answer," she

exclaimed loud enough to be heard by the court and congregation, "don't answer me." The Queen remained silent, dreading further scandal, but she did not forget that day's incident.*

A year afterwards, during the autumn of 1709, another altercation took place still more deplorable. Anne was in the habit of allowing a bottle of wine to be daily carried to one of her laundrymaids who was ailing, without previously asking leave of the Mistress of the Robes. This coming to the knowledge of the Duchess, she ran after the Queen one day as Anne was proceeding on her charitable errand, reproached her for having usurped her functions, and behaved with such violence that the lackeys at the bottom of the stairs could overhear what she said. Indignant at this, Anne rose to leave the room, but the Duchess prevented her by placing her back against the door, and, during an hour, exhausted herself by launching invectives against her sovereign. Having sufficiently vented her rage, the angry woman ended by saying that doubtless she should never see her again, but she cared very little about that. "I think," calmly replied Anne, "the seldomer the better." The Duchess at length quitted the room, but from that day the links of their hitherto close friendship were rudely broken, their correspondence interrupted, and the Queen gave her entire confidence to Mrs. Masham.

The subtle Abigail was ever on the watch to closely observe the frequent disagreements between her Majesty and the Mistress of the Robes, and did not fail to turn them to

* The extent of her insolence towards the Queen on this occasion is scarcely conceivable. "The Duchess gave her her gloves to hold," relates Walpole; "and, on taking them back, suddenly turned away her head, as though the breath of her royal mistress had imparted a disagreeable odour."

skilful account. When the storm had subsided, and the Queen poured into her friendly ear confidential complaints of the absent Duchess, Abigail's sympathy, acquiescence, and responsive condolences, were ever ready, and effected their purpose. The lady-dresser thus gradually wormed herself into the Queen's affections, and as gradually undermined what remained of friendly feeling between her powerful kinswoman and their royal mistress. Every one at court had become aware of the influence of the new favourite before the Duchess herself perceived it; but it was not in the power of the artful relative, nor of her tool, the Queen, much longer to blind the woman whom they had, with true vulgarity of mind, gloried in deceiving.*

From the time of Mrs. Masham's admittance to close attendance on the Queen, the Duchess seemed in a constant state of irritation and annoyance. Her letters to Anne showed the mortification and vexation she endured, and prove the petty and ungrateful conduct of the bedchamber-woman, whose hold on the Queen's regard was sustained by a thousand mean and paltry instances of treachery to her benefactress. That Queen Anne, who had once been really attached to a woman like the Duchess of Marlborough, could condescend to replace her by such a rival is not a little surprising, and shows the true bent of her character to have been such as to render her unworthy of the friendship of an honest and high-minded woman. That the Duchess herself entered into details of petty injuries, and descends to justify herself, cannot be wondered at; for such subjects were forced upon her, and much as it galled her feelings to be obliged to notice what she held in contempt, still she had no other course to pursue.

* MSS. Brit. Mus., Coxe Papers, vol. xliv.

At length, the Duchess perceived clearly enough that she had been hoodwinked in certain matters by the Queen and Mrs. Masham, and that without any reasonable cause for resorting to mystery or deception. Having discovered that not only was Mrs. Hill's marriage known to the Queen, though she had denied any knowledge of the event, but that her Majesty had been herself at the wedding, and given a large dower to the bride, the Duchess immediately wrote to Mrs. Masham, to desire an explanation of her reasons for concealing so important an occurrence from one whom she had every reason to consider her only friend. The cautious answer which she received to her question was dictated, as she easily perceived, by no other than Harley, whose tool she now saw, too late, her unworthy cousin was; and it became sufficiently plain that her empire over the mind of the weak Queen was gone.

The Duchess was, whatever her faults, upright, honest, truthtelling, and fearless; and *she* was long before she could suspect the treachery and meanness of a dependent; and still longer in believing that the woman who had for so many years been her pupil, and had been accustomed to her frankness, could condescend to a low cabal, and, displacing her from her councils, solace herself with the society of a person so immeasurably her inferior.

The betrayed Mistress of the Robes could now trace the whole system of deception which had been carried on to her injury for a considerable time; her relative and former dependent being the chief agent—her sovereign the accomplice. She could account for the interest which Harley had now acquired at court by means of this new instrument. She could explain to her astonished and irritated mind certain incidents, which had seemed of little moment when they occurred, but which afforded an unquestionable confirmation of all that she had learned.

When the Duchess could no longer doubt the mortifying truth, she communicated the fact to her friend, Lord Godolphin, and to her husband, then abroad. Marlborough wearied with these, as he considered them, petty dissensions, wrote a somewhat stern letter to his wife. The great soldier was annoyed and distressed at the details of paltry wrongs which he was obliged to hear, and grown impatient, forgot that sometimes,—

"Dire events from little causes spring ; "

he did not contemplate his own, his wife's, and his friend's disgrace, from the contemptible quarrels among the women about the court.

"If you have good reasons," he writes, "for what you write of the kindness and esteem the Queen has for Mrs. Masham and Mr. Harley, my opinion should be, that my Lord Treasurer and I should tell her Majesty what is good for herself; and if that will not prevail, to be quiet, and to let Mr. Harley and Mrs. Masham do what they please; for I own I am quite tired, and if the Queen can be safe I shall be glad. I hope the Lord Treasurer will be of my mind; and then we shall be much happier than by being in a perpetual struggle."

At length the mask of affected humility assumed by Mrs. Masham was thrown off entirely; and, confident in the support of her royal mistress, the upstart favourite exhibited all the scorn and insolence which was in her nature. The Duchess expatiates with feminine pertinacity upon the stinging impertinences and insulting condescensions she had to endure from her lately exalted cousin. One instance she dwells on with bitter recollection, for it was the first time the minion of the Queen had dared to show her how little she regarded her.

When having with difficulty obtained an interview with Mrs. Masham, the Duchess upbraided her with her treachery, and observed, that she was certain no good intentions towards herself could have influenced her actions, Abigail replied :—

"... very gravely, that she was sure the Queen, who had always loved me extremely, would *always be very kind to me.* I was some minutes before I could recover from the surprise with which so extraordinary an answer struck me. To see a woman whom I had raised out of the dust put on such a superior air, and to hear her assure me, by way of consolation, that the Queen would always be very kind to me !—I was stunned to hear her say so strange a thing ! "

The Duchess of Marlborough was now, therefore, at open variance with her cousin. Towards her Majesty she stood in a predicament the most curious and unprecedented that perhaps ever existed between sovereign and subject. The amused and astonished court beheld Anne cautiously creeping out of that subjection in which the Duchess had, according to her enemies, long held the timid sovereign.

A confidential friend of the Duchess, Mr. Mainwaring, remarks of her, in one of his letters, that she was totally deficient in that "part of craft which Mr. Hobbes very prettily calls crooked wisdom." * Apt, as she herself expresses it, " to tumble out her mind," her openness and honesty were appreciated, when at an advanced age, and after she had run the career of five courts—by that experienced judge, the Lady Mary Wortley Montagu, who often

* Private Correspondence, vol. i., p. 105.

presumed upon the venerable Duchess's candour in telling
her unpalatable truths, which none but the honest could
have borne to hear. It was this uprightness and singleness
of mind which rendered the Duchess unwilling to believe
in the duplicity and the influence of her cousin. Warned
of it by Mr. Mainwaring, it was not until she found in the
Queen a defender of Mrs. Masham's secret marriage, that
the Duchess was roused into suspicion. It was then that
she communicated her conviction to Lord Godolphin and to
Marlborough, and besought their advice and assistance.

The Duke had just then prepared measures for carrying
on the war, and had completed every arrangement for his
voyage into Holland; the only thing which detained him in
England was, says Cunningham, "the quarrel among the
women about the court." He desired his often-offended
Duchess "to put an end to those controversies, and to
avoid all occasions of suspicion and disgust; and not to
suffer herself to grow insolent upon the favour of fortune;
"otherwise," said he, "I shall hardly be able hereafter to
excuse your fault, or to justify my own actions, however
meritorious." To which the Duchess replied, "I will take
care of those things, so that you need not be in any fear
about me; but whoever shall think to remove me out of
the Queen's favour, let them take care lest they remove
themselves."

It was not long before Marlborough perceived that the
Duchess was not mistaken in her apprehensions; nor
before he became painfully aware of the fact, that services
of the greatest magnitude are often not to be weighed
against slights and petty provocations.

Queen Anne, however, had some pangs of conscience, in
spite of her joy at being emancipated from the thraldom of

her haughty Mistress of the Robes, in ill-treating the great general who had filled her reign with glory; but the uninterrupted gossip which she delighted now to indulge in with her waiting-woman compensated for all.

Soon after Marlborough had won the sanguinary battle of Malplaquet, the celebrated trial of the noted Doctor Sacheverell took place; on which occasion an incident occurred which completed the downfall of the Duchess. The prosecution of Sacheverell had been advised by the Duke, lest he should preach him and his party out of the kingdom.

CHAPTER III.

THE result of the trial of Sacheverell made Harley and the favourite sure of the temper of the nation, and they resolved to hesitate no longer. The cabal had succeeded, and the Queen, a tool in the hands of others, by degrees gave up every appearance of regard for the Duchess, or of gratitude to the Duke. Though still fighting his country's battles and gaining immortal honours, the cabal sought to overwhelm him with unkindness and mortification at home. On the death of Lord Essex, the Queen was urged to give the Duke's regiment to Major Hill, Mrs. Masham's brother. Marlborough, highly indignant, insisted on Abigail being dismissed, or else he would resign; but the efforts of Godol- phin and other friends accommodated the matter, and he was contented with the disposal of the regiment being left with him. To prove, as it were, the influence of the favourite, the Queen soon after gave Hill a pension of £1,000 a year; and she made the Duke consent to raise him to the rank of brigadier.

It was Harley's plan to overthrow the Ministry by degrees; and when Lord Godolphin was dismissed from office, the triumph of the adverse party was complete. Thus fell the most able, and perhaps the most patriotic administration that England had possessed since the days of Elizabeth. It fell by disunion in itself, by the imprudent impeachment of a contemptible divine, and by the intrigues of the bedchamber, where a weak woman, whom the constitution had invested with power, was domineered over by one attendant and wheedled and flattered by another.

It was thus that, after seven-and-twenty years' service and professed friendship, Anne emancipated herself from all obligations, and shook off the yoke which pressed too heavily on her mind, regardless of the confusion into which her weak compliance with interested persons cast the country.

It was now that all the malice which had been long repressed burst out, and poured forth its vengeance on the disgraced favourite. Among other libellers in the service of the new Ministry Swift employed his great talents to cover her with ridicule and obloquy. In the celebrated journal called " The Examiner," his unjust insinuations must have been even more galling than his abuse. He represents the Duke and Duchess as extortioners and dissipators of the public money, insatiable in their avarice, and greedily swallowing all that they could get into their power, disposing of places, and seizing on rewards in a manner the most odious. " Even the Duke's courage," says Smollet, " was called in question, and this consummate general was represented as the lowest of mankind." Yet he did not resign; for Godolphin and the Whigs, the Emperor, and all the allies implored him to retain the command of the army, as otherwise all their hopes would be gone.

The clamour raised by Dr. Sacheverell's affair, not less than the acrimonious temper of the Duchess, contributed to ruin the Whigs in the Queen's favour, who was present *incognita* during every debate. During the course of Sacheverell's trial, the government advocate, in order to establish the true Whig doctrine, calumniated by the Doctor, uttered words which seemed revolutionary to the royal ears. It will be readily understood that the theory of absolute obedience, preached by Sacheverell and adopted by certain Tories, was more consonant with the Queen's taste than the maxims of the Whigs, who asserted the dogma of the sovereignty of nations and recognised their right of insurrection against royalty. Anne was a zealous Protestant, and sincerely attached to the Anglican Church, of which she was the head. She blamed the tolerance of the Whigs, and thought with Sacheverell that it was necessary to defend the Church both against Popery and indifferentism.

The Tories fomented these dissensions in an underhand way, turning them dexterously against their enemies. The negotiations then set on foot in Holland occurred still more favourably to advance their projects. Anne had a horror of bloodshed : since her accession she had not permitted a single political execution. She sighed deeply on hearing of the continual levies for the war, and shed tears on receiving the long lists of dead and wounded from the Low Countries. One day, having to sign certain papers relative to the army, her tears were seen to blot the paper, as she exclaimed, " Great God! when will this horrible effusion of blood cease ? " The Tories, who, like herself, wished for peace with all their hearts, adroitly fostered her grief. With her, they deplored the butchery of Malplaquet, the increase of taxation, the misery entailed by the interminable campaigns, and repeated that it was time to put an end to the sufferings of the people. Such hideous carnage seemed at last to cry aloud to Heaven for cessation. Pity and conscience, so long stifled and tyrannised over, claimed at length to be heard. Weighing well also a consideration no less potent over the Queen's heart, they represented that the Whigs were her brother's most implacable enemies—that they had set a price upon his head—that they (the Whigs) would never recognise, as her successor, any other king than the Elector of Hanover; that they (the Tories), on the contrary, felt neither repulsion nor hatred for the Pretender, and that if the good of the country demanded it, they would willingly favour his return. Finally they dwelt upon the odious tyranny of the Duchess of Marlborough,* especially in the scenes enacted at St. Paul's and Windsor, and promised the Queen to deliver her from a woman whom she had ceased to love, and who had begun to terrify her.

Lending a willing ear to such arguments, Anne gave herself up entirely to Mrs. Masham, and the misunderstanding between the Queen and the Duchess had become public, when a fresh outbreak of violence on the part of the latter precipitated her disgrace.

On the occasion of a christening, at which Marlborough was to stand godfather, the Duchess vowed that she would never consent to it if the child were to bear the name of Anne, and she made use of an epithet which neither a queen nor a woman could ever pardon. The word was duly reported at St. James's. Anne heard it with the deepest indignation, and so gross an outrage extinguished any latent spark of tenderness left in her heart. The downfall of the Duchess and the Whigs was resolved upon.

Recognising her error when too late, the Duchess requested an audience of the Queen, in the hope of exculpating herself. Anne, who dreaded her furious violence, replied that she

---

* Bolingbroke says so in express terms : "The true cause (of the change of Ministry) was her discontent," &c.—Secret Memoirs of Lord Bolingbroke, p. 18.

could justify herself by letter, and to avoid the chance of an interview, left London for Kensington Palace.

Explicit, however, as was this step, it did not stop the Duchess. She despatched a letter to the Queen, in which she excused herself, on the score of the impossibility of writing such a justification, and requested an interview—a proposition the most alarming conceivable to the poor Queen, on account of the advantage which her antagonist possessed in powers of tongue. She therefore parried it as long as possible, and would evidently have not assented at all, had not the Duchess extorted the permission by stratagem. Unfortunately, however, for her success, she had told the Queen, in a letter which preceded it, that she only desired to be seen and be heard by her Majesty. There was no necessity, she said, for the Queen to answer. The Queen, in fact, had answered so many of her tormentor's letters in the negative, that the Duchess, not foreseeing what would be the consequence of this general preclusion of response in her Majesty's favour, was resolved to prevent further epistolary acknowledgment by following up her last letter in person. She says, in the foolish " Account " which she gave to the world of her " Conduct," and which had the reverse effect of what she intended (which is the usual case with violent relaters of their own story):—

" I followed this letter to Kensington, and by that means prevented the Queen's writing again to me, as she was preparing to do. The page who went in to acquaint the Queen that I was come to wait upon her stayed longer than usual; long enough, it is to be supposed, to give time to deliberate whether the favour of admission should be granted, and to settle the measure of behaviour if I were admitted. But, at last, he came out and told me I might go in."

The Queen was alone, engaged in writing. "I did not open your letter till just now," she said, "and I was going to write to you."

"Was there anything in it, Madam, that you had a mind to answer?"

"I think," continued poor Anne, who even now endeavoured to stop the coming torrent of words, "I think there is nothing you can have to say but you may write it."

But as this was the very thing over which the Duchess thought she had triumphed, she must have heard the proposal with contemptuous delight; and she proceeded accordingly to pour forth her complaints.

"I cannot write such things," exclaimed the haughty Sarah, alluding to the grossness of the language attributed to her, adding, "Won't your Majesty give me leave to tell it you?"

"Whatever you have to say, you may write it," was the royal answer.

"I believe your Majesty never did so hard a thing to anybody as to refuse to hear them speak—even the meanest person that ever desired it."

"Yes," said the Queen, "I *do* bid people put what they have to say in writing, when I have a mind to it."

"I have nothing to say, Madam," replied the Duchess, "upon the subject that is so uneasy to you. That person (Lady Masham) is not, that I know of, at all concerned in the account that I would give you."

"You can put it into writing," reiterated the Queen, who, desirous at any cost of avoiding a quarrel, which, from the temper of her quondam favourite, seemed inevitable, repeated the same words several times, purposely interrupting the Duchess, who was already beginning to defend herself.

In spite of the Queen's injunctions, Sarah continued to affirm that she was no more capable of making such disrespectful mention of her Majesty than she was of killing her own children, to which Anne coolly remarked, " There are, doubtless, many lies told on ' both sides.' "

During a whole hour, nevertheless, the Duchess strove to establish her innocence by protestations or prayers. But the Queen's heart was irrevocably closed. Desirous of terminating an interview that grew more and more embarrassing, and remembering the scene in St. Paul's, when her Mistress of the Robes had told her to be silent and make no answer, and that lately, in writing to her, the Duchess had said that she required no answer, or that she would not trouble the Queen to give her one, Anne said, " You did not require an answer from me, and I will give you none." This frigid resistance exasperated the Duchess, who, astounded to find herself caught in her own trap, and taken at her word, declared, of course, that the phrase was not intended to imply what it did; but the Queen, she says, repeated it again and again, " without ever receding."

The Duchess protesting that her only design was to clear herself, the Queen repeated over and over again, " You desired no answer, and shall have none."

The angry but still politic Sarah next passed from prayers to reproaches. " I will leave the room," said Anne, with dignity.

" I then begged to know if her Majesty would tell me some other time."

" You desired no answer, and you shall have none."

On hearing these words, which left no further hope, the Duchess burst into tears ; then, as though ashamed of her weakness, she withdrew into the gallery to suppress her passionate fit of weeping. Returning after the lapse of a few minutes, she tried a last and decisive application:

"I have been thinking," said the Duchess, "whilst I sat there, that if your Majesty came to the Castle at Windsor, where I heard you were soon expected, it would not be easy to see me in public now, I am afraid. I will therefore take care to avoid being at the Lodge at the same time, to prevent any unreasonable clamour or stories that might originate in my being so near your Majesty without waiting on you."

"Oh," said the Queen, promptly, "you may come to me at the Castle: it will not make me uneasy."

The Duchess, however, still persevered. "I then appealed to her Majesty again, if she did not herself know, &c. And whether she did not know me to be of a temper incapable of, &c."

"You desired no answer, and you shall have none."

Finding Anne thus inflexible, the Duchess rose up in a towering rage at having vainly humiliated herself, and gave vent to her passion in a storm of recrimination.

"This usage," concludes the Duchess, "was so severe, and these words, so often repeated, were so shocking, &c., that I could not conquer myself, but said the most disrespectful thing I ever spoke to the Queen in my life; and that was, that I was confident her Majesty would suffer for such an instance of inhumanity."

She quitted the presence, in fact, exclaiming, "God will punish you, Madam, for your inhumanity."

"That only concerns myself," drily answered the Queen.

"And thus ended," says the Duchess, "this remarkable conversation, the last I ever had with her Majesty." (April 6th, 1710.)

Such, too, was the end of a thirty years' friendship, and

the last interview between Anne and her once-cherished favourite.* The Duchess remained in the household for a short time afterwards, but never saw her royal mistress save on public occasions ; and from that day the Queen never spoke to her again.

* Private Correspondence of the Duchess of Marlborough, vol. 1, p. 301.

CHAPTER IV.

THE DISGRACE OF THE DUCHESS.

THE disgrace of the Duchess involved the fall of the Whigs. A few days after the scene at Kensington, Anne named two Tories to court appointments, and next dismissed successively all the Whigs from the Ministry—Boyle, Russell, Godolphin, and Walpole. They were replaced by Bolingbroke, Harley, the Earl of Jersey, and the Dukes of Ormonde and Shrewsbury. Anne spared only the Duke and Duchess of Marlborough—not from compassion but through fear. The irate Mistress of the Robes drove about London daily in her splendid equipage, and repeated at every visit she made that she would publish the Queen's letters, and that some day the infamous motives which had brought about her disgrace would be disclosed. Whilst the timid Anne grew terrified at these menaces, the formidable Sarah remained at St. James's, holding her head aloft and dealing out bitter denunciations against her enemies the victorious Tories.

When the Duke of Marlborough came back from Flanders, during the Christmas holidays, he met with the coldest reception possible. The usual motion of thanks to him had been dropped by his friends for fear of its being negatived by the Tory majority. The new ministers, however, waited upon him, promising that he should have all his present military commands, and also the nomination of the generals who were to serve under him. His wife had never ceased making efforts at court, by means of "*one* person" there, who happened to be in good favour with the Queen, and to whom the Duchess wrote long accounts of the past, justifying herself, and exposing the ingratitude, as well as malice, of her enemies. All these accounts that gentleman read to Anne; but he might as well have read them to a stock or stone. According to her Grace, the Queen never offered a word, good or ill, except on one particular point. Lady Masham and Harley had employed Swift and other writers to accuse the Duchess of having grossly cheated her royal mistress of vast sums of money; and on that occasion her Majesty was pleased to say, "Everybody knows cheating is not the Duchess of Marlborough's crime." Where there was so much received in what was deemed an honourable as well as regular way,* there was no great temptation to embezzle and cheat; and the Duchess was in all respects a higher-minded person than her husband, in whom love of money became at last the ruling passion to such a degree as to make him stoop to all kinds of mean and paltry actions. The Duchess, as Mistress of the Robes, boasts that she had dressed the Queen for nine years for thirty-two thousand and some odd hundred pounds; and she asks if ever Queen of England had spent so little in robes! "It evidently appears," says her Grace, "that, by my economy in the nine years I served her Majesty, I saved her near ninety thousand pounds † in clothes alone. "Notwithstanding this," continues the Duchess, "my Lord-Treasurer (Harley) has thought fit to order the *Examiner* (Swift) to represent me in

---

* The Marlborough family were said to be in the receipt of £90,000 a year, including all their places and pensions.

† Anne's sister, Queen Mary, had been charged £12,600 for her dresses one year, and £11,000 another year.

print as a pick-pocket all over England; and for that honest service, and some others, her Majesty has lately made him a Dean."

Just at this moment, the Duchess thought herself obliged to appear at Court "on account of some new clothes which, as Groom of the Stole, she had by her mistress's orders bought for her;" but the Queen charged the only friend her Grace had there to advise her, as from himself, not to come. It was scarcely possible, after this to think of retaining her office; and it appears that the Duchess, of her own accord, sent in her resignation. Lord Dartmouth, however, gives another version of the matter, as follows :—

Emboldened and urged by her Ministers, Anne requested Marlborough to demand the return of the golden Keys which were the symbols of her office. The Duke, who dreaded the consequences of such a step, entreated the Queen to wait till the end of the campaign, promising that he would then retire with his wife. But Anne was driven to extremity by calumnies that reddened her cheek with shame, and she demanded the immediate return of the Keys. Marlborough threw himself on his knees, and entreated her to give him at least ten days' respite. Anne consented to three days, and that interval having expired, renewed her commands. The Duke hastened to the palace, and demanded to be ushered into the presence. But Anne refused to receive him until she received back her gold Keys from the Duchess, and Marlborough at length resigned himself to encounter his wife's anger. On reaching home, he told the Mistress of the Robes that she must give up the golden insignia of office, which she at first refused; but on his persistently intimating the necessity of her resignation, she threw her gold Key on the floor, and told him to do what he liked with it; and that then Marlborough caught it up and carried it to the Queen.*

About one point there is no doubt—Anne accepted the resignation with eagerness and joyfulness, and divided the Duchess's Court places between Lady Masham and the Duchess of Somerset. It astonished most people to see the Duke consent to serve when his wife was dismissed—to see him continue to hold command of the troops under the Ministry which had sprung out of a bed-chamber squabble, and which was sure to thwart him in all his measures. His enemies have generally accounted for this by assuming that the Duke's avarice was at the bottom of it; but his lady assigns very different reasons. " The Duke of Marlborough," she says, " notwithstanding an infinite variety of mortifications, by which it was endeavoured to *make* him resign his commission, that there might be a pretence to raise an outcry against him, as having quitted his Queen's and his country's service merely because he could not govern in the cabinet as well as in the field, continued to serve yet another campaign. All •his friends here, moved by a true concern for the public welfare, pressed him to it, the confederates called him with the utmost importunity, and Prince Eugene entreated him to come with all the earnestness and passion that could be expressed." These were certainly powerful inducements, and they may have mingled (together with that passionate fondness for a fine army which every good general must contract) with Marlborough's love of money.

Mr. Hallam says, with strong and proper feeling, " It seems rather a humiliating proof of the sway which the

---

* The Duchess herself says, "When, after a very successful campaign, the Duke of Marlborough was returned to London, the Queen most readily accepted the resignation that *he* carried *from me* of my offices."—*Account.*

feeblest prince enjoys even in a limited monarchy, that the
fortunes of Europe should have been changed by nothing
more noble than the insolence of one waiting woman and the
cunning of another. It is true that this was effected by
throwing the weight of the crown into the scale of a powerful *faction;* yet the House of Bourbon would probably not
have reigned beyond the Pyrenees but for Sarah and Abigail
at Queen Anne's toilette."*

The Queen, altogether unmindful of her former warm
attachment to her Mistress of the Robes, overjoyed to find
herself free, wrote, with her own hand, the dismissal of the
Duchess, and gave herself up to her enemies.

The Duchess, quite beside herself with chagrin and fury,
only thought of some means or other of revenge. As a first
step she demanded payment of the arrears of her pension—
a boon she had with great high-mindedness refused on
Anne's accession. But that was not all. When she was
about to quit the sphere of her palace triumphs, she gave
directions for the removal of the locks from the doors and
the marble chimney-pieces she had put up at her own cost
in her apartments. "It is all very well," remarked the
Queen to her Secretary of State, "but tell the Duchess if
she demolishes the fittings-up of my palace, she may depend
upon it that I will not build hers at Woodstock." The
Duchess consented to abandon the chimney-pieces, and
withdrew at once to her country seat, near St. Alban's,
where she lived in a style of great magnificence.

In the retirement of private life, Marlborough, worn out
with the harass attendant upon such a lengthened succession
of arduous campaigns, and wearied with political intrigue,
now hoped to enjoy that which he had for years longed for—

* Hallam—Constitutional History

the society of those so dear to him, from whom he had been so many years separated. But it was not to be. Quiet happiness in the evening of his eventful life was not destined to be his lot. His wife, for whom he had ever shown such strong and unalterable affection, was a woman thwarted in all her designs—outraged, injured, mortified, and disgusted with the court and with the world. She was no longer young, nor possessed of the great attractions which had formerly thrown a veil over the deformities of her temper, which, always violent, had now become soured by adversity. She had no indulgence left for others. Dissatisfied with her friends, her children, and everything about her, she was disposed to wrangle and dispute on the slightest provocation.

Next came a great affliction—more deeply felt by both, perhaps, than either the fickleness of the Queen or the virulence of their political enemies—the death under their own roof at St. Alban's of their long-tried, attached, and amiable friend, Lord Godolphin. This sad event determined Marlborough to reside abroad until happier days dawned—their ungrateful country no longer offering any charms for them. His long-cherished desire for rural leisure, retirement, and the quiet enjoyments of private life had ended in disappointment. The master of wealth and great possessions, palatial edifices rising around him, and rank, glory, and well-earned honour his own; yet was he the mark of envy, hatred, and jealousy. Not even could he and the Duchess enjoy and return the ordinary courtesies of society without incurring observation and provoking suspicion. His enemies had triumphed, his Queen was cold and unjust, and now his dearly-loved friend, his adviser and confidant, the sharer of his sorrows, his consoler and encourager, was no more. A blight had fallen upon his existence.

Marlborough sailed from Dover to Ostend in October, 1712, and his wife followed him in a few months afterwards, she having remained behind to arrange his or her own affairs. The Duke was furnished with a passport, it is said, by the instrumentality of his early favourite and secret friend Bolingbroke. His request to see the Queen before his departure from her dominions was refused; and the apathetic Anne never again saw her great general, or the woman for whom she once professed so strong an attachment. When it was told her that both he and the Duchess had left England, she coolly remarked to the Duchess of Hamilton—" the Duke of Marlborough has done wisely to go abroad.''

Thus was the illustrious soldier, then sixty-two years of age, and the Duchess in her fifty-second year, driven from their country by the machinations of a party too strong for them to resist without the especial favour of the Queen.

BOOK III.

CHAPTER I.

MADAME DES URSINS had long continued fearlessly to
face the storm that growled all around her, and by degrees
the horizon showed signs of clearing. As it often happens in
the course of human affairs, the occupation of the capital by
the enemy had an effect contrary to that which it was very
natural to expect. The allies, who had entered Madrid as
conquerors, found within that city none of the elements
necessary for the definitive establishment of the Archduke
who was proclaimed amidst a chilling silence. If the
grandees almost to a man evinced their sympathy for the
House of Austria, if the staff of the administration and the
personal machinery of all the public departments, remained
at their posts at the price of an oath which did not seem to
cost more in those days than at present, the populace of
Madrid showed an aversion to the foreigners which soon
manifested itself in numerous assassinations. How could it
be otherwise than that the ancient soil of Castile should
heave on finding itself trampled on by the partisans of a
loyalty hailed with acclamation at Saragossa and Barcelona ;
on witnessing those outbursts of insolent triumph on the
part of the Portuguese, who, in the eyes of every Spaniard,
were still rebels ; and the contemptuous phlegm of Lord
Galloway's army, commanded, as it was, by a heretic *condot-
tiere ?* Outside the official spheres, the isolation was there-

fore complete, and during that three months' crisis the
errant royalty of Philip V., represented by his courageous
consort, struck indestructible roots in the hearts of his subjects. The northern shores and the great province of Andalusia, joining to those divers motives the hatred with which
England inspired the maritime population, resolutely declared for the House of Bourbon, to such an extent that,
beyond the territories of the ancient realm of Arragon, the
moral conquest of the kingdom was very nearly consum-
mated, despite the foreign occupation, and through the effect
of that very same occupation. The position of the foreigners
at Madrid had never been anything else than provisory;
and it was with transports of joy that the Anglo-Portuguese
troops were seen to hastily evacuate the capital on the
approach of another French army, which advanced through
Navarre under the command of the Duke of Berwick.*
Philip V. was soon able to re-enter Madrid as a liberator,
and a galleon from Mexico brought him most opportunely a
million of crowns. On the 25th of April, 1707, Berwick
completely defeated the allies near Almanza, and the Duke
of Orleans covered himself with glory by the capture of
Lerida, which had previously resisted the great Condé.

The influence of Madame des Ursins became greatly
enhanced after these unhoped-for successes, and both
Philip V. and the cabinet of Versailles equally testified their
gratitude to her. She had manifested an inflexible devotedness in the midst of reverses, and adversity had taken its
full measure of her. Never, throughout the course of her
chequered career, had Madame des Ursins shown more
activity than during the six months which intervened

---

* Natural son of James II. of England, by Arabella Churchill, sister of
the Duke of Marlborough.

between the return of the Court to Madrid and the battle of
Almanza. Her position was as delicate as it was perilous.
It was necessary to stigmatise flagrant defections, but
without driving anyone altogether to desperation. She profited by the confidence she had won to bring about happily
an important reform. Spain, composed of divers kingdoms
successively annexed, had not yet attained unity. More
than ever, after the experiences of 1706, was seen the necessity of a centralisation which should re-unite in the hands
of the new dynasty the entire strength of the government,
which should extinguish injurious rivalries between province and province, which should facilitate administrative
relations, and allow of an equal action in the different parts
of the monarchy. Each kingdom hitherto had had its laws,
its customs, its constitution (*fueros*). Already in 1705 certain restrictions had been imposed by Castile upon Arragon:
no more dared be attempted. The battle of Almanza and
the successes of 1707 inspired still further energy. In the
council, the party of Madame des Ursins, leaning on the
assent of Berwick, overcame the opposition of Montellano
and the friends of the old system; and the pragmatic sanction, or constitution of Castile, became the sole law of Spain.

The victory of Almanza was, in fact, the last service rendered to Philip V. by his native country. From that day
forward, France, menaced upon its frontiers, constrained to
appropriate all its resources to its own safety, became an
obstacle and a permanent peril to Spain. The former compromised the Spanish monarchy by its military operations,
and far more gravely still by its diplomatic negotiations. In
this new phase, signalised by the almost constant antagonism
of the two courts, the position of Madame des Ursins was
one of the most critical nature; but we are about to see her,

with her habitual rectitude of judgment, take unhesitatingly
the part alike dictated by honour as by sound policy.

It was at this juncture that the gravity of events determined Louis XIV. upon being represented in Spain by his
nephew, the Duke of Orleans. That prince, in two campaigns, had subdued the kingdom of Valentia and the
greatest part of Arragon, after taking fortresses in Catalonia
hitherto deemed impregnable. Inspired by the ambition of
the chief of his race, he had made his military services sub-
servient to the extension of monarchical authority, and had
solemnly abolished, in the name of Philip V. in Arragon,
the anarchical privileges which weakened the royal power
without efficaciously strengthening the liberties of Spain.
Distrusted by those he came ostensibly to defend, and, from
the first, an object of suspicion to Madame des Ursins, still
the correspondence of the Princess with Madame de Maintenon and the Maréchale de Noailles from April, 1707, to
November, 1708, the date of the duke's departure, shows
that the relations of the latter with the *camerara-mayor* were
for a long time maintained on the best footing, the dissolute
habits of the Duke of Orleans proving less disgusting to
Madame des Ursins than the accuracy of his insight into
public affairs appears to have charmed her. The rupture of
this good understanding, which, however, took place silently,
was one among other results greatly to be regretted of the
dark intrigue into which certain obscure agents momentarily
led astray the ambition of Anne of Austria's grandson—a
machination the more disastrous to the prince, whose
honour it impugned, than to the King of Spain, who received
no injury from it during the Duke of Orleans' sojourn
within his territories; the movements of Flotte and Renault,

his emissaries, having only assumed some small degree of importance after his departure.

It is a knotty point of history altogether; but the fact is clear that the Duke was the centre of the faction opposed to the Princess, and that around him were banded those with whom she had either clashed or whom she had overcome. The moment was badly chosen for intriguing; to save the state should have been the sole aim of the Duke of Orleans. The allies, for an instant discouraged after Almanza, had not lost all hope. Their successes in Italy and in Germany soon consoled them for that reverse, and their armies became once more menacing. It was then that the Duke of Orleans, it is said, conceived the hope, if not of governing all Spain, at least of obtaining the kingdoms of Murcia, Valentia, and Navarre. He himself avowed later to the Duke de Saint-Simon that, seeing Philip V. tottering, "he had allowed himself to indulge the hope of being put in his place;" hence his double-faced conduct and strange manœuvres. He might not have been willing, doubtless, to pull down the King of Spain with his own hand, but he did not, of course, steadfastly desire a triumph which marred his own fortunes. That which, however, may be affirmed with certainty is, that he maintained with different foreign generals, among others with the Earl of Stanhope, very suspicious negotiations; that he designedly did all he could to impede the progress of the Spanish Government, and seemed, in all he did, solely concerned in not overstepping that loosely-defined line at which treason begins. However that might be, Madame des Ursins, strenuously opposed to the policy which the Duke of Orleans desired to see prevail, and moreover scarcely able to endure the hostile attitude of that Prince, demanded his recall and obtained it.

After his departure she pursued him in the persons of his two agents, Renault and Flotte, whom she had arrested. As for his friend, Marshal de Bezons, whose hasty retreat upon the banks of the Segra excited the indignation of the Spanish court, he lost his command. She even denounced the Duke of Orleans to his royal uncle, and the erring nephew had very great difficulty in escaping a scandalous trial. He was forced, therefore, to renounce his ambitious hopes with regard to Spain, if ever he had seriously nourished them. Such an exposure, rendered his return to the Peninsula impossible. His faction was speedily dispersed. One of the noblemen with whom he had had very intimate relations, the Duke of Medina-Cœli, minister for foreign affairs and head of the grandee party, was suddenly arrested and taken to the Castle of Segovia. Whether, as Saint Simon intimates, it was that " weary of the yoke of Madame des Ursins, he desired *pointer de son chef,"* whether that, favourable to the Duke of Orleans, perhaps even to the allies, he had voluntarily caused the failure of the expedition which the Spanish government meditated against Sardinia, or whether he had dreamed of an anti-French reaction, he ended his days in a state prison.

Whilst the government of Philip V., was working its way very laboriously through that maze of conspiracies and intrigues, the allies regained the ground which Almanza had lost them. " Despite all the efforts of Madame des Ursins," wrote the Chevalier du Bourk, her agent, at Versailles, " matters are going badly at Madrid." France, discouraged and weighed down, moreover by its own reverses, seemed no longer able to defend Philip V.; Louis XIV., whatever might have been his secret intentions, was not willing to appear to support his grandson; the Austrians thoroughly defeated Philip at Saragossa. The severe winter of 1709 had brought the general distress to a climax ; and the Archduke Charles made his entrance into Madrid. The court of Versailles became terror-stricken. Madame de Maintenon, outwearied with this everlasting strife, changed the tone of her letters to a cold and sometimes ironic vein. She went so far as to say to the Princess, " It is not agreeable to us here that women should busy themselves with state affairs." * Louis XIV., himself, advised his grandson to abandon Spain in order to keep Italy.

Madame des Ursins had thus to choose between the French policy, imposed upon Louis XIV. by cruel necessity, and the Spanish policy, for which Philip V. was resolved to die. On one hand, the young mother, who had just confided to her care an infant son she had conceived in anguish, appealed most touchingly to her attachment and courage ; on the other, Madame de Maintenon, whose sole solicitude was to insure repose to Louis XIV., by plucking out one after another all the thorns from his crown, reminded her that she was born a Frenchwoman, and that she owed too much to the Great King to arrogate to herself the right of contradicting him. A subject of Louis XIV., did she dare combat at Madrid the plans decided upon at Versailles ? The governess of the heir to the crown of Spain, could she concur by her advice in despoiling the infant whose first caresses she was receiving ? Madame des Ursins could only escape by a prompt departure from the difficulties of such an alternative. Incon-

* Recueil de M. Geffroy, p. 395.

testable facts prove that she so understood her position, and that she was fully determined to quit Spain towards the close of 1709 ; but the despair of the Queen, the state of whose health at that time gave but too serious grounds for alarm, alone hindered her from following out a project which promised more flattering results than any other in the deep depression into which the resolves of France had plunged her.

Madame des Ursins had no sooner taken the resolution of remaining upon the theatre of events, and of sustaining the King of Spain in the noble career to which his conscience and the national will alike bound him, than she threw herself headlong into the *mêlée*, caring nothing more for the Versailles policy, and burning her ships with a boldness of which her gentleness of character seemed to have rendered her incapable. Her epistolary style undergoes also a marked change, and rises with the loftiness of her part and character. In reproaching Madame de Maintenon for preferring the King's ease to that of his honour, she launches shafts against her which, though tipped with elegance, are none the less sharp-pointed, sometimes in the shape of studied reproaches, but more frequently still with the spontaneous overflowings of a towering wrath. The writer then reveals herself from beneath the guise of the woman of the world, and it is clearly seen that in that encompassed life the heart has for a moment triumphed over the intelligence.

Madame des Ursins alone, however, remained unshaken. She might well have, it is true, some moments of misgiving ; such as when she wrote to Madame de Noailles, "I have foreseen, for a long time, the precipice over which they would hurl us, and to the brink of which we ourselves are hurrying, and I know not, by Heaven, who can save us from it." With admirable eloquence she encouraged Madame de Maintenon, who appeared to despair of the divine protection; and she inspired Philip V. with an energy truly worthy of the throne, shown in that noble letter in which the King of Spain declared to his grandfather " that, in spite of the misfortune which confronted him, he would never abandon his subjects." Madame des Ursins in all probability dictated the phraseology, and all the glory of it resulted from her firmness.

She thoroughly comprehended that it became sovereigns worthy of their position to speak loftily, were it from the depth of an abyss, and that that supreme courage is itself the first indication of a return of good fortune. She soon found that it was so; for from the moment that the King's cause seemed to be lost, the animosities of the grandees gave way before their patriotism. Whether they were at length inspired by so much energy, whether the expulsion of the French from every post throughout the state, decreed by Philip V. under the advice of Madame des Ursins, had well disposed their minds, " almost all, by a sudden awakening of chivalrous fidelity," submitted to the House of Bourbon. The Archduke awaited in vain their homage and their oaths. At the moment of his entrance into the capital, curiosity itself failed to attract any one to cross his path ; a solitude and sullen gloom pervaded all the public places. He did not even proceed so far as the royal palace, but went out by the Alcala gate, muttering, " It is a deserted city."

Without hesitation, therefore, Madame des Ursins placed herself at the head of the national movement, seeking to pluck the safety of Spain from the very abandonment in which France had left that monarchy. Without breaking off confidential relations with her usual correspondents at Versailles, she enveloped them in the thickest possible veil, her sole idea being to stimulate Castilian patriotism, appearing to adopt everything Spanish from its popular costumes, even to its hatreds and its prejudices. By the aid of a *sombrero* and a *gollil* * Don Luis d'Aubigny had become a perfect *caballero;* the like transformation being effected throughout the entire staff of the palace household, and shortly afterwards a very decided step characterised the novel attitude assumed by Philip and his court. Madame des Ursins, who reckoned her chief enemies amongst the monarch's French household, decided that prince upon the dismissal in mass of all his non-Spanish domestics—an unexpected resolve which produced an immense sensation on both sides of the Pyrenees; because, whilst subserving a personal vengeance skilfully dissimulated, it gave sanction to a policy the harshness of which was pushed even to ingratitude.

To throw Philip V. into the arms of the Spaniards, was to flatter alike the democracy and the grandees. To the populace Madame des Ursins presented, amidst the most fervent benediction, the Prince of Asturias; to the grandees, of whom she had long been the declared enemy, she caused to be given a striking proof of the royal confidence. The Duke de Bedmar, appointed to the ministry of war, was charged with the organization of the new levies, and the direction of the troops in all parts of the kingdom. To transform the grandson of Louis XIV. into a peninsula king was to furnish the best argument to the partisans of peace,

---

* A sort of collar.

already numerous in the British parliament. On the other hand, that same policy could not very seriously disquiet the cabinet of Versailles. The King knew that he might count upon every sacrifice from the respectful attachment of his grandson, save that of the throne; and although he had adhered officially to the principle of the dispossessing of Philip V., he could not regret, either as sovereign or as grandsire, the obstacles which the more resolute attitude of Spain then opposed to the enemies of the two crowns. Louis XIV. therefore continued, notwithstanding his diplomatic engagements, to secretly assist in the Peninsula what might be called the party of *fara da se.* Madame des Ursins had recovered her influence at Versailles from the moment at which it was found necessary to depend, in order to prolong the struggle, rather upon the military resources of Spain than upon those of France at bay. To impart more gravity to the national movement, to which she gave the impulse in order to remain the moderatrix, she had required the recall of Amelot, who had long assumed at Madrid the attitude of a prime minister rather than that of an ambassador; and Louis XIV., deferring to that wish, had, replaced that experienced agent by a simple *chargé d'affaires.* Orry was in like manner sacrificed, despite his invaluable services; but, at the same time that she gave satisfaction by the withdrawal of her friends in deference to the popular susceptibilities, the Princess earnestly implored that the Duke de Vendôme might be sent to take command of the Spanish forces; and Louis XIV., on his part, at the moment that he was compelled to withdraw from Spain the last French soldier, despatched thither the general who was destined to save his grandson's crown.

Arriving in Spain sometime during the summer of 1710,

Vendôme displayed an activity which did not seem to comport with his habits, in order to reunite and arm the volunteers, who, from the summit of the Sierras, descended in swarms upon the plains of the two Castiles at the summons of a monarch become the personification of a patriot. He speedily transformed into a powerful and well-trained army the undisciplined *guerillas* whose bravery had hitherto been useless; in a few months, the Anglo-Austrian army, at the head of which the prince who called himself Charles III. had been able to show himself for a few hours in the deserted capital, was confronted by disciplined troops prepared to retake territories which until then had not been seriously disputed. Under the irresistible impulse of a noble patriotism which had at last recovered itself, the English force of Lord Stanhope capitulated at Brihuega after a terrible carnage, and Stahrenberg, crushed in his turn at Villaviciosa, carried away by his flight the last hopes of the House of Austria.

By the victory of Villaviciosa the House of Bourbon was definitively seated on the throne of Charles the Fifth. Philip V. slept that night (10th December, 1710) upon a couch of standards taken from the enemy: the Austrian cause was lost; and Madame des Ursins, who, in spite of Europe coalesced, in spite of Louis XIV. hesitating and disquieted, in spite of so many disasters, had never trembled, received the title of HIGHNESS, and saw her steadfast policy at length crowned by accomplished facts.

Spain had thus solved by her own efforts solely the great question which had kept Europe so long in arms. At the commencement of 1711, Philip V. had acquired for his throne a security that Louis XIV. had not yet obtained for the integrity of his own frontiers, and without mistaking the

influence of the victory of Denain, so wonderfully oppor-
tune, it is just, we think, to allow a far larger share than is
customary to the thoroughly Spanish victory of Villaviciosa in the unhoped-for conditions obtained by France at
the peace of Utrecht.

CHAPTER II.

IF the new ministry of Queen Anne succeeded in inducing the English nation to support the treaty of Utrecht, that was nothing less than to prove undeniably, without fear of contradiction, that the establishment of the French dynasty in the Peninsula had there acquired the authority of a fact irrevocably accomplished. The resuscitation of the Spanish nation had, therefore, a decisive effect upon European affairs; and whilst, by leaving France almost intact, the treaties of Utrecht had parcelled out the monarchy of the catholic kings, the authors of the great popular movement crowned by the victory of Villaviciosa might consider without prejudice their country as sacrificed, notwithstanding the weight which it had flung into the scales.

In this work Madame des Ursins had had certainly a very considerable share, and it was with a very legitimate pride that through it she was enabled to prevail at Versailles as at Madrid. A perseverance unexampled both in idea and conduct, a rare suppleness in the means, had made her the principal instrument of an enterprise in which a virile ambition, united to a deep devotedness, sustained her. Undismayed by reverses, never intoxicated by success, she tempered by her equanimity the at times imprudent ardour of the young Queen, and reanimated by her firmness the frequent retrocessions of her morose consort. She rejoiced, therefore, with a scarcely veiled pride in that security for the future which Spain had conquered before France, and in her correspondence with Madame de Maintenon her letters began to assume a somewhat protective tone. It was at this culminating point of her greatness that fate was preparing to inflict upon her the humiliating catastrophe which again obscured the remembrance of her services and even the honour of her name.

It is unnecessary to recapitulate the means by which peace was re-established, how the fall of the Whig ministry and the elevation of the Archduke to the imperial throne after the death of Joseph I. brought England and the other allied powers into the treaties which confirmed Philip V. in the peaceable possession of the Spanish monarchy. We will not dwell upon these details, nor upon divers acts of interior policy which followed upon the victory of Villaviciosa. Let us confine our attention solely to those in which the Princess des Ursins took an active part. The first was the pursuance of the administrative centralisation of which we have spoken; the abolition of the council exclusively called the Council of Castile, for which she caused to be substituted a council of state, the members of which should be chosen from every part of Spain, and which became the centre of the government. The second was a reform in the finance department; Orry being in these measures the Princess's instrument, and he justified the long-continued esteem with which she had honoured his talents. It was thus that after having successively saved the monarchy from a policy exclusively French, and from the factious pretensions of the grandees, after having contributed to the defeat of Austria, Madame des Ursins sought to consolidate on firm bases the power of Philip V. and prepare a happier future for Spain.

She was not destined, however, to long enjoy the fruits of her triumph. It was a symptomatic sign of this new phase of her life, the universally unfavourable interpretation given to an affair which should rather be looked upon in the light of a check than of a fault. It is well known that Philip, desirous of recognising the devotedness of his son's governess, and of assuring to that noble lady an independent position which should not be below her birth, had stipulated, at the time of the preliminaries of peace, for the reservation of a territory in the Spanish low countries ceded to Austria, which he destined to form into a sovereignty for Marie Anne de la Trémouille. This negotiation, which bore successively upon the county of Limbourg and the small seigniory of La Roche-en-Ardennes, had been received at first at Versailles with the most entire approbation, for the reproach of *"playing the queen"* only occurred as an after-thought. The gratitude of their Catholic Majesties was found to be quite natural, and was warmly praised, especially by Madame de Maintenon. It is not at all to be wondered at, consequently, if Madame des Ursins should blandly contemplate such a prospect, especially in anticipation of the approaching demise of her well-beloved protectress, who could not fail to be soon replaced in the confidence and couch of her consort. The Court of France did not change its opinion until that affair of La Roche, very annoyingly taken by the Dutch, had become the occasion of a delay in the signing of the general peace. Then Madame des Ursins was overwhelmed by reproaches on all sides, and those which came from Saint Cyr were of a peculiarly acrimonious character, which we must not join the Duke de Saint Simon in attributing to a jealousy of which there exists no trace, but which is explained by Madame de Maintenon's desire to secure repose to Louis XIV. at any cost. These reproaches, moreover, were without foundation, for the accusers of the Princess should have considered that, if France had the right to await with lively impatience the signature of a treaty which secured to her almost all her conquests, it was quite otherwise with Spain, called upon by that same treaty to pay alone the costs of the pacification. The measures of 1713, the conclusion of which was in fact retarded for a few months by the interest and intervention of Madame des Ursins, had been received with a very natural indignation in the monarchy of Charles V., from which they tore away the Milanese, the Two Sicilies, Sardinia, the Low Countries, Port Mahon, and Gibraltar. So France can now easily decide whether it had been in 1815 an unpardonable crime in her eyes to cause by a dilatory question the adjournment of the signing of the treaties of Vienna.

That check was the first in a series of misfortunes which death alone was henceforward destined to bring to a close. Early in 1714 died very suddenly, at the age of twenty-six, Marie Louise of Savoy, her delicate frame worn out by an ardent temperament, which had sustained it whilst the storm raged, and which declined when the breath of the hurricane had ceased to kindle it further. The remains of the young Queen had scarcely descended into the vaults of the Escurial ere the nation demanded to know who was to be the new queen-consort; and the same question was addressed to Madame des Ursins by the Court of Versailles, so well were known there both the requirements and the austerity of the King of Spain. What passed during the eight months of that widowhood so painfully borne ? What mysteries did the Medina Cœli palace witness, in which Madame des Ursins shut up closely Philip V. from the gaze of every prying eye ? Such questions can never now be answered with certainty, for the reports put into circulation in France by Saint Simon and Duclos, in Italy by Poggiali, and in England by Fitz-Maurice, had their common source in the conversations of Alberoni, one of the least scrupulous actors in the drama of the *Quadruple Alliance.* Did the elderly *camerara mayor,* already threescore and ten, dare to spread alluring snares wherein to entrap an amorous prince of thirty ? And did such tentative, more strange than audacious, succeed to the extent of binding Philip's conscience in some way ? History will never answer the question. Instead, therefore, of hazarding conjectures, it will be well to confine our attention to the well-authenticated political acts of the Princess at this, to her, serious conjuncture.

In losing her royal mistress, the powerful favourite lost along with her the greatest portion of her strength. It was the remote signal which heralded her fall. At the same time it did not appear that her energy had become diminished, or her intelligence clouded, but that her ordinary prudence had abandoned her. Perhaps, having attained such an elevation, she dreaded no further reverse, and believed herself secure enough, in the universal esteem and admiration in which she was held, to venture upon anything. However that might be, as though her brain had grown dizzy, she destroyed with her own hands, not her skilfully raised political edifice, but the structure of her individual fortunes.

Her first imprudence was to attack the Spanish Inquisition. Spain was not then ripe for that reform accomplished only a century later. Much less, as it appears to us, should Madame des Ursins, under the influence of a preconceived religious opinion, with the object of strengthening the royal authority, have attempted its sudden suppression. Far be it from us, certainly, to think of defending the Spanish Inquisition. But it cannot be denied that that institution had vigorously defended Philip V., and in the eyes of the people was part and parcel, as it were, of Spain itself. It seemed as though French ideas alone demanded such a reform, and hence popular suspicion was excited. The Princess failed in her attempt; but she had voluntarily created for herself a host of enemies, who from that moment laboured to effect her ruin.

We have already said that, cherishing the hope of obtaining for herself an independent sovereignty, the difficulties arising from her pretensions had delayed the conclusion of the treaty of peace. Louis XIV. was indignant at finding his negotiations fettered and himself involved in an unavoidable opposition to the wishes of his grandson. As for Madame de Maintenon, whether the interests of France, compromised by these delays, had alone provoked her resistance, or whether, as Saint Simon declares, that that independent sovereignty which she herself felt was so little beyond her reach offended her pride by making her feel the distance between their several ranks and births, she opposed the desire of her old friend, and peace was concluded by the authority of Louis XIV. But the King had a grudge against the Princess for having driven him to such extremity, Besides, just then his own dynasty had been fatally stricken. The Duke of Burgundy and his eldest son, the Duke of Brittany, had died. The heir to the throne was an infant only three years old. The

Court foresaw the Regency of the Duke of Orleans, a personal enemy of Madame des Ursins, and it was dangerous, by leaving her at the head of affairs in Spain, to prepare, probably, for the future a disastrous rivalry.

The storm thus darkened thickly over the head of this imperious woman, who, supported against her enemies so long as she had been useful, was subject to the common law of favourites, and began to totter when she appeared no longer so. One resource remained to her—to remarry Philip V. She was anxious to find a consort who could replace in her interests Marie Louise, and restore her waning influence. Her incertitude was great: she felt truly that in spite of past services her future fate depended upon her choice. At length she cast her eyes upon Elizabeth Farnese, daughter of the last Duke of Parma, and niece of the then existent Duke, and thought that gratitude for such an extraordinary turn of fortune would for ever secure the attachment of a princess who, without her influence, could never have had pretensions to such an union. But she was anxious to ascertain whether Elizabeth Farnese was one of those who would submit to be ruled, and she opened her mind upon the subject to a man then obscure but afterwards celebrated—Alberoni, who had been sent as consular agent from Parma to Madrid. He had frequent conversations with the great favourite, and readily succeeded in insinuating himself into her good graces. He described the Princess of Parma as simple minded, religious, ignorant of the world from which she had always lived secluded—in short, perfectly fitting to forward the design of the Princess. In making such statements he reckoned at the same time upon pleasing his own Court, and bringing about the fall of Madame des Ursins; for he knew well that Elizabeth, whose character

was very different from that which he had represented,
would not submit to be governed by any one. Dazzled,
therefore, with the smiling vista which chance had so unexpectedly opened to him, and understanding all the importance which he might derive from the negotiation of such
marriage, and finding, moreover, Madame des Ursins well
disposed beforehand towards him, and, by a singular blind-
ness, inclined to put implicit confidence in one whose interest
it was to conceal the truth, he secretly set off for Parma on
his delicate mission. By this first move the Princess's game
was lost.

CHAPTER III.

IT was the peculiar misfortune of Madame des Ursins to scarcely meet with a single sincere friend in Spain : she was submitted to there, rather than accepted. She had been sought after through interest or fear rather than through sympathy ; but especially since the Queen's decease, since no one save herself was seen by the King's side, and that the strokes of her power were dealt without any apparent intermediator, she was no longer tolerated, save with infinite difficulty. Neither can it be concealed that, at this period, she had not acted in a way to diminish the number of her enemies, or to conciliate them. She was of opinion that the Duke of Berwick had not sufficiently defended her at Versailles against their machinations : she broke with him in 1714, before he returned from Catalonia. She did her utmost to have Tessé chosen to replace him, whom she pronounced quite capable of taking Barcelona ; and, on learning that Berwick was nevertheless appointed, she hastened to banish Ronquillo, for something he had uttered against the Government, but in reality because he was the intimate friend of that general.* Two nobles were also imprisoned at this time—Don Manuel de Sylva, commandant of the galleys of Sicily, already temporarily exiled in 1709 for having (so said the sentence) "spoken ill of her," and Don

* Memoirs of Saint Philippe, tom. iii., p. 88.

Valerio d'Aspetia, Lieutenant-General. Both were declared enemies of Madame des Ursins, and the first had moreover the fault of being closely connected with the Duke d'Uzeda. Valerio d'Aspetia died in prison, at the age of seventy, and after fifty years of service, a lamentable loss, and which involved that of his still young and lovely wife, whose days were cut short through grief and poverty. Besides all this, must be noticed a suspicious jealousy of domination over Philip V., which was fearfully developed when that prince found himself a widower, and which betrayed itself in very disagreeable actions.

Saint Simon tells us that, after the death of Marie Louise of Savoy, Madame des Ursins usually supped with the King, and had him transferred from the palace of the Buen-Retiro, in which the Queen had died, to that of Medina Cœli. There she caused a corridor to be constructed, leading from the King's cabinet to the apartments of the young princes, wherein she was lodged ; and it was not, as may be imagined, to facilitate communications between a bereaved father and his children, who had become doubly dear to him, but, according to our authority, in order that it might never be known whether the King was alone or with her. She was in such haste to see this secret passage completed, that, to the great scandal of Catholic Spain, she had the work carried on during Sundays and saints' days as well as upon ordinary days. This was pushed to such an extent, that a great number of pious persons no less than thrice asked Father Robinet, the most exemplary of the confessors Philip V. ever had, if he were not aware of such unlawful labour, and when it was that he intended it should cease. To which the subtle Jesuit, who was unwilling to be accused of laxity in morals, replied that the King had not spoken to him upon the subject, alluding to his relations with Philip as his Confessor, in which relation alone he wished it to be understood that he was to be considered—always adding, for their satisfaction, that if he had been consulted in the matter, he would not have failed to say that, to complete that criminal corridor, work should never have been so permitted, but that to effect its destruction, the labourers might have worked at it even on Easter Day.*

This statement of Saint Simon, quite insupportable as it is, would nevertheless leave subsisting, in the melancholy position of the children and their father, a means of justification to Madame des Ursins, did not Duclos deprive her of it; and who, less charitable than the authority whom he generally cites when treating of this celebrated woman, tells us purely and simply that she desired to facilitate the communication of her own apartments with those of the King, which leaves ample room for slander and suspicion. He goes still further. Improving upon Saint Simon, and showing himself better acquainted with the particulars than the Duke, he mentions a very aggravating fact, which was, that, in order to construct that very suspicious means of communication, it was necessary to demolish a monastery of Capuchins, and that in consequence " dead bodies were disinterred, the Holy Sacrament dislodged from the church, the monks quitting it in procession, amidst exclamations of " Oh, sacrilege! Oh, profanation!" from all Madrid.†

Happily, Duclos is merely in this the servile copyist of a Spanish author, whose contradictions and bad feeling it would be very easy to expose. He has reproduced word for word the version to be found in the *Mémoires sur l'Espagne*, printed as

---

* Mémoires de Saint Simon, tom. xx., p. 171, 172.

† Memoirs of Duclos (Petitot's Collection), tom. i., p. 230.

a sequel to the letters of Fitz-Maurice. What! to make a
simple corridor from one apartment to another, nothing less
was required than to demolish an entire monastery, large as
they were, in Spain especially, with its church and everything devoted to its religious purposes, and the dwellings of
the monks? And Saint Simon knew nothing of all this?
For, had he known it, most assuredly he would not have
failed to fling it in the face of Madame des Ursins. That
the Marquis de Saint Philippe, who was upon the spot, a
man so religious, and who could not endure Madame des
Ursins, should say not one word, without fear of derogating
from his customary gravity, of that impious scandal, of such
a Vandalism as had revolted all Madrid! We think that if
M. Duclos had better informed himself upon the point and
of the source whence he derived it, he, too, would have complained of exaggeration, and would not have given it out as
a fact.

The part played by Madame des Ursins would assuredly
have been grander if she had herself renounced the regal
boon proffered by Philip V., as soon as it promised to be an
obstacle to the pacification of Europe; if she had preferred
the general good to her own particular advantage, and sustained her lofty character to the end, she would have preserved by so doing the prestige of grandeur and disinterestedness which had constantly surrounded her. A love of power
would have been pardoned in her, always foreign to considerations of personal advantage; and, as ambition, like
other human passions, may become a source of crime, though
it is not itself a crime, in her case it would have been praised,
because she would have unceasingly shunned the vanity
which lessens it, the self-interest which debases it, and that
continual recurrence to egotism which travesties it in

intrigue. But she failed to crown her career by that true
glory. Seeing the King and Queen of Spain very much
offended at the retrograde step of Louis XIV., she further
irritated them by her peevish attitude and marked discontent. The Marquis de Brancas, sent by Louis into Spain,
proceeded to represent the articles of the Treaty of Utrecht
to Philip V. in such wise as the Emperor and his allies
wished them to stand; Philip replied that he would not sign
them, unless there was a special clause added in favour of
Madame des Ursins. That ambassador returned furious,
crying out against the Spanish Government, and especially
against Madame des Ursins, who directed everything, he
said, and who had played at cross-purposes in order to cause
his mission to miscarry. He succeeded in drawing down upon
the Court of Madrid the heavy rebuke of Louis XIV. This,
however, proved altogether useless; for Philip persisted in
his resolution, and contented himself with sending the
Cardinal del Guidice to his grandfather, whilst Madame des
Ursins employed with the same monarch the customary influence of Madame de Maintenon. The latter, in fact, so
the Marquis de Saint Philippe tells us, made excuses for
Madame des Ursins to Louis XIV., and the other advocate
of the Court of Madrid obtained the order for the march of
the troops destined for the siege of Barcelona, whose success,
looked upon as certain, ought likewise to render the Austrians more disposed to treat upon the question of her
principality.

But that was not the only expedient employed by Madame
des Ursins. The English ambassador, Lord Lexington, besides Gibraltar and Port Mahon, relied upon obtaining for
the English a free trade in the brandies of Tarragon; this
the Princess conceded to him. He desired also that they

might be allowed to construct, upon the River de la Plata, a fort for their protection, and as a depôt for negroes, in order that in future they might alone supply the Spanish colonies with slaves : this monopoly was also accorded. In return, Lord Lexington signed a convention with her, in which Queen Anne "*engaged to secure her a sovereignty.*" *
At such price the adhesion of England seemed secured. She reckoned also on obtaining that of Holland by analogous commercial advantages, and, in fact, she obtained them. But how to win back Louis XIV. was the question! For that she had a secret project, which, as she thought, ought to rehabilitate her in that monarch's eyes, in representing her as guided by a love of France more than by vanity. Louis XIV. was not to derive any territorial advantage from the Treaty of Utrecht. But Madame des Ursins was desirous so soon as the cession was made of the said principality of giving it up immediately to that King, in exchange for an equivalent life-interest in Touraine, within French territory. With that view she had a clause inserted in the letters-patent of Philip V., empowering her to alienate during her lifetime that principality in whatever way she chose. Such was her design; and that it had evidently been divined by the sagacious Madame de Maintenon would appear from the following passage in a letter of about that date addressed to the Princess : " Side by side with all your merits, you have *a concealed project,* which, if I guess aright, has got the uppermost of all those qualities." †

But that was just what the allies most feared. The faculty given to Madame des Ursins in Philip's deed of gift

* So runs the textual engagement of Queen Anne, taken from the Royal Archives of the Hague, and communicated to M. Geffroy.

† Lettres de Madame de Maintenon et de Madame des Ursins, tom. ii., pp. 7, 8.

had made them suspect that intention of a surrender or an exchange, and they were on the watch for everything which might arise to support their suppositions. In such conjuncture, Madame des Ursins was wanting, as it appears to us, in prudence and address. Instead of postponing, until the cession had become an accomplished fact, the question of the exchange, she pursued the two objects simultaneously. To negotiate the second with Torcy, she sent D'Aubigny secretly to France, and the latter, after some overtures, gave her hopes of entire success. Transported with delight, she gave herself up to all the illusions of what the future had in store for her of happiness. She was not, therefore, destined to descend either in rank or honours after quitting the Court of Madrid. Here she had ruled beneath the shadow of a phantom King; there she would command directly and in person. In Spain, she had only been a subordinate; in France she would have no superior, and would be more mistress of herself. All these satisfactions were increased a hundredfold by the proud feeling of returning to her native country as a sovereign princess, in a state so strictly levelled by royalty, wherein no one would have a condition equal to her own, and in which she would display with jesting haughtiness the pomp inseparable from her title before her abashed enemies. She had so much faith in the hopes with which d'Aubigny inspired her, and by which that cunning favourite thought perhaps already to profit, that she instructed him to go into Touraine and to purchase land in the neighbourhood of Amboise whereon to erect a chateau, which should be called the manor of Chanteloup.* It was something like selling the skin of the bear before slaying her bruin; but with the formal and written engagement of

* Mémoires de Saint Simon, tom. xviii., p. 104.

England, with the support of Holland, which she also had, with Louis XIV., whom she sought to win back through the influence of Madame de Maintenon, and by the calculated nobleness of her intentions, she would overcome the resistance of Austria, and her victory was certain.

Unfortunately, that which she ought to have anticipated actually came to pass. England first discovered the occult negotiations of d'Aubigny at Versailles, and, unwilling that the Princess des Ursins should bestow anything upon France, she changed her tone, and became almost a defaulter to her. A Valentian gentleman, Clemente Generoso, says Duclos, still copying textually from Fitz-Maurice, blamed Lord Lexington, whose agent and interpreter he had been from the beginning of the war, for having committed the Queen of England so far to Madame des Ursins, and advised him to tear up the convention.* By the intervention of that lady, England had obtained all it required, and the written consent of Philip V. rendered the concessions irrevocable; there was no danger, therefore, of want of good faith on the part of Madame des Ursins.

The towering rage of the latter may be imagined when she heard this news. She made the most earnest entreaties to Queen Anne not to abandon her. All that she could obtain was that that Princess " would use her good offices " to procure her the object of her desires. An elastic and somewhat embarrassing promise of protection was substituted for a formal and signed engagement, which bound Queen Anne to the interests of Madame des Ursins as to those of a contracting power. The English had tricked her; they had surpassed her in cunning. A short time afterwards, if we may believe Fitz-Maurice and his Spanish

* Memoirs of Duclos, tom. i., p. 190.

interlocutors, she made Clemente Generoso pay dearly for his evil counsel. One day when he was returning from London to Madrid, with instructions for Lord Lexington, some Irishmen, in the service of Philip V., attacked him, and, as he was endeavouring to take refuge in a church, they killed him, conformably to the orders which they had received, it is said, from the Princess des Ursins and Orry.

We only give this statement, be it well understood, under reservation, because nowhere else have we found any confirmation or even indication of it. But thus much is certain, that the chances which Madame des Ursins had on the part of the Queen of England were greatly diminished, and that it was necessary to look elsewhere for more reliable aid. She quickly despatched, therefore, her favourite d'Aubigny to Utrecht. " But," says Saint Simon, " *c'était un trop petit Sire;* he was not admitted beyond the antechambers." But Saint Simon often falls into error through excessive contempt for those below his own level. By certain documents recently discovered at the Hague and communicated to M. Geffroy, it may be seen that the members of the congress of Utrecht deliberated with d'Aubigny, and that they designated him *the plenipotentiary* of Madame des Ursins. However that may be, d'Aubigny did not obtain much; in fact, he spoilt everything by offering the Dutch greater advantages than had been accorded to the English. So the latter at least pretended, in order, no doubt, to have a pretext for wholly abandoning Madame des Ursins and for resuming their haughty attitude towards her, after having courted her for awhile. Queen Anne feigned, in fact, to be hurt that the Dutch had been more favoured than her own subjects, and exclaimed, with a readiness that betrayed an inward satisfaction : " Since the Princess des Ursins has recourse to others, I abandon her."* D'Aubigny, as the sole result, obtained only vague hopes on the part of the Dutch, who were as inimical as the English as to any exchange with France.

Without being angry with her " man of business," whom she allowed even to return to Amboise to complete the erections already begun, Madame des Ursins selected, to continue the negotiations, a more important personage—a young nephew of Madame de Noailles, named de Bournon-ville, Baron de Capres. But he covered himself with ridi-cule at this game of private intrigue rather than real diplo-matic negotiation ; and, notwithstanding all the trouble he took, he obtained nothing by it, " the gratitude of Madame des Ursins excepted, who made Philip V. give him the Golden Fleece, the rank of grandee, the Walloon com-pany of the bodyguard—everything, in fact, he could desire." †

The successive check of her two diplomatists was not, however, a sufficient warning to Madame des Ursins. Ever in pursuit of a position, which had become nothing more than a chimera after having served as a lure on the part of the English, she relied for success upon the persistent and obsti-nate will of Philip V., who made it a question of *amour propre* for himself as much as a just recompense for Madame des Ursins. It was under these circumstances that this Prince refused to sign the treaty of Utrecht, that treaty which Louis XIV. had signed and sealed with his own royal hand, and engaged to make him accept it, even though the allied powers should not grant him what he desired to bequeath to

---

* Memoirs of Duclos, tom. i., p. 191.

† MS. Letters of the Baron de Capres to Mad. des Ursins, xxxi., xxxii.

Madame des Ursins.* Such a firm attitude proved plainly enough that there was good reason for reliance upon him.

But this affair "hung up" the peace, to use Saint Simon's phrase—the peace that Louis XIV. could now sign, because it was honourable. His displeasure was extreme. It was all very well for Madame des Ursins to say that she had nothing to do with the matter, that the King of Spain was only following his own inclination, and that after all she despised the malevolent designs of his enemies; still the delay experienced in the conclusion of the general peace was imputed to her. She was accused of occupying herself too exclusively with her own interests, and of placing in the scales the repose of Europe entire : it was said that she abused Philip's good-nature, and that she ought not to have availed herself of her ascendancy over that conscientious prince save to release him from his promise, to free him from all trammel, and incline him towards the wishes of his grandfather.

It was from the French ministry that these complaints came, and Torcy, so greatly humiliated in 1704, at length had his revenge. Madame de Maintenon herself made remarks upon her, based upon the same motives; only that she threw more form into them, contenting herself with giving the Princess to infer that of which the others did not spare her the harshest expression. "You have good reason to let folks chatter ;" she wrote, " *provided that you have nothing to reproach yourself with.* . . . for, you must know, we here look upon the treaty of Spain with Holland, such as it is, as equally necessary, *as you think it shameful at Madrid.* . . . Make up your mind, therefore, Madam, and do not allow it to be said *that you are the*

* Memoirs of Duke of Berwick, tom. ii., pp. 164—169.

sole cause of the prolongation of the war. I cannot believe it, and think it very scandalous that others should."*

But these warnings and exhortations, imparted with such delicate tact, had no more effect at Madrid than the harsh severity of the ministerial reprimands. Louis XIV. then made his solemn voice heard. " Sign," said he, tartly, to his grandson, " or no aid from me. Berwick is on his march for Barcelona—I will recall him ; then I will make peace privately with the Dutch and with the Emperor ; I will leave Spain at war with those two powers, and I will not mix myself up further in any of your affairs, because I do not choose, for the private interest of Madame des Ursins, to defer securing the repose of my people, and perhaps plunge them into fresh sufferings." †

When Louis XIV. had thus proffered his last word, Philip V. even yet urged some objections, and the Princess des Ursins on her part, moved her friends into action ; but there was no means of converting Louis XIV. to what the Court of Madrid demanded, since not one of the allies was willing either ; and, as for the acquisition of those few manors in Luxembourg, in exchange for an equivalent in Touraine, he preferred personally to have nothing upon any frontier, than to gain so little, and owe such feeble legacy to an intrigue, unworthy of his character, unworthy of a great nation, and only fit to serve as a text for the biting irony of foreigners or that of his own subjects.

Madame des Ursins is indeed no longer comprehensible throughout this affair. She, hitherto so noble-minded, so devoted to high-class politics, so prudent, so full of tact.

* Letters of Madame des Ursins to Madame de Maintenon, tom. ii., 7th Aug., 1713 ; 3rd Sept., 1713 ; 16th June, 1714.

† Mémoires de Saint Philippe, tom. iii., p. 91, and Duclos, tom. i., p. 100.

Oh! how far off are we from realising that lofty sentiment of hers:—

" Sans peine je passerais de la dictature à la charrue ! "

There was nothing left, however, but to give way. The treaty of Utrecht was signed by Philip V., and unconditionally. The net gain in the business fell to d'Aubigny; he received for his trouble as a negotiator, and for his constancy in another way, the manor of Chanteloup, revealed the motive of its construction—yet an enigma to everybody in France, says Saint Simon *—installed himself therein, and, for the rest, made himself loved and esteemed there. To Madame des Ursins there only remained the mortification of having failed, a mortification the greater that her pretensions had been so lofty and tenacious. It was further increased, also, by having turned the Court of France against her, and engendered a coolness towards her on the part of Madame de Maintenon herself, who up to that juncture had always approved of her manner of acting and her system of government, but who now, seizing the occasion of Orry having established some imposts upon the Catalans, did not hesitate to say very harshly and laconically : " We do not think Orry fit for his post, for Spain is very badly governed."†

Those were accents which must have deeply grieved the heart of the Princess. Next came Berwick, who was by no means, as we have seen, to be ranked amongst her friends— Berwick, whom Louis XIV. had sent in spite of her, in spite of what she had said of Tessé, who, by his own account, had failed the first time before Barcelona only because he had been prevented from commencing the siege

* Mémoires de Saint Simon, tom. xviii., p. 104.
† Lettres, tom. iii., p. 448, year 1714.

soon enough. Her influence, it was impossible to longer doubt, had been greatly lessened at Versailles, if it had not perished altogether.

Trembling for herself, she continued naturally to lean upon the King of Spain, who was devoted to her. In order that this plank of safety should not escape her grasp, she permitted only those she liked to have access to him; she regulated all his proceedings; she kept him from all private audience; she seemed jealous of it, whilst she was only so as regarded her own preservation. Scandal, as may be imagined, was again busy with her name. It was again whispered that she was in hopes that the King, scarcely yet thirty-two, would not be repelled by the faded charms of a septuagenarian; that he would marry her, that was certain; and in every saloon throughout the world of fashion in France, circulated the following anecdote, which Saint Simon duly registered in his Memoirs, and in which further figured, to render it more piquante and authentic, the Reverend Father Robinet. The King certainly had one evening withdrawn with his confessor into the embrasure of a window. The latter appearing reserved and mysterious, the curiosity of Philip V. was excited, and the King questioned his confessor as to the meaning of the unwonted mood in which he found him. Upon which Father Robinet replied, that since the King forced him to it, he would confess that nobody either in France or Spain doubted but that he would do Madame des Ursins the honour of espousing her. "I marry her!" hastily rejoined the King. "Oh! as to that, certainly not!" and he turned upon his heel as he uttered the sentence. It was the pendant of "*Oh! pour mariée, non!*" of the famous letter of the Abbé d'Estrées, related by the same historian. Saint

Simon's two pictures are delightful; in either of the two, the priest, whether cunning or malignant, figures conspicuously, attracts attention, and keeps up one's curiosity.

For some time, Philip V. treated these reports as mere inventions and calumnies, "the offspring of envy, hatred, and ambition." All that was said concerning the omnipotence of Madame des Ursins, of her empire over him, of her hopes, her designs, of that same corridor, of their private interviews, left him unmoved and indifferent. The Count de Bergueick, until then a stanch adherent of the Princess des Ursins, himself declared that that omnipotence had become insupportable, and he asked permission to return to Flanders, whence he had been summoned. Philip V. allowed him to depart, and Madame des Ursins lost not one jot of her authority. But the complaints, the murmurs, the idle talk continued, the incessant repetition of which could not fail at last to make an impression upon a weak mind. In the end the King grew wearied, and vexed, especially at the reports relating to such a ridiculous marriage, to a matrimonial project which wounded his self-love as a man as well as his royal dignity, and tormented besides by the exigencies of a temperament, in which the flesh was far too predominant over the spirit—" Find me a wife," said he, one day to Madame des Ursins, " our *tête-à-têtes* scandalise the people." *

* Mémoire de Duclos, tom. i., p. 230.

CHAPTER IV.

"FIND me a wife!" The sentence was like a thunder-clap in the ears of Madame des Ursins, so long accustomed as she had been to govern and domineer. Where to find one—one like Marie Louise of Savoy, who would consent to retain her in the same functions, and who, like her, with intelligence and firmness of mind, would have a boundless confidence in her *camerara mayor*, and a docility proof against everything? Louis XIV., being consulted, replied to his grandson that he gave him his choice between a princess of Portugal, a princess of Bavaria, and a princess of Parma. The first was greatly to the taste of the Casti-lians; they had always had reason to praise their Portu-guese queens, and they attached to such choice hopes of renewed political unity for the Spanish peninsula to the profit of Castile, which thus, by marriages, would absorb, on the left, Portugal, as it had appropriated on the right, the kingdom of Arragon. But the Court of the King of Portugal, the brother of that princess, had been the rendez-vous and the asylum of aristocratic and Austrian opposi-tion. These antecedents alarmed Madame des Ursins on her own account, and did not appear much more assuring for Philip V. Was it not known, on the other hand, that Portugal—especially since the treaty of Utrecht, since the Bourbons had become, in spite of that nation, the immutable possessors of Spain—dreaded those neighbouring kings, after having previously loved them so much as liberators, and on that account had placed herself under the protection of England, the enemy of all the reigning branches of that powerful and ambitious house ?

A marriage with the daughter of the Elector of Bavaria, of a firm ally of Louis XIV. and Philip V., might well be the boon and the bónd of an old friendship, but could not procure for Spain any compensation for the sacrifices imposed upon her by the terms of the recent peace.

The Princess of Parma, as a guarantee of security, if not of material advantage, did not at the first glance seem more eligible. " Besides that she was the issue of a double bastardy, of a pope on her father's side, of a natural daughter of Charles V. on her mother's side, she was the daughter of a petty duke of Parma and a thoroughly Austrian mother, who was herself the sister of the dowager-empress, of the dowager-queen of Spain, who was so unpopular that she was exiled ; and further of the Queen of Portugal, who had persuaded her husband to receive the Archduke at Lisbon, and to carry the war into Spain."* On that account such was not an eligible choice for the King of Spain. It was certain, moreover, although Madame des Ursins was unaware of it, that "she was of a haughty disposition, and that she had been brought up at Parma with the same thoroughly French freedom which reigned at Turin." †
But by her uncle, the reigning Duke of Parma, who had no children, and was no longer of an age to have any, she was heiress to the duchies of Parma, Plaisance, and Guastalla,

---

* Memoirs of St. Simon, tom. xx., p. 175.
† Histoire Secrete de la Cour de Madrid, année 1714, p. 315.

and by another uncle, the aged Gaston de Medicis, Duke of
Tuscany, she had the expectation of Tuscany itself, and the
isle of Elba, a dependance of it. United to Philip V. she
might therefore some day, and perhaps shortly, bring Spain
into Italy, alongside of its ancient possessions, from which
the treaty of Utrecht had driven her. This consideration
had much weight with Madame des Ursins, to whom that
treaty, as we have seen from a letter of Madame de Maintenon, had appeared disgraceful for Spain, as well as detri-
mental to herself. Doubtless there was something disquieting in the family alliances of this princess; but it might be
thought that the perspective of an union with one of the
most illustrious crowned houses of Europe, and moreover
the crown of a queen which would bind her brow, would
render her favourable to Madame des Ursins, upon whom a
marriage so brilliant depended, and which far surpassed
Elizabeth's utmost expectations. The former thought to
find in the Farnese, brought up in a modest and virtuous
court, a simple-minded, timorous girl. Gratitude for such
a service appeared to Madame des Ursins a certain security
for her future tranquillity; but a skilful intriguer who had
but very slightly rendered himself agreeable to the princess—
Alberoni, a native of Parma—afterwards celebrated throughout Europe as the Cardinal Alberoni, but then occupying a
subordinate position in Spain, conceived at that moment
one of those vast plans to which his fertile genius was wont
to give birth, and which would have placed him in the foremost rank of great men had a like success equally crowned
them all. He concealed, as already said, the real character
of the Princess of Parma, who, moreover, could not then
have been known to be what she afterwards turned out.
The marriage was concluded, the new Queen set out for

Spain, and Madame des Ursins went forward to meet her at Xadraque, a small town some few leagues from Madrid.

A dispensation from the Pope—for the future Queen was a near relative of Gabrielle of Savoy—had been promptly obtained. Already did the favourite indulge herself with the contemplation of the illimitable prospect of domination which the future seemed to open up for her, when she received more truthful information relative to the character of Elizabeth Farnese. Her letters during the latter part of 1714, notwithstanding their great reserve, reveal a manifest uneasiness, and it is with an ill-concealed emotion that she relates, without precisely detailing them, the contradictory reports which reach her relative to the Princess. It seems impossible to doubt that, during the few months which preceded the arrival of the Princess of Parma, the presence of Madame des Ursins had not become a torment to the Spanish King, and that he had not secretly lent his hand to a *coup d'état* carried out subsequently with a barbarous determination by his new consort. It was, in fact, by showing to the officers of the guard a plenary power from the King that Elizabeth triumphed over their hesitation, and that she secured their assistance in the execution of a measure which perhaps would have been less cruel if it had been more sanguinary; but if, since the death of Marie Louise of Savoy, the relations of the King of Spain with Madame des Ursins had assumed an obscure character, the active intervention of the latter in the second marriage of that Prince at least excludes the idea that she could have dreamed of a royal position for herself, as her enemies accused her. Granted that the Abbé Alberoni may have transformed the most ambitious princess in Europe into " a

jolly *Parmesane* fattened upon cheese and butter,"* and that
the habitual circumspection of Madame des Ursins did not
protect her against the clumsiness of such a snare may be
true, however unlikely ; but it is at least doubtful that the
camerara mayor could have cherished such illusion when she
presented herself for the first time before the new Queen at
the interview at Xadraque.

Whether the indiscretions of others had revealed to her
the true character of Elizabeth Farnese, whether she had
foreseen the manœuvres of the Inquisition with the future
Queen, whether she had dreaded the anger of Louis XIV.,
who had not been consulted ; whether the triumphant attitude of her enemies had opened her eyes, certain it is, however, that the Princess attempted to break off the match.
But it was in vain that she despatched a confidential agent
to Parma for that purpose.   On his arrival, the messenger
was thrown into prison and threatened with death, and so
failed in his mission.   The marriage by procuration was
celebrated on the 16th of August, 1714.   That unskilful and
tardy opposition released the Princess Farnese from all feelings of gratitude, furnished the enemies of Madame des
Ursins with a deadly weapon, by appearing to justify their
accusations in a striking manner, and so prepared her ruin.

Her disgrace was prompt, cruel, decisive.   The plan had
evidently been concerted long beforehand.†   Confirmed in

---

* "Questo abbate pur freddamente, e come a mezza voce la nomino,
aggiugnendo per altro, ch' ella era una buona Lombarda, impastata da
buttero et fromagio picentino, elevata alla casalingua, ed avezza di non
sentirsi di altro parlare che di mertelli ricami e tele."—*Memorie Istoriche* di
Poggiali, p. 279.

† "I only ask one thing of you," wrote Elizabeth Farnese to Philip V. ;
"that is the dismissal of Madame des Ursins ;" and the king had replied—
" At least do not spare your blow ; for if she only talk to you for a couple

her design by her interview at Saint Jean de Luz with the Queen Dowager, widow of Charles II. and her relative, and at Pampeluna with Alberoni, Elizabeth held on her way to Madrid. The King advanced to meet her on the road to Burgos, and Madame des Ursins, as has been said, went on before as far as the little town of Xadraque. When the Queen arrived there on the 23rd of December, 1714, Madame des Ursins received her with the customary reverences. Afterwards, having followed her into a cabinet, she perceived her instantly change her tone. By some it is said that Madame des Ursins, being desirous of finding fault with something about the Queen's head-dress, whilst she was at her toilette, the latter treated it as an impertinence, and immediately flew into a rage. Others relate (and these different accounts tally with each other in the main) that Madame des Ursins having protested her devotedness to the new Queen, and assured her Majesty "that She might always reckon upon finding her stand between the King and herself, to keep matters in the state in which they ought to be on her account, and procuring her all the gratifications which she had a right to expect—the Queen, who had listened quietly enough so far, took fire at these last words, and replied that she did not want anyone near the King; that it was an impertinence to make her such an offer, and that it was presuming too much to dare to address her in such a fashion." Thus much is certain, that the Queen, outrageously thrusting Madame des Ursins out of her cabinet,* summoned M. d'Amezaga, lieutenant of the body-

---

of hours, she wi enchain you, and hinder us from sleeping together, as happened to the late Queen."—Duclos.

* Madame des Ursins, stupified, sought to make excuses. "La Reine alors, redoublant de furie et de menaces, se mit à crier qu'on fît sortir cette

guard, who commanded the escort, and ordered him to arrest the Princess, to make her get immediately into a carriage, and have her driven to the French frontiers by the shortest road, and without halting anywhere. As d'Amezaga hesitated, the Queen asked him whether he had not received a special command from the King of Spain to obey her in everything and without reserve—which was quite true. Madame des Ursins was arrested, therefore, and carried off instantaneously, just as she was, in her full dress of ceremony, and hurried across Spain as fast as six horses could drag her. It was mid-winter—no provisions to be found in the inns of Spain ; no beds; not a change of clothes—the ground covered with frost and snow ; and the Princess was then in her seventy-second year. A lady's maid and two officers of the guard accompanied her in the carriage.

" I know not how I managed to endure all the fatigue of that journey," she wrote Madame de Maintenon, whilst wandering about the French frontiers, eighteen days after the scene at Xadraque. " They compelled me to sleep upon straw, and to breakfast in a very different style to the repast to which I had been accustomed. I have not forgotten in the details which I have taken the liberty to send the King (Louis XIV.) that I ate only two stale eggs daily ; it struck me that such a fact would excite him to take pity upon a faithful subject who has not deserved, it seems to me, in any way such contemptuous treatment. I am going to Saint Jean de Luz to take a little repose and learn what it may please the King to do in my behalf."

And from this last-named town—at which she was set at liberty—and up to her arrival at which she had unfalteringly

folle de sa présence et de son logis, et l'en fit mettre dehors par les épaules."
—Saint Simon.

maintained the strength and constancy of her character, neither a tear nor a complaint escaping her—a few days later she wrote again to Madame de Maintenon:

"Here I shall await the King's commands. I am in a small house—the ocean before me, sometimes calm, sometimes agitated: it is an image of what passes in courts. You know what has happened to me ; I shall not implore in vain your generous compassion. I agree perfectly with you that stability is only to be found in God. Assuredly it is not to be found in the human breast ; for who could be more certain than I was of the King of Spain's heart ? "

Everything leads us to infer, in fact, that it was Philip V. who, forgetting the long and faithful services of Madame des Ursins, and wearied of a domination from which he had not the courage to free himself, gave authority to his new consort to take everything upon herself; and the latter, who, like Alberoni, her crafty adviser, belonged to the intrepid race of political gamesters, did not hesitate for a single instant to commence her regal play with the execution of such a master-stroke. Elizabeth of Parma felt herself to be too first-rate a personage to condescend to figure side by side on the same stage with Madame des Ursins.

It was of this same Elizabeth, born for a throne, that Frederick the Great said : " The pride of a Spartan, the obstinacy of a Briton, added to Italian finesse and French vivacity, formed the character of this singular woman. She advanced audaciously to the accomplishment of her designs; nothing astonished her, nothing could stop her." Possessed of such qualities it is not surprising to find that she profited by the smallest opening to sweep the ground clear on her arrival.

Recovering from this stunning downfall, Madame des

Ursins, after the first moments of surprise, recovered all her strength, her sang-froid, her wonted equanimity. Not a complaint or unbecoming reproach or weak word escaped her lips. She had formed a just estimate beforehand of all that human instability; she said to herself, on beholding her enemies triumphant and her friends in consternation, that there was no reason to be greatly astonished. That this world was only a stage over which many very poor actors strutted, that she had thereon played her part better than many others perhaps, and that her enemies ought not to have expected to see her so humiliated that she could no longer perform it: "It is in the eye of heaven that I should be humbled," said she, "and I am so."

Every reader of Saint Simon must be deeply impressed with his narrative of that terrible night of December 24th, 1714. Who can fail to picture to himself the rude expulsion of the Princess des Ursins from the Queen's apartment in her full dress of ceremony, suddenly packed off in a carriage, without proper clothing or change of linen, and without money, to be whirled away through a winter's night so severe that her driver lost one of his hands from frost-bite, over mountain passes where the roads had disappeared beneath the snow, towards an unknown destination? Who cannot picture to himself hunger coming to add fresh tortures to those of the prolonged nightmare under which that unfortunate lady must have suffered the keenest pangs of incertitude, of astonishment, and of humiliation? Such, however, was the fate reserved for a woman who had inscribed her name among those of the founders of a dynasty and the liberators of a great kingdom!

For some time previous to the occurrence of that strange event—so unlooked for, so inconceivable—the Princess had

not been free from inquietude with respect to the preservation of her prestige and authority, as also on the score
of constantly recurring difficulties with the Court of Versailles, wherein she had numerous enemies keeping up an
active correspondence with the still more numerous enemies
by whom she was surrounded at Madrid ; the affairs of the
sovereignty, the isolation in which Philip was kept ; the
marriage of that Prince, determined upon and almost concluded without the consent of his grandfather—all which
had deeply angered Louis the Fourteenth.

Though all this tended by turns to inspire the Princess
with fear and disgust, still, she could not anticipate an
ignominious treatment coming from that quarter. Soon,
however, her wonted courage got the uppermost in her
bosom ; besides, she had hopes both from her justification
and from the King of Spain, whose confidence she thought
unshakeable, of a return to Court, difficult, nevertheless,
after such a shock. Meanwhile, the Queen vouchsafed no
replies to her letters ; the King announced to her that he
was unable to refuse the maintenance of the measure taken
at the instance of the Queen, but assured her that pensions
would be conferred upon her. Having reached St. Jean de
Luz, Madame des Ursins wrote to Versailles, and shortly
afterwards despatched thither one of her nephews. The Great
Monarch was compelled to be guided by the decision of his
grandson ; Madame de Maintenon replied by evasive compliments. The Princess could then see that all was at an
end, as regarded her resumption of power. She pursued her
way through France, and arrived in Paris. The King received her coldly ; her stay in France was not prolonged
without difficulty. Moreover, she foresaw the approaching
decease of Louis the Fourteenth, and a regency under the

Duke of Orleans. Their old quarrels, the open hatred which had since existed between them, causing her uneasiness and misgivings, she resolved to quit France. She wished to visit the Low Countries, but was not permitted. She proceeded to Savoy, thence to Genoa, and at last returned to Rome, where she once more fixed her abode. There a suitable existence was secured to her, for Philip kept his promise, and caused her pension to be punctually paid.

Habituated to the stir of courts and the excitement of state affairs, she could not condemn herself, notwithstanding her age, to an absolute repose. Prince James Stuart, called *the Pretender,* having withdrawn to Rome, Madame des Ursins attached herself to him and his fortunes; she did the honours of his house : and thus she remained until her death, which took place December 5th, 1722, at the age of fourscore and upwards.

It has been sought to divine the real authors of the Princess's disgrace; for it has been considered, not without good reason, that it was very improbable that no other cause save a sudden impulse arising from a feeling of anger, barely justifiable on the Queen's part, had urged her to put in execution a resolution which brought about nothing less than an actual political revolution.

BOOK IV.

———•———

CLOSING SCENES.

CHAPTER I.

THE Princess des Ursins, as it will be seen, shared the fate of Portocarrero, of Medina-Cœli, and of all those whose power she had broken or whose designs she had frustrated; and who, after their decease, were immediately buried in silence and oblivion. Divided into two parts by the death of Marie-Louise of Savoy, her political life in Spain had not always assumed the same character, a like aspect. The first had been marked by useful or glorious actions, and was of real grandeur; the second was more remarkable for its weakness. Side by side with a bold and honourable, although unsuitable enterprise, ridiculous and extravagant pretensions were coupled. Finding herself alone at the right hand of Philip the Fifth, she became puffed up with her exclusive influence, her new rank and title. She exaggerated her personal importance. She was possessed with the secret desire of being in Spain, with a young sovereign, and he too on the eve of marriage, what Madame de Maintenon was in France, with an aged monarch, and for a while she attained that object, as flattering to her feminine vanity as to her ambition.

In this there was only one difference, a difference arising from the respective characters of these two ladies and of those two kings; which was that the ascendant of the one, taking the form of friendship the most discreet, was lasting, whilst the other, exercising a direct, immediate, and too overt

domination, was destined, sooner or later, to end in tiring
out a monarch infinitely less capable than Louis the Fourteenth, but quite as jealous of sway.   The Princess bore,
therefore, rather the semblance of an intriguante, as people
remarked, than of a serious woman, having large views, of
will alike firm and prompt, of enlightened and, in a certain
sense, liberal mind, with an entire abnegation of self—seeking the welfare of the State alone, and the interests only
of the two great countries.   Except those whom she had
served, or who had sent her to Spain, few had approved
her acts at any period of her favour.   The misfortunes and
the abuses that marked her possession of power, when it
had reached its apogee, confirmed them in their opinion,
especially when they saw, in France, the severest censure
launched against her even from high places, whence until
then praise had descended.   Others, to whom her previous
conduct was less known, judged her only by what seemed
ridiculous or faulty at that period of her life, and the last
impression received was that which they retained, which
has been transmitted to posterity ; which was regarded as
that most to be relied upon, and which the almost exclusive
perusal of Saint Simon, far from modifying in any way that
impression, only served to confirm it.   That consummate
courtier has well said, in his Memoirs, that " her history
deserved to be written," implying the deep interest which
would be derivable from it.   The narrative, apart from its interest, is valuable for the lesson it conveys of the fruitlessness
of the devotion of a most gifted woman's life to the pursuit
of politics on the grandest and most elevated scale.   During
twelve years the Princess des Ursins exercised a power almost
absolute.   If, however, the beneficent traces of her influence
and sway are sought for, the search proves futile ; though

doubtless, after so many crises and revolutions Spain has experienced since her time, that ungovernable country must
have lost all such advantages; but at any rate posterity would
have preserved a remembrance of them. We must not, however, accuse Madame des Ursins too severely. One of those
vigorous geniuses was needed which but too seldom make
their appearance upon the scene of events to resuscitate and
sustain the Spanish monarchy amidst circumstances so
untoward and difficult. After civil and foreign war which
had driven Philip to the brink of a precipice, he had succeeded in reducing to obedience the last city of his kingdom, only a few days before the fall of Madame des Ursins.
And then began a peaceful sway, which allowed useful
reforms and beneficent ameliorations to be thought of.

The subject of so many accusations, and probably miscon-
ceptions, the Princess possessed a large, fine, and cultivated
mind, a rare aptitude for business, a force of character little
common among persons of her sex. Warm in her affections,
she was naturally so in her hatreds; and though but too
easily accessible to unjust prejudices, was prompt also to
seek out and encourage merit. She has been reproached
for her intrigues, but the same weapons with which she was
assailed she turned against her enemies, and their number
was great. How manifold must have been the animosities
excited by the position of a woman who, standing only at the
foot of the throne, governed both its possessors and their
Court, created and directed its ministers, generals, and ambassadors! Fervent attachment to her sovereigns, eminent
services rendered to them and their countries, an astonish-
ing capacity, a profound knowledge of mankind, a rare presence of mind, and an unshakeable firmness in situations
the most perilous and misfortunes the most unlooked-for,

such attributes cannot be denied without injustice to the Princess des Ursins, and which, however futile the result of her political career, ought to consecrate the memory of her labours and her name.

It was a generous impulse which prompted Madame des Ursins to commence a fresh attack upon the Spanish Inquisition. Can it be said that the war she waged against it remained without any result? Assuredly not. By her active intervention the English Government obtained the privilege that the palace of its ambassador at Madrid should enjoy the right of an asylum against all the proceedings of the Inquisition, and the same privilege was acquired for British vessels in the ports of Spain. A Protestant nation thus opened in the capital of the Catholic King a perpetual refuge against the rigours of the Holy Office. It was a great innovation; it was the first blow dealt by the spirit of modern times against that of those Spanish institutions which represented the most faithfully the blind and almost barbarous religion of the Middle Ages.

It is difficult to decide whether it was a misfortune or an advantage to her to figure in the gallery of the ducal memoir-writer, Saint Simon. That portrait, sketched with a breadth and freedom by which her womanly character has somewhat suffered, depicts her as devoured by a thirst for power, without even allowing the important services which she rendered to the two nations to be so much as suspected. The great master has not given us a bust-portrait of Madame des Ursins, but a full-length likeness, with that lavish excess of colour flung upon the canvas which imparts more life than truth, more of relief than perspective to the majority of his pictures. If in that brilliant delineation the great lady shines with a somewhat theatrical majesty, the national object which she pursued is in no wise indicated—a grave though natural omission on the part of a man in whom a passionate fondness for details almost always blinds him to the collective point of view, and who is not the first of portraitists only because he is the least reliable of historical painters. He, nevertheless, in her case, always manifests the feeling that she is worthy of a careful, special, and patient study, and he points out such study for the edification of posterity. " She reigned in Spain," he remarks, " and her history deserves to be written."

We will now reproduce his elaborate portrait of the Princess. " Rather tall than short of stature, she was a brunette with blue eyes whose expression incessantly responded to everything that pleased her; with a perfect shape, a lovely bosom, and a countenance which, without regularity of feature, was more charming even than the purely symmetrical. Her air was extremely noble, and there was something majestic in her whole demeanour, and a grace so natural and continual in all she did, even in things the most trivial and indifferent, that I have never seen anyone approach to, either in form or mind. Her wit was copious and of all kinds. She was flattering, caressing, insinuating, moderate, desirous to please for pleasing sake, and with charms irresistible when she strove to persuade and win over. Accompanying all this, she possessed a grandeur that encouraged rather than repelled. A delightful tone of conversation, inexhaustible and always most amusing—for she had seen many countries and peoples. A voice and way of speaking extremely agreeable and full of sweetness. She had read much and reflected much. She knew how to choose the best society, how to receive it, and could even have held a Court; was polite and distinguished; and, above all, careful never to take a step in advance without dignity and discretion. She was eminently fitted for intrigue, in which, from taste, she had passed her time at Rome. With much ambition, but of that vast kind far above her sex and the common run of men—a desire to occupy a great position and to govern. An inclination to gallantry and personal vanity were her foibles, and these clung to her until her latest days; consequently she dressed in a way that no longer became her, and as she advanced in life departed further from propriety in this particular. She was an ardent and excellent friend—of a friendship that time and absence never enfeebled; and therefore an implacable enemy, pursuing her hatred even to the infernal regions. Whilst caring little for the means by which she gained her ends, she tried as much as possible to reach them by honest means. Secret, not only for herself, but for her friends, she was yet of a decorous gaiety, and so governed her humours, that at all times and in everything she was mistress of herself."

Such was the Princess des Ursins, as sketched by that painstaking limner, Saint-Simon; throughout whose " Memoirs " many other scattered traits are to be found of this celebrated woman, who so long and so publicly governed the Court and Crown of Spain, and whose fate it was to make so much stir in the world alike by her reign and her fall.

CHAPTER II.

THROUGHOUT the political conflicts which agitated the Court of England since the Duke and Duchess of Marlborough had left their native shores, the Duke maintained a steady correspondence with his friends, but expressed a firm refusal to deviate from those principles which had occasioned his exile, or to approve of the Peace of Utrecht, or to abandon his desire for the Hanoverian succession. Distrusting the sincerity of Harley's pretended exertions, he resolutely refused to hold intercourse with a Minister of whose hollowness he had already received many proofs. Nor was the Duchess less determined never to pardon the injuries which she conceived herself and her husband to have sustained from Harley. All offers of his aid, all attempts to lend to him the influence which Marlborough's military and personal character still commanded, were absolutely rejected.

At the Court of Hanover, the Duke and Duchess saw, as it were, reflected the cabals of their native country. Little, indeed, that was reassuring reached them in their foreign retreat, relative to public affairs. The existing policy of Anne's Ministers seemed likely to destroy all that his labours had effected during a long life of toil and danger ; and the sacrifice of thousands of lives had gained no advantage which the malice of his enemies could not undo. In short, the friendly relations which were brought about between France and England threatened to change the face of things altogether.

The result of the shrewd Duchess's experience of political life and royal favour was embodied in the sound advice she gave her illustrious husband on his return to England, shortly after the death of Anne, and previous to the arrival of her successor, George I. " I begged of the Duke upon my knees," relates the Duchess, " that he would never accept any employment. I said everybody that liked the Revolution and the security of the law had a great esteem for him, that he had a greater fortune than he wanted, and that a man who had had such success, with such an estate, would be of more use to any court than they could be to him; that I would live civilly with them, if they were so to me, but would never put it into the power of any King to use me ill. He was entirely of this opinion, and determined to quit all, and serve them only when he could act honestly and do his country service at the same time."

Though the Duchess witnessed the triumph of the Whigs on their return to power at the accession of George I., she was very far from possessing the influence she had enjoyed during Anne's reign. Her feverish thirst for political and courtly intrigues had returned upon her, despite so many bitter deceptions and the advance of old age. She scolded incessantly her husband for his indolence, when he had really become incapable of any longer taking an active part in public affairs. He confined himself to the enjoyment of his opulence and his high position. In May, 1716, he experienced a violent attack of paralysis, which for some time deprived him of speech and recollection. His health continued to decline more and more to the close of his life in June, 1722, though the notion of his imbecility appears to have been erroneous.

The Duke of Marlborough was one of the bravest and

most kindly-tempered of men. His gentleness and devotion towards his wife and love of his children were not the only proofs which he gave of a kindly nature, and many curious anecdotes are related of the way in which he governed his imperious consort when he had to encounter her tears, sulks, and torrents of passionate reproaches, which were among the favourite and irresistible features of her conjugal eloquence. The fiery Duchess survived her illustrious husband the long period of twenty-two years. Notwithstanding her age, and probably on account of her immense fortune, she was sought in marriage by the Duke of Somerset and Lord Coningsby. The reply she made to the offer of the first-named, an old friend, the " proud Duke," was admirable. She declined a second marriage as unsuitable to her age; but added— " Were I only thirty, and were you able to lay the empire of the world at my feet, I would not allow you to succeed to that heart and hand which has always been devoted wholly to John, Duke of Marlborough." A proof of her good judgment and true dignity ! At the same time, it must be owned that, alike through pride and gratitude, she truly owed such a testimony of respect to the memory of a husband who had left behind so great a name, and who was throughout his married life full of amiability, deference, and tenderness towards her, and who had suffered with an exemplary patience all the capriciousness of her imperious character.

The instructive lesson derivable from the extraordinary career and signal disgrace of this remarkable political woman is emphatically given by the Duchess herself, on her retirement, as the results of her own experience of royal favour.

" After what has passed, I do solemnly protest, that if it

were in my power I would not be a favourite, which few will believe; and since I shall never be able to give any demonstration of that truth, I had as good say no more of it. But as fond as people are of power, I fancy that anybody that had been shut up so many tedious hours as I have been with a person that had no conversation, and yet must be treated with respect, would feel something of what I did, and be very glad when their circumstances did not want it, to be freed from such a slavery, which must be uneasy at all times; though I do protest, that upon the account of her loving me, and trusting me so entirely as she did, I had a concern for her, which is more than you will easily believe, and I would have served her with the hazard of my life upon any occasion; but after she put me at liberty by using me ill, I was very easy, and liked better that anybody should have her favour than myself, at the price of flattery without which I believe nobody can be well with a King or Queen, unless the world should come to be less corrupt or they wiser than any I have seen since I was born."

In another place she says: "Women signify nothing unless they are the mistresses of a Prince or a Prime Minister, which I would not be if I were young; and I think there are very few, if any, women that have understanding or impartiality enough to serve well those they really wish to serve."

The wife of the great captain and hero of Queen Anne's time—the most remarkable woman of her own, or perhaps of any epoch—lived to the age of eighty-four.

"So singular was the fate of this extraordinary woman in private life," it has been truly observed, "that scarcely did she possess a tie which was not severed or embittered by worldly or political considerations."

Those who hopelessly covet wealth, honour, and celebrity through the avenues of political strife may contemplate the career of Sarah Duchess of Marlborough with profit, and rise from the study reconciled to a calmer course of life and resigned to a humbler fate.

INDEX.

ALBERONI, Julio Abbé (afterwards cardinal), Prime Minister of Spain, deceives Madame des Ursins as to the character of Elizabeth Farnese, 270–289 ; his representation of that most ambitious princess as "a jolly Parmesane fattened upon cheese and butter," 291 ; concerts with the Princess of Parma the ruin of Madame des Ursins, 292 ; belonged to the intrepid race of political gamesters, 294.

AMELOT, the President, nominated ambassador for Spain by Madame des Ursins, 191.

ANNE of AUSTRIA (mother of Louis XIV.), an example among all queens, and almost among all women, of constancy in adversity, 17 ; her reception of Mazarin after his exile, 18.

ANNE, Queen of England, her feeling towards the Whigs purely official, and not a genuine sympathy, 206 ; she secretly leans towards the Tories, as defender of the royal prerogative, 206 ; indolent and taciturn, she yields without resistance to the ascendency of Sarah Jennings, 215 ; her unhappy married life, 215 ; the Queen and Sarah treat each other as equals, writing under assumed names, 215 ; state of parties on her accession, 218 ; chooses a ministry combining both Whigs and Tories, 218 ; entertains the Archduke Charles with truly royal magnificence, 218 ; the Duchess of Marlborough surrounds the Queen with the chiefs of the Whigs against her will, 222 ; an endless succession of jars and piques between the Queen and the Duchess, 222 ; the insolence of the Mistress of the Robes towards the Queen, 226 ; gives her favour and confidence to Mrs. Masham, 227 ; Anne cautiously creeps out of her subjection to the Duchess, 230 ; has some pangs of conscience in ill-treating Marlborough, 232 ; gives up all regard for the Duchess or gratitude to the Duke, 233 ; emancipates herself from obligations regardless of the confusion into which she casts the country, 234 ; intrigues of the bed-chamber, 234 ; a weak woman domineered over by one attendant and wheedled and flattered by another, 234 ; gives herself up entirely to Mrs. Masham, 236 ; dreading the furious violence of the Duchess, Anne leaves London, 237 ; spares the Duke and Duchess not from compassion but fear, 242 ; terrified at the Duchess's threat to publish her letters, 242 ; exonerates the Duchess from the charge of cheating, 243 ; demands the return of the gold key from the Duchess, 244 ; divides her Court places between Mrs. Masham and the Duchess of Somerset, 245 ; writes with her own hand the dismissal of the Duchess, and gives herself up to her enemies, 246 ; her apathetic remark on hearing that the Duke and Duchess had left England, 248 ; she never sees again her great general or the woman to whom she was once so strongly attached, 248 ; her conduct towards Madame des Ursins in the repudiation of Lexington's convention, 281.

AUBIGNY, Louis d', equerry of Madame des Ursins, 178 ; his character and

Luxembourg, 78; her creditable position among French writers and her encouragement of literary men, 79.

MONTELLANO, Duke de, replaces Archbishop Arias in the presidency of Castile, 172; counterbalances the authority of Porto-Carrero, 172; offended at the attitude of the princess, he resigns, 196.

NEMOURS, Charles Amadeus of Savoy, Duke de, wounded in the Fronde war, is visited in various disguises by the Duchess de Châtillon, 4; wounded in several places in the combat at the Faubourg St. Antoine, 9; is killed in a duel with his brother-in-law, Beaufort, 14.

NOIRMOUTIER, Duke de, circulates his sister's annotated letter throughout Paris, 179.

ORLEANS, Gaston, Duke d', but for his daughter, his inaction would have allowed Condé to perish, 10; his interview with Condé after the fight, 12; exiled to Blois, 15; passes there the remainder of his contemptible existence, 25.

ORLEANS, Henrietta of England, daughter of Charles I., Duchess d', admits Louise Quérouaille into her household as maid-of-honour, 96; intrusted with the negotiating of detaching England from the interests of Holland, 97; her character and personal attributes at five-and-twenty, 97; her unbounded power over her brother, Charles II., 97; the secret of Louis XIV.'s progress to Flanders, known only to her, 99; embarks from Dunkirk for Dover, with La Quérouaille and initiates the secret negotiation with her brother, 99; Charles falls into the snare and Henrietta carries most of the points of that disgraceful treaty, 99; takes her maid-of-honour back to France to incite Charles's desire to retain her in his Court, 100; the Duchess thought more of augmenting the greatness of Charles than of benefiting England, 100; her motives for

undertaking all this shameful bargaining, 102; on her return to Paris, a cabal in her household seeks to effect her destruction, 102; the motives originating the plot, 103; she is seized with a mortal illness at St. Cloud, 104; the heartless indifference of all around her, save Madlle. de Montpensier, 105; her dying declaration that she was poisoned, 105; Bossuet consoles her in her last moments, 106; the cause of her death falsely attributed to *cholera-morbus*, 106; St. Simon's statement of the poison being sent from Italy by the Chevalier de Lorraine, 107; the intrigues which led to the murder present a scene of accumulated horrors and iniquity, 107; the last political act of the Duchess calculated to secure the subjection of the English nation, 107.

ORLEANS, Philip II. (nephew of Louis XIV. and afterwards Regent), Duke d', represents Louis XIV. in Spain, 254; distrusted by, but remains on the best footing with Mad. des Ursins, 254; indulged the hope of being put in the place of Philip V., 255; his suspicious negotiations with the Earl of Stanhope, 255; Mad. des Ursins demands his recall and obtains it, 255; denounced by Mad. des Ursins, and with difficulty escapes a scandalous trial, 256.

ORRY, Jean Louville's accusations against him, 177; Mad. des Ursins' letter with friendly remembrances to d'Aubigny's wife, 183; recalled to France, 187; reinstated by Mad. des Ursins, 190.

PALATINE, Anne de Gonzagua, Princess, if the Fronde could have been saved, her advice would have saved it, 18; is associated with Mazarin's triumph, 19; her political importance dates from the imprisonment of the Princess, 54; uses the feminine factionists as so many wires by which to move the men whom they governed, 54; the opinions of De

THE END.